# Giant
# Steps

# Giant Steps

## Daily Devotions from
## Spiritual Giants of the Past

Warren W. Wiersbe, editor

BAKER BOOK HOUSE
Grand Rapids, Michigan 49506

Copyright 1981 by
Baker Book House Company

ISBN: 0-8010-9648-0

First printing, December 1981
Second printing, January 1982
Third printing, August 1984

Printed in the United States of America

The editor wishes to express his appreciation for permission to reprint excerpts from:
*The Diary and Life of David Brainerd* by Jonathan Edwards, edited by Philip Howard,
copyright 1949, Moody Press, Moody Bible Institute of Chicago. Used by permission.

*Lectures on Colossians*, by H. A. Ironside, published by Loizeaux Brothers, Neptune,
New Jersey.

Specified excerpts (totaling approximately 1150 words) from *A Testament of
Devotion*, by Thomas R. Kelly. Copyright 1941 by Harper and Row, Publishers, Inc.
Reprinted by permission of the publisher.

*The Divine Conquest* by A. W. Tozer copyright © 1950 by Fleming H. Revell Company.
Used by permission.

To my wife

*Betty*

who has lovingly accepted me as
I am (a bookworm), has never
complained as the library grew,
and who has been my greatest
encouragement in my ministry
of preaching and writing.

# Contents

# *Preface*

The purpose of this book is the spiritual enrichment of the serious-minded believer who is not afraid of truth.

The format of the book is simple. I have selected fifty-two of the spiritual giants of the past, and have chosen from their writings seven significant excerpts. These selections are not typical devotional thoughts. I have deliberately chosen material that is meaty, that will make you think, and, in some cases, may make you disagree. I am sure the result will be intellectual and spiritual growth, if you are willing to face truth honestly.

The Scripture quotations that introduce each selection were, for the most part, chosen by me. However, in some cases these quotations were the text of the sermon or chapter from which I have quoted. A few verses have been used more than once, but this will give you opportunity to compare the way different men approach the Word of God. When the writer refers to a verse of Scripture, but does not quote it, I suggest you look it up and read it. When he quotes but does not give the reference, I suggest you use your concordance. Don't be a *passive* reader!

The fact that any preacher or writer is included in this book is not necessarily an endorsement of everything he has said, done, or written. The fact that many other persons are *not* included does not mean I am ignorant of them or think them unworthy of attention. It is obvious that no book can include everybody whose spiritual contribution is meaningful. We all have our favorites.

*Giant Steps* is the third volume of a series that includes *Walking with the Giants* and *Listening to the Giants*, both published by Baker Book House. My research into the lives and ministries of the great preachers and leaders of the church put me in contact with their writings, and over the years I have marked passages that have helped me in a special way. Many of these favorite passages are in this volume.

The reader can use the book as a daily devotional or as an anthology for occasional reading and pondering. The authors and the selections are arranged chronologically. (They are listed alphabetically in the table of contents.) Two of the selections (from Alexander Maclaren and C. H. Spurgeon, pp. 147 and 181) are appropriate as devotions for New Year's Day.

An annotated list of sources at the end of the book gives information about the books from which these selections are taken. The sources are listed alphabetically according to the format of the table of contents.

I could not have completed this book without the help of my daughter, Judy, who typed the manuscript; I want to record here my appreciation for her assistance. I also want to thank Linda Triemstra, the project editor, for her careful editing of my manuscript.

My prayer is that the truths in these pages will help us all to take many "giant steps" in our faith and Christian living.

*Warren W. Wiersbe*

# *Prologue*

To study the lives, to meditate the sorrows, to commune with the thoughts, of the great and holy men and women of this rich world, is a sacred discipline, which deserves at least to rank as the forecourt of the temple of true worship, and may train the tastes, ere we pass the very gate of heaven. We forfeit the chief source of dignity and sweetness in life, next to the direct communication with God, if we do not seek converse with the greater minds that have left their vestiges on the world.

James Martineau

---

From Mary W. Tileston, comp., *Daily Strength for Daily Needs* (New York: Grosset and Dunlap, 1928), p. 6.

# Thomas à Kempis

## (1380?–1471)

While learned professors debate whether Thomas à Kempis actually wrote *The Imitation of Christ*, millions of devout souls continue to use this manual of devotion for spiritual profit.

Thomas, a German mystic, was a member of the Brethren of the Common Life. One of his tasks was to serve as a copyist; in fact, he is supposed to have copied the Bible four times. He wrote a great many letters, poems, sermons, and devotional pieces.

*The Imitation of Christ* certainly is one of the most popular devotional books in the world. One authority claims that it has been issued in more than two thousand different editions and printings. It is a book for all Christians (in spite of its strong sacramentalism in some sections) because the writer seeks to glorify Jesus Christ.

Looking unto Jesus the author and
finisher of our faith. . . . (Heb. 12:2)

He that followeth Me, walketh not in darkness, saith the Lord. These are the words of Christ, by which we are admonished how we ought to imitate His life and manners, if we will be truly enlightened, and be delivered from all blindness of heart.

Let therefore our chiefest endeavour be, to meditate upon the life of Jesus Christ.

2. The doctrine of Christ exceedeth all the doctrines of holy men; and he that hath the Spirit, will find therein an hidden manna.

But it falleth out, that many who often hear the Gospel of Christ, are yet but little affected, because they are void of the Spirit of Christ.

But whosoever would fully and feelingly understand the words of Christ, must endeavour to conform his life wholly to the life of Christ.

3. What will it avail thee to dispute profoundly of the Trinity, if thou be void of humility, and art thereby displeasing to the Trinity?

Surely high words do not make a man holy and just; but a virtuous life maketh him dear to God.

I had rather feel compunction, than understand the definition thereof.

If thou didst know the whole Bible by heart, and the sayings of all the philosophers, what would all that profit thee without the love of God and without grace?

Vanity of vanities, and all is vanity, except to love God, and to serve Him only.

This is the highest wisdom, by contempt of the world to tend towards the kingdom of Heaven.

> In the multitude of words there
> wanteth not sin: but he that re-
> fraineth his lips is wise. (Prov. 10:19)

Lay not thy heart open to every one; but treat of thy affairs with the wise, and such as fear God.

Converse not much with young people and strangers.

Flatter not the rich: neither do thou appear willingly before great personages.

Keep company with the humble and plain ones, with the devout and virtuous; and confer with them of those things that may edify. Be not familiar with any woman; but in general commend all good women to God.

Desire to be familiar with God alone and His Angels, and avoid the acquaintance of men.

2. We must have charity towards all, but familiarity with all is not expedient.

Sometimes it falleth out, that a person unknown to us, is much esteemed of, from the good report given him by others; whose presence notwithstanding is not grateful to the eyes of the beholders.

We think sometimes to please others by our company, and we rather distaste them with those bad qualities which they discover in us.

Behold, to obey is better than sacrifice. . . . (I Sam. 15:22)

It is a great matter to live in obedience, to be under a superior, and not to be at our own disposing.

It is much safer to obey, than to govern.

Many live under obedience, rather for necessity than for charity; such are discontented, and do easily repine. Neither can they attain to freedom of mind, unless they willingly and heartily put themselves under obedience for the love of God.

Go whither thou wilt, thou shalt find no rest, but in humble subjection under the government of a superior. The imagination and change of places have deceived many.

2. True it is, that every one willingly doth that which agreeth with his own sense, and is apt to affect those most that are of his own mind;

But if God be amongst us, we must sometimes cease to adhere to our own opinion for the sake of peace.

Who is so wise that he can fully know all things; Be not therefore too confident in thine own opinion; but be willing to hear the judgment of others.

If that which thou thinkest be not amiss, and yet thou

partest with it for God, and followest the opinion of another, it shall be better for thee.

3. I have often heard, that it is safer to hear and take counsel, than to give it.

It may also fall out, that each one's opinion may be good; but to refuse to yield to others when reason or a special cause requireth it, is a sign of pride and stiffness.

> Thou hypocrite, first cast out the
> beam out of thine own eye; and then
> shalt thou see clearly to cast out the
> mote out of thy brother's eye.
> (Matt. 7:5)

Those things that a man cannot amend in himself or in others, he ought to suffer patiently, until God order things otherwise.

Think that perhaps it is better so for thy trial and patience, without which all our good deeds are not much to be esteemed.

Thou oughtest to pray notwithstanding when thou hast such impediments, that God would vouchsafe to help thee, and that thou mayest bear them kindly.

2. If one that is once or twice warned will not give over, contend not with him: but commit all to God, that His will may be fulfilled, and His name honoured in all His servants, who well knoweth how to turn evil into good.

Endeavour to be patient in bearing with the defects and infirmities of others, of what sort soever they be; for that thyself also hast many failings which must be borne with by others.

If thou canst not make thyself such an one as thou wouldest, how canst thou expect to have another in all things to thy liking?

We would willingly have others perfect, and yet we amend not our own faults.

3. We will have others severely corrected, and will not be corrected ourselves.

The large liberty of others displeaseth us; and yet we will not have our own desires denied us.

We will have others kept under by strict laws; but in no sort will ourselves be restrained.

And thus it appeareth, how seldom we weigh our neighbor in the same balance with ourselves.

If all men were perfect, what should we have to suffer of our neighbor for God?

> Moreover it is required in stewards,
> that a man be found faithful.
> (I Cor. 4:2)

Regard not much who is for thee, or against thee, but mind what thou art about, and take care that God may be with thee in every thing thou doest.

Have a good conscience, and God will well defend thee.

For whom God will help, no man's perverseness shall be able to hurt.

If thou canst be silent and suffer, without doubt thou shalt see that the Lord will help thee.

He knoweth the time and manner how to deliver thee, and therefore thou oughtest to resign thyself unto Him.

It belongs to God to help, and to deliver from all confusion.

It is often very profitable, to keep us more humble, that others know and rebuke our faults.

2. When a man humbleth himself for his failings, then he easily pacifieth others, and quickly satisfieth those that are offended with him.

God protecteth the humble and delivereth him; the humble He loveth and comforteth; unto the humble man He inclineth Himself; unto the humble He giveth great grace; and after his humiliation He raiseth him to glory.

15

Unto the humble He revealeth His secrets, and sweetly draweth and inviteth him unto Himself.

The humble person, though he suffer confusion, is yet tolerably well in peace; for that he resteth on God, and not on the world.

Do not think that thou hast made any progress, unless thou esteem thyself inferior to all.

> Forasmuch as this people draw near
> me with their mouth, and with their
> lips do honour me, but have
> removed their heart far from me,
> and their fear toward me is taught
> by the precept of men. (Isa. 29:13)

Let the eternal Truth be above all things pleasing to thee. Let thy own extreme unworthiness be always displeasing to thee.

Fear nothing, blame nothing, flee nothing, so much as thy vices and sins; which ought to be more unpleasing to thee than any losses whatsoever of things earthly.

Some walk not sincerely in My sight, but led by a certain curiosity and pride wish to know My secrets, and to understand the high things of God, neglecting themselves and their own salvation.

These oftentimes, when I resist them, for their pride and curiosity do fall into great temptations and sins.

4. Fear thou the judgments of God, and dread the wrath of the Almighty. Do not however discuss the works of the Most High, but search diligently thine own iniquities, in how great things thou hast offended, and how many good things thou hast neglected.

Some carry their devotion only in books, some in pictures, some in outward signs and figures.

Some have Me in their mouths, but little in their hearts.

Others there are who, being illuminated in their under-

16

standings, and purged in their affection, do always breathe after things eternal, are unwilling to hear of the things of this world, and do serve the necessities of nature with grief; and these perceive what the Spirit of Truth speaketh in them.

For He teacheth them to despise earthly, and to love heavenly things, to neglect the world, and to desire Heaven all the day and night.

For sin, taking occasion by the commandment, deceived me, and by it slew me. (Rom. 7:11)

My son, mark diligently the motions of Nature and of Grace; for in a very contrary and subtle manner do they move, and can hardly be distinguished but by him that is spiritually and inwardly enlightened.

All men indeed desire that which is good, and pretend somewhat good in their words and deeds; and therefore under the show of good, many are deceived.

Nature is crafty, and seduceth many, ensnareth and deceiveth them, and hath always self for her end and object:

But Grace walketh in simplicity, abstaineth from all show of evil, sheltereth not herself under deceits, doeth all things purely for God's sake, in whom also she finally resteth.

2. Nature is reluctant and loth to die, or to be kept down, or to be overcome, or to be in subjection, or readily to be subdued:

But Grace studieth self-mortification, resisteth sensuality, seeketh to be in subjection, longeth to be defeated, hath no wish to use her own liberty; she loves to be kept under discipline, and desires not to rule over any, but always to live, remain, and be under God, and for God's sake is ready humbly to bow down to every ordinance of man.

Nature striveth for her own advantage, and considereth what profit she may reap by another:

Grace considereth not what is profitable and commodious

unto herself, but rather what may be for the good of many.

Nature willingly receiveth honour and reverence:

But Grace faithfully attributeth all honour and glory unto God.

# *John Calvin*
## (1509–1564)

John Calvin was born in France and studied to be a lawyer. In 1534 he was converted and began to associate with the Reformers. Calvin always wanted to be a quiet scholar who served God by his studies, but the Lord had other plans. He was called to Geneva where he sought to establish a true Christian commonwealth. He preached and lectured daily and perfected his expository approach to the Word of God. His many commentaries bear witness to his long hours of prayerful study and meditation.

In 1536 Calvin published the first edition of his *Institutes of the Christian Religion,* a book he kept editing and enlarging until its final edition in 1559. This is perhaps the most influential volume of the Reformation period. Some scholars have called it the most important theological work in the history of the church.

Behold, the LORD's hand is not short-
ened, that it cannot save; neither his
ear heavy, that it cannot hear.
(Isa. 59:1)

It is, therefore, by the benefit of prayer that we reach those riches which are laid up for us with the Heavenly Father. For there is a communion of men with God by which, having entered the heavenly sanctuary, they appeal to him in person concerning his promises in order to experience, where necessity so demands, that what they believed was not vain,

19

although he had promised it in word alone. Therefore we see that to us nothing is promised to be expected from the Lord, which we are not also bidden to ask of him in prayers. So true is it that we dig up by prayer the treasures that were pointed out by the Lord's gospel, and which our faith has gazed upon.

Words fail to explain how necessary prayer is, and in how many ways the exercise of prayer is profitable. Surely, with good reason the Heavenly Father affirms that the only stronghold of safety is in calling upon his name (cf. Joel 2:32). By so doing we invoke the presence both of his providence, through which he watches over and guards our affairs, and of his power, through which he sustains us, weak as we are and well-nigh overcome, and of his goodness, through which he receives us, miserably burdened with sins, unto grace; and, in short, it is by prayer that we call him to reveal himself as wholly present to us. Hence comes an extraordinary peace and repose to our consciences. For having disclosed to the Lord the necessity that was pressing upon us, we even rest fully in the thought that none of our ills is hid from him who, we are convinced, has both the will and the power to take the best care of us.

> LORD, thou hast heard the desire of
> the humble: thou wilt prepare their
> heart, thou wilt cause thine ear to
> hear. (Ps. 10:17)

Now for framing prayer duly and properly, let this be the first rule: that we be disposed in mind and heart as befits those who enter conversation with God. This we shall indeed attain with respect to the mind if it is freed from carnal cares and thoughts by which it can be called or led away from right and pure contemplation of God, and then not only devotes itself completely to prayer but also, in so far as this is possible, is lifted and carried beyond itself. Now I do not here require the mind to be so detached as never to be pricked or gnawed by vexations, since, on the contrary, great anxiety should kindle in us the desire to pray. Thus we see that God's saintly servants give proof of huge torments, not to say vexations, when they speak of uttering their plaintive cry to the Lord from the deep abyss, and from the very jaws of death (cf. Ps. 130:1). But I say that we are to rid ourselves of all alien and outside cares, by which the mind, itself a wanderer, is borne about hither and thither, drawn away from heaven, and pressed down to earth. I mean that it ought to be raised above itself that it may not bring into God's sight anything our blind and stupid reason is wont to devise, nor hold itself within the limits of its own vanity, but rise to a purity worthy of God.

> Let us therefore come boldly unto
> the throne of grace, that we may
> obtain mercy, and find grace to help
> in time of need. (Heb. 4:16)

Since no man is worthy to present himself to God and come into his sight, the Heavenly Father himself, to free us at once from shame and fear, which might well have thrown our hearts into despair, has given us his Son, Jesus Christ our Lord, to be our advocate (I John 2:1) and mediator with him (I Tim. 2:5; cf. Heb. 8:6 and 9:15), by whose guidance we may confidently come to him, and with such an intercessor, trusting nothing we ask in his name will be denied us, as nothing can be denied to him by the Father. And to this must be referred all that we previously taught about faith. For just as the promise commends Christ the Mediator to us, so, unless the hope of obtaining our requests depends upon him, it cuts itself off from the benefit of prayer.

For as soon as God's dread majesty comes to mind, we cannot but tremble and be driven far away by the recognition of our own unworthiness, until Christ comes forward as intermediary, to change the throne of dreadful glory into the throne of grace. As the apostle also teaches how we should dare with all confidence to appear, to receive mercy, and to find grace in timely help (Heb. 4:16). And as a rule has been established to call upon God, and a promise given that those who call upon him shall be heard, so too we are particularly bidden to call upon him in Christ's name; and we have the promise made that we shall obtain what we have asked in his name. "Hitherto," he says, "you have asked nothing in my name; ask and you will receive." (John 16:24). "In that day you will ask in my name" (John 16:26), "and whatever you ask . . . I will do it that the Father may be glorified in the Son" (John 14:13).

> Endeavoring to keep the unity of the
> Spirit in the bond of peace. (Eph. 4:3)

Βut because a small and contemptible number are hidden in a huge multitude and a few grains of wheat are covered by a pile of chaff, we must leave to God alone the knowledge of his church, whose foundation is his secret election. It is not sufficient, indeed, for us to comprehend in mind and thought the multitude of the elect, unless we consider the unity of the church as that into which we are convinced we have been truly engrafted. For no hope of future inheritance remains to us unless we have been united with all other members under Christ, our Head.

The church is called "catholic," or "universal," because there could not be two or three churches unless Christ be torn asunder (cf. I Cor. 1:13)—which cannot happen! But all the elect are so united in Christ (cf. Eph. 1:22–23) that as they are dependent on one Head, they also grow together into one body, being joined and knit together (cf. Eph. 4:16) as are the limbs of a body (Rom. 12:5; I Cor. 10:17; 12:12, 27). They are made truly one since they live together in one faith, hope, and love, and in the same Spirit of God. For they have been called not only into the same inheritance of eternal life but also to participate in one God and Christ (Eph. 5:30). Although the melancholy desolation which confronts us on every side may cry that no remnant of the church is left, let us know that Christ's death is fruitful, and that God miraculously keeps his church as in hiding places. So it was said to Elijah, "I have kept for myself seven thousand men who have not bowed the knee before Baal" (I Kings 19:18).

> . . . the house of God, which is the
> church of the living God, the pillar
> and ground of the truth. (I Tim. 3:15)

We have laid down as distinguishing marks of the church the preaching of the Word and the observance of the sacraments. These can never exist without bringing forth fruit and prospering by God's blessing. I do not say that wherever the Word is preached there will be immediate fruit; but wherever it is received and has a fixed abode, it shows its effectiveness. However it may be, where the preaching of the gospel is reverently heard and the sacraments are not neglected, there for the time being no deceitful or ambiguous form of the church is seen; and no one is permitted to spurn its authority, flout its warnings, resist its counsels, or make light of its chastisements—much less to desert it and break its unity. For the Lord esteems the communion of his church so highly that he counts as a traitor and apostate from Christianity anyone who arrogantly leaves any Christian society, provided it cherishes the true ministry of Word and sacraments. He so esteems the authority of the church that when it is violated he believes his own diminished.

It is of no small importance that it is called "the pillar and ground of the truth" and "the house of God" (I Tim. 3:15, KJV). By these words Paul means that the church is the faithful keeper of God's truth in order that it may not perish in the world. For by its ministry and labor God willed to have the preaching of his Word kept pure and to show himself the

Father of a family, while he feeds us with spiritual food and provides everything that makes for our salvation.

> One Lord, one faith, one baptism,
> One God and Father of all, who is
> above all, and through all, and in
> you all. (Eph. 4:5–6)

The pure ministry of the Word and pure mode of celebrating the sacraments are, as we say, sufficient pledge and guarantee that we may safely embrace as church any society in which both these marks exist. The principle extends to the point that we must not reject it so long as it retains them, even if it otherwise swarms with many faults.

What is more, some fault may creep into the administration of either doctrine or sacraments, but this ought not to estrange us from communion with the church. For not all the articles of true doctrine are of the same sort. Some are so necessary to know that they should be certain and unquestioned by all men as the proper principles of religion. Such are: God is one; Christ is God and the Son of God; our salvation rests in God's mercy; and the like. Among the churches there are other articles of doctrine disputed which still do not break the unity of faith. Suppose that one church believes—short of unbridled contention and opinionated stubbornness—that souls upon leaving bodies fly to heaven; while another, not daring to define the place, is convinced nevertheless that they live to the Lord. What churches would disagree on this one point? Here are the apostle's words: "Let us therefore, as many as are perfect, be of the same mind; and if you be differently minded in anything, God shall reveal this also to you" (Phil. 3:15). Does this not sufficiently indicate that a difference of opinion over these nonessential matters should in no wise be the basis of schism among Christians? First and foremost, we should agree on all points. But since all men are somewhat beclouded with ignorance, either we must leave no church remaining, or we must condone delusion in those matters which can go unknown without harm to the sum of religion and without loss of salvation.

> Brethren, if a man be overtaken in a
> fault, ye which are spiritual, restore
> such an one in the spirit of
> meekness; considering thyself, lest
> thou also be tempted. (Gal. 6:1)

In bearing with imperfections of life we ought to be far more considerate. For here the descent is very slippery and Satan ambushes us with no ordinary devices. For there have always been those who, imbued with a false conviction of their own perfect sanctity, as if they had already become a sort of airy spirits, spurned association with all men in whom they discern any remnant of human nature.

There are others who sin more out of ill-advised zeal for righteousness than out of that insane pride. When they do not see a quality of life corresponding to the doctrine of the gospel among those to whom it is announced, they immediately judge that no church exists in that place. This is a very legitimate complaint, and we give all too much occasion for it in this most miserable age. And our cursed sloth is not to be excused, for the Lord will not allow it to go unpunished, seeing that he has already begun to chastise it with heavy stripes. Woe to us, then, who act with such dissolute and criminal license that weak consciences are wounded because of us! But on their part those of whom we have spoken sin in that they do not know how to restrain their disfavor. For where the Lord requires kindness, they neglect it and give themselves over completely to immoderate severity. Indeed, because they think no church exists where there are not perfect purity and integrity of life, they depart out of hatred of wickedness from the lawful church, while they fancy themselves turning aside from the faction of the wicked.

25

# Thomas Manton
## (1620–1677)

Thomas Manton was a brilliant student at Oxford and was ordained at the age of twenty. In his early ministry, he flaunted his learning by including Greek and Latin quotations in his sermons. That ended when a shabbily-dressed man said to him, "I came hoping to get some good for my soul, but I could understand very little of what you said."

Manton opposed the execution of Charles I, which alienated him from some of the Puritan clergy. He was pastor of a number of churches and preached with grace and power. He spent six months in jail for his convictions, and he served as one of three scribes at the famous Westminster Assembly.

Manton's preaching was typically Puritan—an attempt to explain everything in the text and apply its truths to everything in life.

I pray for them: I pray not for the
world, but for them which thou hast
given me; for they are thine.
(John 17:9)

Oh! it is a sad thing not to have a name in Christ's prayer. There is a great number left out; and if you will know who they are, they are called 'the world.' It presseth us to come out of that state where we are in this danger. Men that are now worldly may be in the roll of God's election, but it is no comfort to them. 'I pray not for the world;' so it is expressed; and as long as thou art worldly, thou canst take no comfort in

Christ's intercession. Certainly this should be an effectual consideration with the people of God, to cause them 'to keep themselves unspotted from the world,' James 1:27. These have the benefit of Christ's prayers. A christian should never be quiet till he be clearly out of that number which is excepted. Christ hath a constant enmity and antipathy against mammon; there must be a separation from the world, and a contempt of earthly things, before we can have an interest in him. The world maketh a sport of these things; but what can be more terrible than to be shut out of Christ's prayers? He curseth those for whom he doth not pray; and that is the reason why men that are besotted with the world do always wax worse and worse.

I am glorified in them. (John 17:10)

Those that mind Christ's glory, he mindeth their salvation. He is interceding for you in heaven when you are glorifying him on earth; he is doing your business in heaven when you are doing his business in the world; he is your advocate, and you are his bailiffs and factors: Matt. 10:32, 'Whosoever shall confess me before men, him will I confess also before my Father which is in heaven.' When you own Christ in the world, and avow his name and truth in the world, you shall lose nothing. When you come to pray, Christ will own you: Father, hear him, this is one of mine. You cannot honor Christ so much as he will honor you. When carnal men come to pray, Christ saith, 'I know them not.' Oh! it is sad to be disowned in the court of heaven, when Christ disclaimeth any interest or intendment in his purchase for us, they are nothing akin to me, are none of mine. When we do all things for by-ends, we disclaim God for a paymaster, and therefore must look for our reward elsewhere.

> . . . but these are in the world, and I
> come to thee. (John 17:11)

We have Christ always for us in heaven; he hath a part of his office to perform there. His absence doth not hinder us from having a right to him, or a spiritual possession of him. He is ours, and he hath his residence in heaven, and hath power to open it to us and give us entrance. His high honor doth not hinder him from the discharge of his office to do us good. He is at God's right hand, and yet 'a minister of the sanctuary.' Christ is not stately: many forget their poor friends when advanced; Christ regardeth his poor church as much as ever. The butler, when he was advanced, forgot Joseph: but he remembereth us; he disdaineth not to look after every poor christian: Heb. 4:15, 'We have not a high priest which cannot be touched with the feeling of our infirmities.' His heart is not changed by his honor, but he is in a greater capacity to do us good.

> For it became him [the
> Father], . . . in bringing many sons
> unto glory, to make the captain of
> their salvation perfect through suf-
> ferings. (Heb. 2:10)

Christ hath had experience of all trials whereinto any of his servants can fall, poverty, forsaking of friends, exile, imprisonment, hunger, nakedness, watching, weariness, pain of body, heaviness of heart, desertion as to sense, wrath and curse of God. Christ hath carried his feeling with him into heaven; he knew what poverty meaneth, what trouble of conscience, what heaviness of spirit meaneth. Christ could not so experimentally pity us, so feelingly pity us, if he were not like us in all things; his heart was entendered by experience, as a man that hath felt the gout and felt the stone. Israel knew the heart of a stranger; Christ knew the heart of a man that is left to the world's frowns and snares. He took a communion of our nature and miseries, as a pawn and pledge that he will pity us and help us.

> The grass withereth, and the flower
> thereof falleth away: But the word
> of the Lord endureth for ever.
> (I Peter 1:24–25)

Be not contented with outward happiness; things are worthy according to their duration. Nature hath such a sense of God's eternity that the more lasting things are, it accounteth them the better. The immortal soul must have an eternal good. Now all things in the world are frail and passing away, therefore they are called 'uncertain riches,' I Tim. 6:17, compared with Prov. 8:18, 'Riches and honour are with me; yea, durable riches and righteousness.' The flower of these things perisheth, their grace passeth away; in the midst of their pride and beauty, like Herod in his royalty, they vanish and are blasted. The better part is not taken away: Luke 10:42, 'Mary hath chosen the better part, which cannot be taken away from her.' A man may outlive his happiness, be stripped of the flower of all. Worldly glory is sure to end with life, that is transitory; and still they are uncertain riches, uncertain whether we shall get them, uncertain whether we shall keep them. By a care of the better part, we may have these things with a blessing: Matt. 6:33, 'Seek ye first the kingdom of God, and the righteousness thereof, and all these things shall be added to you.'

> I in them, and thou in me, that they
> may be made perfect in one; and
> that the world may know that thou
> hast sent me, and hast loved them,
> as thou hast loved me. (John 17:23)

He loveth us because he loved Christ. Therefore it is said: Eph. 1:6, 'He hath made us accepted in the beloved.' The elect are made lovely, and fit to be accepted by God, only by Jesus Christ; accepted both in our state and actions as we are reconciled to him; and all that we do is taken in good part for Christ's sake, who was sent and intrusted by the Father to procure this favour for us, and did all which was necessary to obtain it. The ground of all that love God beareth to us is for Christ's sake. There is indeed an antecedent love showed in giving us to Christ, and Christ to us: John 3:16, 'For God so loved the world, that he gave his only-begotten Son—That whosoever believeth in him should not perish, but have everlasting life.' The first cause of Christ's love to us was obedience to the Father; the Son loved us, because the Father required it; though afterwards God loved us because Christ merited it. All consequent benefits are procured by the merit of Christ.

> That they all may be one; as thou,
> Father, art in me, and I in thee, that
> they also may be one in us: that the
> world may believe that thou hast
> sent me. (John 17:21)

Though it be secret and mystical, yet it [our union with Christ] is real; because a thing is spiritual, it doth not cease to be real. These are not words, or poor empty notions only, that we are united to Christ; but they imply a real truth. Why should the Holy Ghost use so many terms; of being planted into Christ? Rom. 6:5, 'For if we have been planted together in the likeness of his death, we shall be also in the likeness of his resurrection;' of being joined to Christ? I Cor. 6:17, 'He that is joined to the Lord is one Spirit;' of being made partakers of Christ? Heb. 3:14, 'For we are made partakers of Christ, if we hold the beginning of our confidence steadfast to the end.' Do these terms only imply a relation between us and Christ? No; then the emphasis of the words is lost. What great mystery in all this. Why is this mystery so often spoken of? Christ is not only ours, but 'he is in us, and we in him.' God is ours, and we dwell in God: I John 4:13, 'Hereby know we that we dwell in him, and he in us, because he hath given us of his Spirit;' and ver. 15, 'Whosoever shall confess that Jesus is the Son of God, God dwelleth in him, and he in God.' It is represented by similitudes, that imply a real union as well as a relative, by head and members, root and branches, as well as by marriage, where man and wife are made one flesh. It is compared here with the mystery of the Trinity, and the unity of the divine persons. It is not a notion of scripture, but a thing wrought by the Spirit.

# *John Bunyan*
## (1628–1688)

Everybody who has any contact with religious books knows that John Bunyan wrote *The Pilgrim's Progress,* which, next to the Bible, is the most widely-distributed religious book in the world. When you visit the Bunyan Museum in Elstow, you see the display of editions in languages perhaps you had never heard of.

Bunyan's complete works are found in three large volumes. This is incredible when you consider that Bunyan had no formal schooling, and his basic library was a Bible and a concordance, along with *Foxe's Book of Martyrs.* He was a Puritan and a courageous man who would rather go to prison than compromise his faith. It was during his nearly twelve years in Bedford jail that he conceived and wrote *The Pilgrim's Progress.*

Bunyan was born into a poor family, and when he married, he was even poorer. A tinker by trade, he came to Christ through the witness of some godly women and the ministry of the local minister, John Gifford. Wherever Bunyan preached, huge crowds gathered to listen. He published at least sixty books, some of which are classics.

And the publican . . . smote upon his
breast, saying, God be merciful to
me a sinner. (Luke 18:13)

In this confession, he implicitly acknowledgeth, that sin is the worst of things, forasmuch as it layeth the soul without the reach of all remedy that can be found under heaven.

Nothing below, or short of the mercy of God, can deliver a poor soul from this fearful malady. This the Pharisee did not see. Doubtless he did conclude, that at some time or other he had sinned; but he never in all his life did arrive to a sight of what sin was: His knowledge of it was but false and counterfeit, as is manifest by his cure; to wit, his own righteousness. For take this for a truth undeniable, that he that thinks himself better before God, because of his reformations, never yet had the true knowledge of his sin: But the poor Publican he had it, he had it in truth, as is manifest, because it drives him to the only sovereign remedy. For indeed, the right knowledge of sin, in the guilt and filth, and damning power thereof, makes a man to understand, that not any thing but grace and mercy by Christ, can secure him from the hellish ruins thereof.

> Now unto him that is able to do
> exceeding abundantly above all that
> we ask or think, according to the
> power that worketh in us. (Eph. 3:20)

It is a text made up of words *picked* and *packed* together by the wisdom of God, *picked* and *packed* together on purpose for the succour and relief of the tempted, that they may when in the midst of their distresses, cast themselves upon the Lord their God. He can do abundantly more than we *ask*. Oh! says the soul, that he would but do *so* much for me as I could *ask* him to do! How happy a man should I then be. Why, what wouldest thou *ask* for, sinner? you may be sure, says the soul, I would ask to *be saved* from my sins; I would ask for *faith* in, and *love* to, Christ; I would ask to be preserved in this evil world, and ask to be glorified with Christ in heaven. He that *asketh* for all this, doth indeed *ask* for much, and for more than Satan would have him believe that God is able or willing to bestow upon him; but mark, the text doth not say, that God is able to do *all* that we can *ask or think*, but that he is able to do *above* all, yea, *abundantly* above all, yea, *exceeding* abundantly above all that we ask or think. What a text is this! What a God have we! God foresaw the sins of his people, and what work the devil would make with their hearts about them, and therefore to prevent their ruin by his temptation, he has thus largely, as you see, expressed his love by his word. Let us therefore, as has been bidden us, make this good use of this doctrine of grace, as to cast ourselves upon this love of God in the times of distress and temptation.

> And God said, Let there be light.
> (Gen. 1:3)

This is the first thing with which God began the order of the creation; to wit, light, 'Let there be light:' From which many profitable notes may be gathered, as to the order of God in the salvation of the soul. As,

. . . When the Holy Ghost worketh upon us, and in us, in order to a new creation; he first toucheth our understanding, that great peace of the heart, with his spiritual illumination: Mat. 4:16. His first word, in order to our conversion, is, Let there be light: light, to see their state by nature; light to see the fruits and effects of sin; light, to see the truth and worth of the merits of Jesus Christ; light to see the truth and faithfulness of God, in keeping promise and covenant with them that embrace salvation upon the blessed terms of the gospel of peace. He. 10:32. Now that this word, Let there be light, was a semblance of the first work of the Holy Ghost upon the heart, compare it with that of Paul to the Corinthians; 'For God, who commanded the light to shine out of darkness,' that is, at the beginning of the world, 'hath shined in our hearts to *give* the light of the knowledge of the glory of God in the face of Jesus Christ.' 2 Co. 4:6.

Let every one that nameth the name
of Christ depart from iniquity.
(II Tim. 2:19)

And, indeed, if a man will depart from iniquity, he must
depart from his darling sin first; for as long as that is enter-
tained, the others, at least those that are most suiting with that
darling, will always be haunting of him. There is a man that
has such and such haunt his house, and spend his substance,
and would be rid of them, but cannot; but now, let him rid
himself of that, for the sake of which they haunt his house,
and then he shall with ease be rid of them. Thus it is with sin.
There is a man that is plagued with many sins, perhaps
because he embraceth one: well, let him turn that one out of
doors, and that is the way to be rid of the rest. Keep thee from
thy darling, thy bosom, thy constitution-sin.

Thou hast enlarged my steps under
me; so that my feet did not slip.
(II Sam. 22:37)

I have often thought that the best Christians are found in the
worst of times: and I have thought again, that one reason why
we are no better, is because God purges us no more. I know
these things are against the grain of the flesh, but they are not
against the graces of the Spirit. Noah and Lot, who so holy as
they, in the day of their affliction? Noah and Lot, who so idle
as they in the day of their prosperity? I might have put in
David too, who, while he was afflicted, had ways of serving
God that were special; but when he was more enlarged, he
had ways that were not so good. Wherefore the first ways of
David are the ways that God has commended: but the rest of
his ways, such as had not pre-eminence. 2 Ch. 17:3.

We have need of all, and of more than all that has yet
befallen us: and are to thank God, since his word and patience
have done no more good to us, that he hath appointed men to

make us better. Wherefore for a conclusion, as we are to receive with meekness the engrafted word of God, so also we are with patience to bear what God, by man, shall lay upon us.

> But and if ye suffer for righteous-
> ness' sake, happy are ye: and be not
> afraid of their terror, neither be
> troubled. (I Peter 3:14)

Dost thou suffer for righteousness' sake? why then, thy righteousness is not diminished, but rather increased by thy sufferings. Righteousness thriveth best in affliction, the more afflicted, the more holy man; the more persecuted, the more shining man. Ac. 6:15. The prison is the furnace, thy graces are the silver and the gold; wherefore, as the silver and the gold are refined by the fire, and so made more to show their native brightness, so the Christian that hath, and that loveth right- eousness, and that suffereth for its sake, is by his sufferings refined and made more righteous, and made more christian, more godly. Zec. 13:9. Some, indeed, when they come there, prove lead, iron, tin, and at the best, but the dross of silver; and so are fit for nothing, but there to be left and consumed, and to bear the badge, if ever they come from thence, of repro- bate silver from the mouth and sentence of their neighbours.

> For whom the Lord loveth he
> chasteneth. . . . (Heb. 12:6)

To believe he loves us when he shows himself terrible to us, is also very much becoming of us. Wherefore has he given us grace? Is it that we should live by sense? Wherefore has he sometimes visited us? Is it that our hearts might be estranged from him, and that we still should love the world? And I say

36

again, wherefore has he so plainly told us of his greatness, and of what he can do? Is it not that we might be still when the world is disturbed; and that we might hope for good things to come out of such providences that, to sense, look as if themselves would eat up and devour all?

Let us wait upon God, walk with God, believe in God, and commit ourselves, our soul, our body, to God, to be kept. Yea, let us be content to be at the disposal of God, and rejoice to see him act according to all his wondrous works. For this is a posture highly becoming them that say of God he is their Father, and that have committed the keeping of their souls to him as unto a Creator. A comely thing it is for the soul that feareth God, to love and reverence him in all his appearances. We should be like the spaniel dog, even lie at the foot of our God, as he at the foot of his master; yea, and should be glad, could we but see his face, though he treads us down with his feet.

# *François Fénelon*
## (1651–1715)

François Fénelon was a French Roman Catholic leader, and his writings come very close to evangelical mysticism. He was a friend of Madame Guyon, tutor to Louis XIV's grandson, and a defender of the infallibility of the church.

Yet Fénelon's *Spiritual Letters* has been a source of encouragement and enlightenment to saints for centuries. Fénelon was a "spiritual director" in the church, and many people conferred with him about the practical problems of Christian living. We face these same problems today and Fénelon's counsel is just as helpful.

He that is faithful in that which is
least is faithful also in much. . . .
(Luke 16:10)

But the most dangerous thing is that the soul, by the neglect of little things, becomes accustomed to unfaithfulness. It saddens the Holy Spirit; it yields to its own impulses; it makes nothing of failing God. On the contrary, true love sees nothing as little. Everything which can please or displease God always seems great to it. It is not that true love throws the soul into fussing and scruples, but it does place no limits to its fidelity. It acts simply with God, and as it is quite untroubled by the things which God does not ask of it, it also never wants to hesitate a single instant in that which God does ask of it. Thus, it is not by fussiness that we become faithful and exact in the smallest things. It is by a feeling of love, which is free from the reflections and fears of the anxious and scrupulous. We are as though carried away by the love of God. We only want to do what we are doing, and we do not want to do anything at all which we are not doing. At the same time that God, jealous, urges the soul, presses it relentlessly in the least details, and seems to withdraw all liberty from it, it finds itself free, and it enjoys a profound peace in him. O, how happy it is!

And to know the love of Christ,
which passeth knowledge. . . .
(Eph. 3:19)

But what blindness to fear to advance too far in the love of God! Let us plunge into it. The more we love him, the more we love also all that which he makes us do. It is this love which consoles us in our losses, which softens our crosses for us, which detaches us from all which it is dangerous to love, which preserves us from a thousand poisons, which shows us a benevolent compassion through all the ills which we suffer, which even in death opens for us an eternal glory and happiness. It is this love which changes all our evils to good. How can we fear to fill ourselves too full of it? Are we afraid of being too happy, too freed from ourselves, from the whims of our pride, from the violence of our passions, and from the tyranny of a deceitful world? Why do we delay to throw ourselves with full confidence into the arms of the Father of Mercies and the God of all consolation? He will love us. We shall love him. His love growing will take the place for us of all the rest. He alone will fill our heart, which the world has intoxicated, agitated, distressed, without being ever able to fill it. He will make us only feel contempt for the world which we already feel contempt for. He will take away from us that which makes us unhappy. He will make us do what we are doing every day, simple and reasonable things which we are doing badly, because we are not doing them for him. He will make us do them well, by inspiring us to do them to obey him. All, even the least activities of a simple and ordinary life, will be turned to satisfaction, to merit and to reward. We shall see in peace the approach of death. It will be changed for us into the beginning of life immortal.

> . . . he that loveth me shall be loved
> of my Father, and I will love him,
> and will manifest myself to him.
> (John 14:21)

Pure love is only in singleness of will. Thus it is not a love of sentiment, because imagination has no part in it. It is a love which loves without feeling, as pure faith believes without seeing. We need not fear that this love may be imaginary, because nothing is less so than the will detached from all imagination. The more the action is purely intellectual and spiritual, the more it is not only reality, but the very perfection for which God asks. Thus the activity in it is the more perfect. At the same time faith exists there, and humility protects it. So the love is chaste because it is God in himself and for himself. It is no longer that he makes us feel to what we are attached. We follow him but not for the many loaves. "What!" we will say, "Does all piety consist only in a will to unite self with God, which may be rather a thought and an imagining than an effective willing?" If this will is not sustained by faithfulness in important things, I believe that it is not true. For the good tree carries good fruit, and this will ought to make us careful to accomplish the will of God. But it is compatible in this life with small weaknesses which God leaves in the soul to humiliate it. If then we only experience these daily weaknesses, we must pick the fruit of humiliation, without losing courage.

> . . . but they measuring themselves
> by themselves, and comparing
> themselves among themselves, are
> not wise. (II Cor. 10:12)

There is an interior idolatry in every moment of life. This idolatry, though covered with the lustre of virtues, is more horrible than many other sins which we think more outrageous. There is only one truth, and only one way to judge it as God himself. Before God, monstrous crimes, committed by weakness, by passion or by ignorance, are less crimes than are the virtues which a soul full of itself practises in order to relate everything to its own excellence, as though it alone were divine. For that is the total reversal of God's whole design for creation. Let us cease then to judge virtues and vices by our own taste, which self-love has made depraved, and by our false standards of greatness. There is no one great except he who makes himself very small before the unique and supreme greatness. You become great by the turning of your heart, and by your habit of turning it. But God wants to abase you and to make you small in his hand. Let him do this.

> For I know that in me (that is, in my
> flesh) dwelleth no good thing.
> (Rom. 7:18)

Do not hope to perform the work of grace with the resources and efforts of nature. Content yourself to giving your will to God without reserve, and never envisage any painful state which you do not accept by yielding to divine Providence. Be careful never to go further than this in your thoughts of the cross; but when God permits them to come to you without your seeking them, never let them go by without result.

Accept, despite the revulsion and horror of nature, all that God presents to your mind, as a proof by which he wants to train your faith. Do not trouble yourself to know if you will have, when the time comes, the strength to carry out what you want to do from a distance. The present opportunity will have its grace, but the grace of the moment in which you visualize these crosses is to accept them with a good heart when God gives them to you. Having laid the foundation of abandonment, go on serenely and with confidence. Provided that this disposition of your will is not changed by voluntary attachments to something against the order of God, it will always last.

> My God, my God, why hast thou
> forsaken me? why art thou so far
> from helping me, and from the
> words of my roaring? (Ps. 22:1)

Often sadness comes because, seeking God, we do not feel his presence enough to satisfy ourselves. To want to feel it is not to want to possess it, but it is to want to assure ourselves, for love of ourselves, that we do possess it, in order to console ourselves. Nature beaten and discouraged is impatient at guiding itself in a state of pure faith. It makes all its efforts to get out of it because there all support is lacking. It is as though up in the air. It would like to feel its advancement. At the sight of its faults, pride is offended, and it takes this hurt pride for a feeling of penitence. We should like, because of love of self, to have the pleasure of seeing ourselves perfect. We scold ourselves for not being so. We are impatient, haughty and in an ill humor against ourselves and against others. Deplorable error! As if the work of God could be accomplished by our chagrin! As if we could unite ourselves to the God of peace by losing the peace within! "Martha, Martha, why art thou troubled about so many things," for the service of Jesus Christ? "One thing only is needful," which is to love him and to keep ourselves motionless at his feet.

When we are really abandoned to God, all that we do we do well, without doing many things. We abandon ourselves with confidence to the future. We want with no reservations all that God wants, and we close our eyes in order not to anticipate the future. Meanwhile we devote ourselves in the present to accomplishing his will. Sufficient to each day is its good and its evil. This daily accomplishment of the will of God is the coming of his kingdom within us, and at the same time our daily bread. We should be unfaithful, and guilty of a pagan distrust, if we wished to penetrate into the future time which God hides from us. We leave it to him. It is for him to make it sweet or bitter, short or long. Let him do what is good in his eyes. The most perfect preparation for this future, whatever it is, is to die to all will of our own, in order to yield ourselves wholly to that of God. As the manna had all flavours, this general disposition encloses all the graces and all the feelings suitable to every state in which God can successively place us.

> Peter answered and said unto him,
> Though all men shall be offended
> because of thee, yet will I never be
> offended. (Matt. 26:33)

O how deceiving this courage of the senses is, which makes everything easy, which does everything and endures everything, which knows itself willing never to hesitate! O, how it feeds our self-confidence and a certain exaltation of heart! This courage, which sometimes edifies the public marvellously, nourishes a certain satisfaction within us, and a witness which we give to ourselves, which is a subtle poison. We get a taste for our own goodness; we are pleased with it; we want to possess it; we are glad to know its strength.

A weak and humble soul, which finds no more resource in itself, which fears, is troubled, is sad unto death, as Jesus Christ was when he was in the garden; which cries at last as he did on the cross, "O God, O my God, why hast thou forsaken me?" is much more purified, underrates itself more, is more annihilated and more dead to all its own desire, than the brave souls which enjoy in peace the fruits of their own virtue.

Happy the soul which God beats down, which God crushes, from which God takes away all force of its own in order no longer to sustain it except in him. One which sees its poverty, which is content with it, which carries, besides the crosses outside, the great inner cross of discouragement, without which all the others would weigh nothing!

# Philip Doddridge
## (1702–1751)

The next time you sing "O Happy Day That Fixed My Choice," note that it was composed by Philip Doddridge. He also wrote "Awake My Soul, Stretch Every Nerve" and "Great God, We Sing That Mighty Hand."

However, Doddridge's life was spent educating young men for the ministry. His academy was at Northampton. He was a great believer in unity among God's people, so he permitted his students to make up their own minds about the controversial doctrines of the faith. Most of his graduates became liberal Presbyterians.

*The Rise and Progress of Religion in the Soul* (written ca. 1745) is Doddridge's most famous work, and it is a spiritual autobiography.

> If we live in the Spirit, let us also
> walk in the Spirit. (Gal. 5:25)

Let me farther lead you into some reflections on "the temper of your heart towards the blessed Spirit." If "we have not the Spirit of Christ, we are none of his." Rom. 8:9. If we are not "led by the Spirit of God, we are not the children of God." Rom. 8:14. You will then, if you are a real Christian, desire that you may "be filled with the Spirit;" (Eph. 5:18.) that you may have every power of your soul subject to his authority; that his agency on your heart may be more constant, more operative, and more delightful. And to cherish these sacred influences, you will often have recourse to serious consideration and meditation: you will abstain from those sins which tend to grieve him; you will improve the tender seasons, in which he seems to breathe upon your soul; you will strive earnestly with God in prayer, that you may have him "shed on you still more abundantly through Jesus Christ;" (Tit. 3:6.) and you will be desirous to fall in with the great end of his mission, which was to "glorify Christ;" (John 16:14.) and to establish his kingdom. "You will desire his influences as the Spirit of adoption," to render your acts of worship free and affectionate, your obedience vigorous, your sorrow for sin overflowing and tender, your resignation meek, and your love ardent: in a word, to carry you through life and death with the temper of a child who delights in his father, and who longs for his more immediate presence.

> Behold, how good and how pleasant
> it is for brethren to dwell together in
> unity! (Ps. 133:1)

If you are a Christian indeed, you will have such a value and esteem for peace, as to endeavour to obtain, and to preserve it, "as much as lieth in you," (Rom. 12:18.) as much as you fairly and honourably can. This will have such an influence upon your conduct, as to make you not only cautious of giving offence, and slow in taking it, but earnestly desirous to regain peace as soon as may be, when it is in any measure broken, that the wound may be healed while it is green, and before it begins to rankle and fester. And more especially, this disposition will engage you "to keep the unity of the Spirit in the bond of peace," (Eph. 4:3.) "with all that in every place call on the name of our Lord Jesus Christ," (1 Cor. 1:2.) whom if you truly love, you will also love all those whom you have reason to believe to be his disciples and servants.

For whom the Lord loveth he
chasteneth. . . . (Heb. 12:6)

Since "man is born unto trouble, as the sparks fly upward,"
(Job, 5:7) and Adam has entailed on all his race the sad
inheritance of calamity in their way to death, it will certainly
be prudent and necessary, that we should all expect to meet
with trials and afflictions; and that you, reader, whoever you
are, should be endeavouring to gird on your armour, and put
yourself in a posture to encounter those trials which will fall
to your lot as a man and a Christian. Prepare yourself to
receive your afflictions, and to endure them, in a manner
agreeable to both these characters. . . .

When at length your turn comes, as it certainly will, from
the first hour in which an affliction seizes you, realize to
yourself the hand of God in it, and lose not the view of him in
any second cause, which may have proved the immediate
occasion. Let it be your first care, to "humble yourself under
the mighty hand of God, that he may exalt you in due time." 1
Pet. 5:6. Own that "he is just in all that is brought upon you,"
(Neh. 9:33.) and that in all these things "he punishes you less
than your iniquities deserve." Ezra, 9:13. Compose yourself to
bear his hand with patience, to glorify his name by a submission to his will, and to fall in with the gracious design of this
visitation, as well as to wait the issue of it quietly, whatsoever
the event may be.

My brethren, count it all joy when
ye fall into divers temptations.
(James 1:2)

God himself has said, "In every thing give thanks," (1 Thess.
5:18.) and he has taught his servants to say, "Yea, also we glory
in tribulation." Rom. 5:3. And most certain it is, that to true
believers afflictions are tokens of divine mercy; for "whom
the Lord loveth he chasteneth, and scourgeth every son

whom he receiveth," with peculiar and distinguishing en-
dearment. Heb. 12:6. View your present afflictions in this light,
as chastisements of love; and then let your own heart say,
whether love does not demand praise. Think with yourself, "It
is thus that God is making me comfortable to his own Son; it is
thus that he is training me up for complete glory. Thus he kills
my corruptions; thus he strengthens my graces; thus he is
wisely contriving to bring me nearer to himself, and to ripen
me for the honours of his heavenly kingdom. It is, if need be,
that 'I am in heaviness,' (1 Pet. 1:6.) and he surely knows what
that need is better than I can pretend to teach him, and knows
what peculiar propriety there is in this affliction to answer my
present necessity and to do me that peculiar good which he is
graciously intending me by it. This tribulation shall 'work
patience, and patience experience, and experience' a more
assured 'hope,' even a hope which 'shall not make ashamed,'
while 'the love of God is shed abroad in my heart,' (Rom.
5:3–5.) and shines through my affliction, like the sun through
a gentle descending cloud, darting in light upon the shade,
and mingling fruitfulness with weeping."

> Trust in him at all times; ye people,
> pour out your heart before him:
> God is a refuge for us. (Ps. 62:8)

Take some time for recollection, and ask your own conscience, seriously, how matters stand between the blessed
God and your soul? Whether they are as they once were, and
as you could wish them to be, if you saw your life just drawing
to a period, and were to pass immediately into the eternal
state? One serious thought of eternity shames a thousand
vain excuses, with which, in the forgetfulness of it, we are
ready to delude our own souls. And when you feel that secret
misgiving of heart, which will naturally arise on this occasion,
do not endeavour to palliate the matter, and to find out slight
and artful coverings, for what you cannot forbear secretly

condemning, but honestly fall under the conviction, and be humbled for it. Pour out your heart before God, and seek the renewed influences of his Spirit and grace. Return with more exactness to secret devotion, and to self-examination. Read the Scripture with yet greater diligence, and especially the more devotional and spiritual parts of it. Labor to ground it in your heart, and to feel what you have reason to believe the sacred penmen felt when they wrote, so far as circumstances may agree. Open your soul, with all simplicity, to every lesson which the word of God would teach you; and guard against those things which you perceive to alienate your mind from inward religion, though there be nothing criminal in the things themselves. They may perhaps in the general be lawful; to some possibly they may be expedient; but if they produce such an effect as was mentioned above, it is certain they are not convenient for you.

Be not overcome of evil, but
overcome evil with good.
(Rom. 12:21)

**R**eflect farther, "How can you bear injuries?" There is a certain hardness of soul in this respect, which argues a confirmed state in piety and virtue. Does every thing of this kind hurry and ruffle you, so as to put you on contrivances how you may recompense, or, at least, how you may disgrace and expose him who has done you the wrong? Or can you stand the shock calmly, and easily divert your mind to other objects, only (when you recollect these things) pitying and praying for those who with the worst tempers and views are assaulting you? This is a Christ-like temper, indeed, and he will own it as such; will own you as one of his soldiers, as one of his heroes; especially if it rises so far, as, instead of being "overcome of evil, to overcome evil with good." Rom. 12:21. Watch over your spirit and over your tongue, when injuries are offered, and see whether you be ready to meditate upon them to aggravate them in your own view, to complain of them to others, and to lay on all the load of blame that you in justice can; or, whether you be ready to put the kindest construction upon the offence, to excuse it as far as reason will allow, and (where, after all, it will wear a black and odious aspect) to forgive it, heartily to forgive it, and that even before any submission is made, or pardon asked; and in token of the sincerity of that forgiveness, to be contriving what can be done, by some benefit or other toward the injurious person, to teach him a better temper.

> For who maketh thee to differ from
> another? and what hast thou that
> thou didst not receive? (I Cor. 4:7)

Again, has God been pleased to raise you to esteem among your fellow-creatures, which is not always in proportion to a man's rank or possession in human life? Are your counsels heard with attention? Is your company sought? Does God give you good acceptance in the eyes of men, so that they do not only put the fairest constructions on your words, but overlook faults of which you are conscious to yourself, and consider your actions and performances in the most indulgent and favourable light? You ought to regard this, not only as a favour of Providence, and as an encouragement to you cheerfully to pursue your duty, in the several branches of it, for the time to come, but also, as giving you much greater opportunities of usefulness than in your present station you could otherwise have had. If your character has any weight in the world, throw it into the right scale. Endeavour to keep virtue and goodness in countenance. Affectionately give your hand to modest worth, where it seems to be depressed or overlooked: though shining, when viewed in its proper light, with a lustre which you may think much superior to your own. Be an advocate for truth; be a counsellor of peace; be an example of candour; and do all you can to reconcile the hearts of men, especially of good men, to each other, however they may differ in their opinions about matters which it is possible for good men to dispute. And let the caution and humility of your behavior, in circumstances of such superior eminence, and amidst so many tokens of general esteem, silently reprove the rashness and haughtiness of those who perhaps are remarkable for little else; or who, if their abilities were indeed considerable, must be despised, and whose talents must be in a great measure lost to the public, till that rashness and haughtiness of spirit be subdued.

# *John Wesley*
## (1703–1791)

John Wesley was born in the manse, the fifteenth child of Samuel and Susanna Wesley. While at Oxford, John and his brother Charles met with other students for times of spiritual fellowship, and the group was nicknamed the "Holy Club." Wesley was ordained an Anglican priest in 1728.

Wesley went to America as part of a missionary ministry to the Indians, but was not sure *he* was converted. The witness of some godly Moravian people on the ship made a great impression on him. Back in London, on May 24, 1738, Wesley went "very unwillingly" to a meeting in Aldersgate Street where Luther's commentary on Romans was being read; and he felt his "heart strangely warmed" as he received assurance of salvation.

The rest is history. God used John and Charles Wesley to bring the gospel to Great Britain and to found the Methodist Church. Historians believe that the Wesleyan revival helped to save England from the great problems that scourged other nations. Certainly Wesley was a forerunner in preaching against social evils.

And Paul said, I would to God, that
not only thou, but also all that hear
me this day, were both almost, and
altogether, such as I am, except
these bonds. (Acts 26:29)

If it be inquired, "What more than this is implied in the being *altogether a Christian?*" I answer, First. The love of God. For thus saith his word, "Thou shalt love the Lord thy God, with all thy heart, and with all thy soul, and with all thy mind, and with all thy strength." Such a love is this, as engrosses the whole heart, as takes up all the affections, as fills the entire capacity of the soul, and employs the utmost extent of all its faculties. He that thus loves the Lord his God, his spirit continually "rejoiceth in God his Saviour." His delight is in the Lord, his Lord and his All, to whom "in everything he gives thanks. All his desire is unto God, and to the remembrance of his name." His heart is ever crying out, "Whom have I in heaven but thee? and there is none upon earth that I desire beside thee."

> . . . the devils also believe, and
> tremble. (James 2:19)

For neither does religion consist in orthodoxy, or right opinions; which, . . . are not in the heart, but the understanding. A man may be orthodox in every point; he may not only espouse right opinions, but zealously defend them against all opposers; he may think justly concerning the incarnation of our Lord, concerning the ever-blessed Trinity, and every other doctrine contained in the oracles of God; he may assent to all the three creeds,—that called the Apostles', the Nicene, and the Athanasian; and yet it is possible he may have no religion at all. . . . He may be almost as orthodox—as the devil . . . and may, all the while, be as great a stranger as he to the religion of the heart.

> For the kingdom of God is not meat
> and drink; but righteousness, and
> peace, and joy in the Holy Ghost.
> (Rom. 14:17)

This holiness and happiness, joined in one, are sometimes styled, in the inspired writings, "the kingdom of God". . . . It is termed "the kingdom of God" because it is the immediate fruit of God's reigning in the soul. So soon as ever he takes unto himself his mighty power, and sets up his throne in our hearts, they are instantly filled with this "righteousness, and peace, and joy in the Holy Ghost." It is called "the kingdom of heaven" because it is (in a degree) heaven opened in the soul. For whosoever they are that experience this, they can aver before angels and men,

> Everlasting life is won,
> Glory is on earth begun[.]

> How can ye believe, which receive
> honour one of another, and seek not
> the honour that cometh from God
> only? (John 5:44)

A sure effect of our having formed this right judgment of the sinfulness and helplessness of our nature, is a disregard of that "honour which cometh of man," which is usually paid to some supposed excellency in us. He who knows himself, neither desires nor values the applause which he knows he deserves not. It is therefore a "very small thing with him, to be judged by man's judgment." He has all reasons to think, by comparing what it has said, either for or against him, with what he feels in his own breast, that the world, as well as the god of this world, was "a liar from the beginning." And even as to those who are not of the world; though he would choose, if it were the will of God, that they should account of him as one desirous to be found a faithful steward of his Lord's goods, if haply this might be a means of enabling him to be of more use to his fellow-servants, yet as this is the one end of his wishing for their approbation, so he does not at all rest upon it: For he is assured, that whatever God wills, he can never want instruments to perform; since he is able, even of these stones, to raise up servants to do his pleasure.

> But every man is tempted, when he is drawn away of his own lust, and enticed. (James 1:14)

Does a child of God first commit sin, and thereby lose his faith? Or does he lose his faith first, before he can commit sin?

I answer, Some sin of omission, at least, must necessarily precede the loss of faith; some inward sin: But the loss of faith must precede the committing outward sin.

The more any believer examines his own heart, the more will he be convinced of this: That faith working by love excludes both inward and outward sin from a soul watching unto prayer; that nevertheless we are even then liable to temptation, particularly to the sin that did easily beset us; that if the loving eye of the soul be steadily fixed on God, the temptation soon vanishes away: But if not, if we are ... *drawn out* of God by our *own desire*, and ... *caught by the bait* of present or promised pleasures; then that desire, conceived in us, brings forth sin; and, having by that inward sin destroyed our faith, it casts us headlong into the snare of the devil, so that we may commit any outward sin whatever.

No man can serve two masters. . . .
Ye cannot serve God and mammon.
(Matt. 6:24)

What he here condemns is, the care of the heart; the anxious, uneasy care; the care that hath torment; all such care as does hurt, either to the soul or body. What he forbids is, that care which, sad experience shows, wastes the blood and drinks up the spirits; which anticipates all the misery it fears, and comes to torment us before the time. He forbids only that care which poisons the blessings of to-day, by fear of what may be to-morrow; which cannot enjoy the present plenty, through apprehensions of future want. This care is not only a sore disease, a grievous sickness of soul, but also a heinous offence against God, a sin of the deepest dye. It is a high affront to the gracious Governor and wise Disposer of all things; necessarily implying, that the great Judge does not do right; that he does not order all things well. It plainly implies that he is wanting, either in wisdom, if he does not know what things we stand in need of; or in goodness, if he does not provide those things for all who put their trust in him. . . . With a single eye to God, do all that in you lies to provide things honest in the sight of all men: And then give up all into better hands; leave the whole event to God.

And John answered him, saying,
Master, we saw one casting out
devils in thy name, and he followeth
not us: and we forbad him, because
he followeth not us. But Jesus said,
Forbid him not. . . . (Mark 9:38–39)

He who differs from us in judgment or practice, may possibly stand at a greater distance from us in affection than in judgment. And this indeed is a very natural and a very common effect of the other. The differences which begin in points of opinion, seldom terminate there. They gradually spread into the affections, and then separate chief friends. Nor are any animosities so deep and irreconcilable as those that spring from disagreement in religion. For this cause the bitterest enemies of a man are those of his own household. For this the father rises against his own children, and the children against the father; and perhaps persecute each other even to the death, thinking all the time they are doing God service. It is therefore nothing more than we may expect, if those who differ from us, either in religious opinions or practice, soon contract a sharpness, yea, a bitterness towards us; if they are more and more prejudiced against us, till they conceive as ill an opinion of our persons as of our principles. An almost necessary consequence of this will be, they will speak in the same manner as they think of us. They will set themselves in opposition to us, and, as far as they are able, hinder our work; seeing it does not appear to them to be the work of God, but either of man or of the devil. He that thinks, speaks, and acts in such a manner as this, in the highest sense, "followeth not us."

# David Brainerd

## (1718–1747)

The Life and Diary of David Brainerd is a devotional classic that has influenced many lives, particularly those of pastors and missionaries. For example, godly Robert Murray McCheyne was challenged by Brainerd's devotion to Christ.

Brainerd was expelled from Yale, but he continued his theological studies and was licensed to preach. In spite of multiplied hardships and physical weakness, he traveled thousands of miles on horseback to minister to the Indians. God did a remarkable work through him.

The great preacher and theologian Jonathan Edwards was his friend and would have become his father-in-law but for Brainerd's untimely death. Edwards edited Brainerd's journal and it was later included in Edwards's *Complete Works.*

Why art thou cast down, O my soul?
and why art thou disquieted in me?
hope thou in God: for I shall yet
praise him for the help of his countenance. (Ps. 42:5)

Monday, April 12. This morning the Lord was pleased to lift up the light of His countenance upon me in secret prayer, and made the season very precious to my soul. Though I have been so depressed of late, respecting my hopes of future serviceableness in the cause of God, yet now I had much encouragement respecting that matter. I was especially assisted to intercede and plead for poor souls and for the enlargement of Christ's kingdom in the world, and for special grace for myself to fit me for special services. I felt exceedingly calm and quite resigned to God, respecting my future employment, when and where He pleased. My faith lifted me above the world and removed all those mountains that I could not look over of late.

I wanted not the favor of man to lean upon; for I knew Christ's favor was infinitely better, and that it was no matter when, nor where, nor how Christ should send me, nor what trials He should still exercise me with, if I might be prepared for His work and will. I now found revived, in my mind, the wonderful discovery of infinite wisdom in all the dispensations of God towards me, which I had a little before I met with my great trial at college; everything appeared full of divine wisdom.

They go from strength to strength,
every one of them in Zion appeareth
before God. (Ps. 84:7)

Lord's Day, April 25. This morning I spent about two hours in secret duties and was enabled more than ordinarily to agonize for immortal souls. Though it was early in the morning and the sun scarcely shined at all, yet my body was quite wet with sweat. I felt much pressed now, as frequently of late, to plead for the meekness and calmness of the Lamb of God in my soul; and through divine goodness felt much of it this morning. Oh, it is a sweet disposition heartily to forgive all injuries done us; to wish our greatest enemies as well as we do our own souls! Blessed Jesus, may I daily be more and more conformed to Thee.

At night I was exceedingly melted with divine love and had some feeling sense of the blessedness of the upper world. Those words hung upon me with much divine sweetness, Psalm 84:7: "They go from strength to strength, every one of them in Zion appeareth before God." Oh, the near access that God sometimes gives us in our addresses to Him! This may well be termed appearing before God: it is so indeed, in the true spiritual sense, and in the sweetest sense. I think I have not had such power of intercession these many months, both for God's children and for dead sinners as I have had this evening. I wished and longed for the coming of my dear Lord: I longed to join the angelic hosts in praises, wholly free from imperfection. Oh, the blessed moment hastens! All I want is to be more holy, more like my dear Lord. Oh, for sanctification! My very soul pants for the complete restoration of the blessed image of my Saviour, that I may be fit for the blessed enjoyments and employments of the heavenly world.

> Wherefore I abhor myself, and
> repent in dust and ashes. (Job 42:6)

Tuesday, October 26. (At West Suffield) Underwent the most dreadful distresses, under a sense of my own unworthiness. It seemed to me I deserved rather to be driven out of the place than to have anybody treat me with any kindness, or come to hear me preach. Verily my spirits were so depressed at this time (as at many others) that it was impossible I should treat immortal souls with faithfulness. I could not deal closely and faithfully with them, I felt so infinitely vile in myself. Oh, what dust and ashes I am, to think of preaching the gospel to others! Indeed I never can be faithful for one moment, but shall certainly "daub with untempered mortar" if God do not grant me special help. In the evening I went to the meeting-house, and it looked to me near as easy for one to rise out of the grave and preach, as for me. However, God afforded me some life and power, both in prayer and sermon, and was pleased to lift me up and show me that He could enable me to preach! Oh, the wonderful goodness of God to so vile a sinner! Returned to my quarters and enjoyed some sweetness in prayer alone, and mourned that I could not live more to God.

... and we beheld his glory ... full
of grace and truth. (John 1:14)

Monday, March 7. This morning when I arose, I found my heart go forth after God in longing desires of conformity to Him, and in secret prayer found myself sweetly quickened and drawn out in praises to God for all He had done to and for me, and for all my inward trials and distresses of late. My heart ascribed glory, glory, glory to the blessed God! and bid welcome to all inward distress again, if God saw meet to exercise me with it. Time appeared but an inch long, and eternity at hand. I thought I could with patience and cheerfulness bear anything for the cause of God; for I saw that a moment would bring me to a world of peace and blessedness. My soul, by the strength of the Lord, rose far above this lower world, and all the vain amusements and frightful disappointments of it. Afterwards, had some sweet meditation on Genesis 5:24, "And Enoch walked with God." This was a comfortable day to my soul.

Blessed are they that keep his testimonies, and that seek him with the whole heart. (Ps. 119:2)

Thursday, August 4. Was enabled to pray much, through the whole day; and through divine goodness found some intenseness of soul in the duty, as I used to do, and some ability to persevere in my supplications. I had some apprehensions of divine things that were engaging and which afforded me some courage and resolution. It is good, I find, to persevere in attempts to pray if I cannot pray with perseverence, that is, continue long in my addresses to the Divine Being. I have generally found that the more I do in secret prayer the more I have delighted to do, and have enjoyed more of a spirit of prayer; and frequently have found the contrary, when with journeying or otherwise I have been much deprived of retirement. A seasonable, steady performance of secret duties in their proper hours, and a careful improvement of all time, filling up every hour with some profitable labor, either of heart, head, or hands, are excellent means of spiritual peace and boldness of access to God. But a good conscience void of offense is an excellent preparation for an approach into the divine presence.

There is a difference between self-confidence or a self-righteous pleasing of ourselves—as with our own duties, attainments, and spiritual enjoyments—which godly souls sometimes are guilty of, and that holy confidence arising from the testimony of a good conscience which good Hezekiah had when he says, "Remember, O Lord, I beseech thee, how I have walked before thee in truth, and with a perfect heart." Then, says the holy Psalmist, "shall I not be ashamed when I have respect to all thy commandments." Filling up our time with and for God is the way to rise up and lie down in peace.

> . . . I will sing unto the LORD, for he
> hath triumphed gloriously. . . .
> (Exod. 15:1)

Thursday, November 3. Spent this day in secret fasting and prayer, from morning till night. Early in the morning, I had some small degree of assistance in prayer. Afterwards, read the story of Elijah the prophet, I Kings 17, 18, and 19, and also II Kings 2 and 4. My soul was much moved observing the faith, zeal, and power of that holy man and how he wrestled with God in prayer. My soul then cried with Elisha, "Where is the Lord God of Elijah!" Oh, I longed for more faith! My soul breathed after God and pleaded with Him that a "double portion of that spirit," which was given to Elijah, might "rest on me."

That which was divinely refreshing and strengthening to my soul was that I saw that God is the same as He was in the days of Elijah. Was enabled to wrestle with God by prayer in a more affectionate, fervent, humble, intense, and importunate manner than I have for many months past. Nothing seemed too hard for God to perform; nothing too great for me to hope for from Him.

I had for many months entirely lost all hopes of being made instrumental of doing any special service for God in the world. It has appeared entirely impossible that one so black and vile should be thus employed for God. But at this time God was pleased to revive this hope.

Afterwards read the third chapter of Exodus and on to the twentieth, and saw more of the glory and majesty of God discovered in those chapters than ever I had seen before. Frequently in the meantime I fell on my knees and cried to God for the faith of Moses and for a manifestation of the divine glory. Especially the third and fourth, and part of the fourteenth and fifteenth chapters, were unspeakably sweet to my soul. My soul blessed God that He had shown Himself so gracious to His servants of old. The fifteenth chapter seemed to be the very language which my soul uttered to God in the season of my first spiritual comfort, when I had just got through the Red Sea, by a way that I had no expectation of.

Oh, how my soul then rejoiced in God! And now those things came fresh and lively to my mind. Now my soul blessed God afresh that He had opened that unthought-of-way to deliver me from the fear of the Egyptians, when I almost despaired of life.

> . . . conformed to the image of his
> Son, that he might be the firstborn
> among many brethren. (Rom. 8:29)

How I was, the first day or two of my illness, with regard to the exercise of reason, I scarcely know; I believe I was somewhat shattered with the violence of the fever, at times. But the third day of my illness, and constantly afterwards for four or five weeks together, I enjoyed as much serenity of mind, and clearness of thought, as perhaps I ever did in my life. I think my mind never penetrated with so much ease and freedom into divine things, as at this time. I never felt so capable of demonstrating the truth of many important doctrines of the gospel as now. And as I saw clearly the truth of those great doctrines, which are justly styled the doctrines of grace; so I saw with no less clearness, that the *essence of religion* consisted in the soul's *conformity to God,* and acting above all selfish views, for *His glory,* longing to be *for Him,* to live *to Him,* and please and honor Him in all things. And this from a clear view of His infinite excellency and worthiness in Himself to be loved, adored, worshiped, and served by all intelligent creatures.

Thus I saw, that when a soul loves God with a supreme love, he there in acts like the blessed God Himself, who most justly loves Himself in that manner. So when God's interest and his are become one, and he longs that God should be glorified and rejoices to think that He is unchangeably possessed of the highest glory and blessedness, herein also he acts in conformity to God. In like manner, when the soul is fully *resigned to,* and rests satisfied and contented *with,* the divine will, here it is also *conformed* to God.

# *John Newton*
## (1725–1807)

The next time you sing "Amazing Grace," recall that its author had lived a profligate life, had been both a slave and a slave trader, and that God wonderfully saved him and called him into the ministry.

John Newton was born in London, and was converted at about age twenty-three. He was greatly influenced by Wesley, Whitefield, and the poet William Cowper. Ordained in the Church of England, Newton ministered in Olney, where he and Cowper collaborated on *The Olney Hymns*. Newton was appointed to a London church, St. Mary's Woolnoth, and he was pastor there for twenty-seven years, until his death.

Besides composing many hymns, Newton wrote a number of books about the Christian life, including *Cardiphonia* ("The Voice of the Heart").

For I bear them record that they
have a zeal of God, but not according to knowledge. (Rom. 10:2)

The grace of God influences both the understanding and the affections. Warm affections, without knowledge, can rise no higher than superstition; and that knowledge which does not influence the heart and affections, will only make a hypocrite. The true believer is rewarded in both respects; yet we may observe, that though [this believer] is not without knowledge, this state is more usually remarkable for the warmth and liveliness of the affections. On the other hand, as the work advances, though the affections are not left out, yet it seems to be carried on principally in the understanding. The old Christian has more solid, judicious, connected views of the Lord Jesus Christ, and the glories of his person and redeeming love; hence his hope is more established, his dependence more simple, and his peace and strength, *caeteris paribus*, more abiding and uniform, than in the case of a young convert; but the latter has, for the most part, the advantage in point of sensible fervency. A tree is most valuable when laden with ripe fruit, but it has a peculiar beauty when in blossom.

> He shall not be afraid of evil tidings:
> his heart is fixed, trusting in the
> LORD. (Ps. 112:7)

A spiritual taste, and a disposition to account all things mean and vain, in comparison of the knowledge and love of God in Christ, are essential to a true Christian. The world can never be his prevailing choice; I John 2:15. Yet we are renewed but in part, and are prone to an undone attachment to worldly things. Our spirits cleave to the dust, in defiance to the dictates of our better judgments; and I believe the Lord seldom gives his people a considerable victory over this evil principle, until he has let them feel how deeply it is rooted in their hearts. We may often see persons entangled and clogged in this respect, of whose sincerity in the main we cannot justly doubt; especially upon some sudden and unexpected turn in life, which brings them into a situation they have not been accustomed to. A considerable part of our trials are mercifully appointed to wean us from this propensity; and it is gradually weakened by the Lord's showing us at one time the vanity of the creature, and at another his own excellence and all-sufficiency. From hence arises a peaceful reliance upon the Lord; he has nothing which he cannot commit into his hands, which he is not habitually aiming to resign to his disposal. Therefore he is not afraid of evil tidings; but when the hearts of others shake like the leaves of a tree, he is fixed, trusting in the Lord, who he believes *can* and *will* make good every loss, sweeten every bitter, and appoint all things to work together for his advantage. He sees that the time is short, lives upon the foretastes of glory, and therefore accounts not his life, or any inferior concernment, dear, so that he may finish his course with joy.

> I in them, and thou in me. . . .
> (John 17:23)

Communion presupposes union. By nature we are strangers, yea, enemies to God; but we are reconciled, brought nigh, and become his children, by faith in Christ Jesus. We can have no true knowledge of God, desire towards him, access unto him, or gracious communications from him, but in and through the Son of his love. He is the medium of this inestimable privilege: for he is the way, the only way, of intercourse between heaven and earth; the sinner's way to God, and God's way of mercy to the sinner. If any pretend to know God, and to have communion with him, otherwise than by the knowledge of Jesus Christ, whom he hath sent, and by faith in his name, it is a proof that they neither know God nor themselves. God, if considered abstracted from the revelation of himself in the person of Jesus, is a consuming fire; and if he should look upon us with respect to his covenant of mercy established in the Mediator, we could expect nothing from him but indignation and wrath. But when his Holy Spirit enables us to receive the record which he had given of his Son, we are delivered and secured from condemnation; we are accepted in the Beloved; we are united to him in whom all the fulness of the Godhead substantially dwells, and all the riches of divine wisdom, power, and love, are treasured up. Thus in him, as the temple wherein the glory of God is manifested, and by him, as the representative and high priest of his people, and through him, as the living head of his mystical body the church, believers maintain communion with God. They have meat to eat which the world knows not of, honour which cometh of God only, joy which a stranger intermeddleth not with. They are for the most part poor and afflicted, frequently scorned and reproached, accounted hypocrites or visionaries, knaves or fools; but this one thing makes amends for all, "They have fellowship with the Father, and with his son Jesus Christ."

> He made known his ways unto
> Moses. . . . (Ps. 103:7)

The secret of the Lord is with them that fear him. He deals familiarly with them. He calls them not servants only, but friends; and he treats them as friends. He affords them more than promises; for he opens to them the plan of his great designs from everlasting to everlasting; shows them the strong foundations and inviolable securities of his favour towards them, the height, and depth, and length, and breadth of his love, which passeth knowledge, and the unsearchable riches of his grace. He instructs them in the mysterious conduct of his providence, the reasons and ends of all his dispensations in which they are concerned; and solves a thousand hard questions to their satisfaction, which are inexplicable to the natural wisdom of man. He teaches them likewise the beauty of his precepts, the path of their duty, and the nature of their warfare. He acquaints them with the plots of their enemies, the snares and dangers they are exposed to, and the best methods of avoiding them. And he permits and enables them to acquaint him with all their cares, fears, wants, and troubles, with more freedom then they can unbosom themselves to their nearest earthly friends. His ear is always open to them; he is never weary of hearing their complaints, and answering their petitions. The men of the world would account it a high honour and privilege to have an unrestrained liberty of access to an earthly king; but what words can express the privilege and honour of believers, who, whenever they please, have audience of the King of kings, whose compassion, mercy, and power, are, like his majesty, infinite. The world wonders at them; that they are so patient in trouble, so inflexible in their conduct, so well satisfied with that state of poverty and obscurity which the Lord, for the most part, allots them, but the wonder would cease if what passes in secret were publicly known. They have obtained the pearl of great price; they have communion with God; they derive their wisdom, strength and comfort from on high, and cast all their cares upon him who, they assuredly know, vouchsafes to take care of them.

> Who, when he was reviled, reviled
> not again . . . but committed himself
> to him that judgeth righteously.
> (I Peter 2:23)

What will it profit a man if he gains his cause, and silences his adversary, if at the same time he loses that humble tender frame of spirit in which the Lord delights, and to which the promise of his presence is made! Your aim, I doubt not, is good; but you have need to watch and pray, for you will find Satan at your right hand to resist you: he will try to debase your views; and though you set out in defence of the cause of God, if you are not continually looking to the Lord to keep you, it may become your own cause, and awaken in you those tempers which are inconsistent with true peace of mind, and will surely obstruct communion with God. Be upon your guard against admitting anything personal into the debate. If you think you have been ill treated, you will have an opportunity of showing that you are a disciple of Jesus, who, "when he was reviled, reviled not again; when he suffered, he threatened not." This is our pattern, thus we are called. The wisdom that is from above is not only pure, but peaceable and gentle; and the want of these qualifications, like the dead fly in the pot of ointment, will spoil the savour and efficacy of our labours. If we act in a wrong spirit, we shall bring little glory to God, do little good to our fellow-creatures and procure neither honour nor comfort to ourselves. If you can be content with showing your wit, and gaining the laugh on your side, you have an easy task; but I hope you have a far nobler aim, and that, sensible of the solemn importance of Gospel-truths, and the compassion due to the souls of men, you would rather be a means of removing prejudices in a single instance, than obtain the empty applause of thousands. Go forth, therefore, in the name and strength of the Lord of Hosts, speaking the truth in love; and may he give you a witness in many hearts, that you are taught of God, and favoured with the unction of his Holy Spirit.

> For sin shall not have dominion over
> you: for ye are not under the law,
> but under grace. (Rom. 6:14)

Though sin wars, it shall not reign; and though it breaks our peace, it cannot separate from his love. Nor is it inconsistent with his holiness and perfection, to manifest his favour to such poor defiled creatures, or to admit them to communion with himself; for they are not considered as in themselves, but as one with Jesus, to whom they have fled for refuge, and by whom they live a life of faith. They are accepted in the Beloved, they have an Advocate with the Father, who once made an atonement for their sins, and ever lives to make intercession for their persons. Though they cannot fulfill the law, he has fulfilled it for them; though the obedience of the members is defiled and imperfect, the obedience of the Head is spotless and complete; and though there is much evil in them, there is something good, the fruit of his own gracious Spirit. They act from a principle of love, they aim at no less

70

than his glory, and their habitual desires are supremely fixed upon himself. There is a difference in kind between the feeblest efforts of faith in a real believer, while he is covered with shame at the thoughts of his miscarriages, and the highest and most specious attainments of those who are wise in their own eyes, and prudent in their own sight. Nor shall this conflict remain long, or the enemy finally prevail over them. They are supported by almighty power, and led on to certain victory. They shall not always be as they are now; yet a little while, and they shall be freed from this vile body, which, like the leprous house, is incurably contaminated, and must be entirely taken down. Then they shall see Jesus as he is, and be like him, and with him for ever.

> O how love I thy law! it is my medi-
> tation all the day. (Ps. 119:97)

To read the Scripture, not as an attorney may read a will, merely to know the sense; but as the heir reads it, as a description and proof of his interest: to hear the Gospel, as the voice of our Beloved, so as to have little leisure either for admiring the abilities, or censuring the defects of the preacher; and, in prayer, to feel a liberty of pouring out our hearts before the Lord, to behold some glances of his goodness passing before us, and to breathe forth before him the tempers of a child, the spirit of adoption: and thus, by beholding his glory, to be conformed more and more to his image, and to renew our strength by drawing water out of the wells of salvation—herein is blessedness. They who have tasted it can say: "It is good for me to draw nigh to God." The soul thus refreshed by the water of life, is preserved from thirsting after the vanities of the world; thus instructed in the sanctuary, comes down from the mount filled with heavenly wisdom, anointed with a holy unction, and thereby qualified to judge, speak, and act in character, in all the relations and occasions of secular life. In this way, besides the pleasure, a spiritual taste is acquired, something analogous to the meaning of the word taste when applied to music or good-breeding, by which discords and improprieties are observed and avoided, as it were by instinct, and what is right is felt and followed, not so much by the force of rules, as by a habit insensibly acquired, and in which the substance of all necessary rules are, if I may so say, digested. O that I knew more of this blessedness, and more of its effects!

# Robert Haldane
## (1764–1842)

A man of independent means, Robert Haldane used what he had to spread and defend the gospel in his native Scotland. He wanted to be a missionary to India, but the leaders of the Church of Scotland refused his request. Instead, Haldane used his wealth to found what were called evangelical tabernacles and to assist seminaries.

From 1816 to 1819, Haldane ministered in Switzerland and France. The great church historian D'Aubigné called this ministry "one of the most beautiful episodes in the history of the church." Haldane ministered to students in Geneva, teaching Paul's Epistle to the Romans, and the result was a revival that affected the churches in both Switzerland and France. D'Aubigné himself was converted at that time, and so were Frederic Monad and Louis Gaussen. Monad became a key leader in the Free Churches in France, and Gaussen a strong Calvinistic leader in Switzerland. Gaussen's book *Theopneustia* ("God-breathed") is a classic defense of the inspiration of the Bible.

> . . . like as Christ was raised up from
> the dead by the glory of the Father,
> even so we also should walk in
> newness of life. (Rom. 6:4)

The resurrection of Jesus Christ, as well as His death, presents the strongest motives for the encouragement and sanctification of believers. His resurrection establishes their faith, as being the heavenly seal with which God has been pleased to confirm the truth of the Gospel. Having been declared to be the Son of God with power by His resurrection from the dead, they regard Him as the Creator of the world, and the eternal Son of the Father. It assures them of the effect of His death in expiating their sins, and obliges them to embrace the blood of His cross as the price of their redemption. His resurrection being the victory which He obtained over the enemies of His Church, they are bound to place all their confidence in Him, and to resign themselves for ever to His guidance. It presents the most powerful motive to have constant recourse to the mercy of the Father, for having Himself raised up the Head and Surety of His people; it is an evident pledge of His eternal purpose to love them, and of their freedom of access to God by His Son.

In the resurrection and exaltation of Jesus Christ, believers are taught the certainty of their immortality and future blessedness. Lazarus, and others who were raised up, received their life in the same state as they possessed it before; and after they arose they died a second time; but Jesus Christ, in His resurrection, obtained a life entirely different. In His birth a life was communicated to Him which was soon to terminate on the cross. His resurrection communicated a life imperishable and immortal. Jesus Christ being raised from the dead, death hath no more dominion over Him.

> That the righteousness of the law
> might be fulfilled in us, who walk
> not after the flesh, but after the
> Spirit. (Rom. 8:4)

In all this we see the Father assuming the place of judge against His Son, in order to become the Father of those who were His enemies. The Father condemns the Son of His love, that He may absolve the children of wrath. If we inquire into the cause that moved God to save us by such means, what can we say, but that it proceeded from His incomprehensible wisdom, His ineffable goodness, and the unfathomable depth of His mercies? For what was there in man that could induce the Creator to act in this manner, since He saw nothing in him, after his rebellion by sin, but what was hateful and offensive? And what was it but His love that passeth knowledge which induced the only-begotten Son of God to take the form of a servant, to humble Himself even to the death of the cross, and to submit to be despised and rejected of men? These are the things into which the angels desire to look.

But besides the love of God, we see the wonderful display of His justice in condemning sin in His Son, rather than allowing it to go unpunished. In this assuredly the work of redemption surpasses that of creation. In creation God had made nothing that was not good, and nothing especially on which He could exercise the rigour of His justice; but here He punishes our sins to the utmost in Jesus Christ. It may be inquired if, when God condemned sin in His Son, we are to understand this of God the Father, so as to exclude the Son; or if we can say that God the Son also condemned sin in Himself. This can undoubtedly be affirmed; for in the Father and the Son there is only one will and one regard for justice; so that, as it was the will of the Father to require satisfaction for sin from the Son, it was also the will of the Son to humble Himself, and to condemn sin in Himself. We must, however, distinguish between Jesus Christ considered as God, and as our Surety and Mediator. As God, He condemns and punishes sin; as Mediator, He is Himself condemned and punished for sin.

> For the law of the Spirit of life in
> Christ Jesus hath made me free
> from the law of sin and death.
> (Rom. 8:2)

When sin was condemned or punished in the Son of God, to suppose that He felt nothing more than bodily pain, would be to conclude that He had less confidence in God than many martyrs who have gone to death cheerfully, and without fear. The extremity of the pain He suffered when He said in the garden, 'My soul is sorrowful even unto death,' was the sentiment of the wrath of God against sin, from which martyrs felt themselves delivered. For the curse of the law is principally spiritual, namely, privation of communion with God in the sense of His wrath. Jesus Christ, therefore, was made a curse for us, as the Apostle says, Gal. 3:13, proving it by the declaration, 'Cursed is every one that hangeth on a tree.' For this punishment of the cross was the figure and symbol of the spiritual curse of God. As in His body, then, He suffered this most accursed punishment, so likewise in His soul He suffered those pains that are most insupportable, such as are suffered by those finally condemned. But that was only for a short time, the infinity of His person rendering that suffering equivalent to that of an infinity of time. Such, then, was the grief which He experienced when on the cross He cried, 'My God, My God, why hast Thou forsaken Me?' What forsaking was this, unless that for a time God left Him to feel the weight of His indignation against sin? This feeling is the sovereign evil of the soul, in which consists the griefs of eternal death; as, on the other hand, the sovereign good of the soul, and that in which the happiness of eternal life consists, is to enjoy gracious communion with God.

> And if Christ be in you, the body is
> dead because of sin; but the Spirit is
> life because of righteousness.
> (Rom. 8:10)

The nature, then, of death, is changed to believers by Jesus Christ, so that 'the day of their death is better than the day of their birth.' Death to them is no more a curse, but a blessing, which puts an end to their sins and troubles, causing them to pass to perfect holiness and happiness, and from being absent from the Lord to carry them into His presence in paradise.

From being strangers on the earth, it introduces them into their heavenly inheritance. From their wanderings and agitations here below, it brings them into the haven of everlasting rest. If the children of Israel, when they arrived at the river Jordan, were dismayed at the overflowings of its waters, had they not reason to rejoice when they beheld on the other side that fertile land which God had promised them, and into which they were about to enter to enjoy its fruits? But, above all, had they not cause of encouragement when they saw that the ark of the covenant was in the midst of Jordan? Death is the passage of Jordan by which believers enter the heavenly Canaan. In order that its waves may not overwhelm them in passing, Jesus Christ arrests them, since He is in His people, and consequently with them. This was David's support, 'Though I walk through the valley of the shadow of death, I will fear no evil; for Thou art with me.' When the devouring lion roars around His people, ready to destroy them, Jesus Himself is still nearer to defend them; and He commands His angels to encamp about them, who have in charge to bear their spirits to the paradise of God.

> And we know that all things work
> together for good to them that love
> God, to them who are the called
> according to his purpose.
> (Rom. 8:28)

That *all things* work together for the good of them that love God, is a truth affording the highest consolation. These words teach believers that whatever may be the number and overwhelming character of adverse circumstances, they are all contributing to conduct them into the possession of the inheritance provided for them in heaven. That they are thus working for the good of the children of God, is manifest from the consideration that God governs the world. The first cause of all is God; second causes are all His creatures, whether angels, good or bad men, animals, or the inanimate creation. Second causes move only under His direction; and when God withdraws His hand, they cannot move at all, as it is written, 'In Him we live, and move, and have our being.' As God, then, the first cause, moves all second causes against His enemies, so, when He is favourable to us, He employs all to move and work for our good, as it is said, 'In that day will I make a covenant for them with the beasts of the field, and with the fowls of heaven, and with the creeping things of the ground; and will break the bow, and the sword, and the battle out of the earth, and will make them to lie down safely,' Hos. 2:18. And as of men it is said, 'When a man's ways please the Lord, He maketh even his enemies to be at peace with him,' Prov. 16:7.

If all things work together for good, there is nothing within the compass of being that is not, in one way or other, advantageous to the children of God. All the attributes of God, all the offices of Christ, all the gifts and graces of the Holy Spirit, are combined for their good. The creation of the world, the fall and the redemption of man, all the dispensations of Providence, whether prosperous or adverse, all occurrences and events—all things, whatsoever they be—work for their good. They work *together* in their efficacy, in their unity, and in their connection. They do not work thus of themselves: it is God that turns all things to the good of His children. The afflictions of believers, in a peculiar manner, contribute to this end.

> For I say, through the grace given
> unto me, to every man that is
> among you, not to think of himself
> more highly than he ought to think;
> but to think soberly, according as
> God hath dealt to every man the
> measure of faith. (Rom. 12:3)

God hath given us here, by the Apostle, a standard by which we may measure ourselves. Of the term 'faith' in this place, various explanations are given; but that it simply means faith in its usual acceptation throughout the Scriptures, as this is the most obvious, so it appears to be its true import. By faith we are united to the Saviour, and by faith is received out of His fulness all that is imparted to us by God. The measure, then, of faith, with which each believer is blessed, whether strong faith or weak, great faith or little, indicates with certainty both his real character before God, and his relative standing among other believers. According, therefore, to his faith, as evidenced by his works, every Christian ought to estimate himself. The man who has the greatest faith is the highest in the school of Christ. We here also learn that not only faith, but every degree of it, is the gift of God; for men believe according as God hath dealt to each of them the measure of faith; and 'unto every one of us is given grace, according to the measure of the gift of Christ.' By the consideration of the manner in which the Apostle thus enforces his admonition, the believer will both be moderated in his own esteem, and also in his desire for the esteem of others. He will consequently be much less exposed to encounter what may inflame his pride, or tend to his discouragement.

> Rejoicing in hope; patient in tribulation; continuing instant in prayer.
> (Rom. 12:12)

Here, in the midst of exhortations to attend to various duties, they are commanded to *rejoice in hope*. Hope is founded on faith, and faith on the Divine testimony. Hope, then, respects what God has declared in His word. We are here exhorted to exercise hope with respect to future glory, and to rejoice in the contemplation of the objects of hope. What can be better calculated to promote joy than the hope of obtaining blessings so glorious in a future world? Were this hope kept in lively exercise, it would raise believers above the fear of man and a concern for the honours of this world. It would also enable them to despise the shame of the cross.

The objects, then, of the believer's hope are the spiritual and celestial blessings which are yet future, to which his eyes should constantly be directed, and which are calculated to fill him with the greatest joy. It is not the prospect of terrestrial possessions in which he is to rejoice, but of a house eternal in the heavens. 'In Thy presence is fulness of joy; at Thy right hand there are pleasures for evermore.' It is that glorious communion with Jesus Christ of which the Apostle speaks, when he says, 'Having a desire to depart, and to be with Christ; which is far better.' It is that state in which believers shall be like Him, for they shall see Him as He is. 'As for me, I will behold Thy face in righteousness; I shall be satisfied when I awake with Thy likeness.' It is the hope of righteousness for which, through the Spirit, believers wait, Gal. 5:5. This hope is founded on the unchangeable promise of God—on His promise accompanied by His oath—on the blood of Christ with which He has sealed His promise—on Him who was not only dead, but is risen again, who is even at the right hand of God, who also maketh intercession for His people. This hope, then, is both sure and stedfast, and entereth into that within the vail, whither the forerunner, even Jesus, is for us entered.

# John Henry Newman
## (1801–1890)

Congregations know John Henry Newman as the author of "Lead, Kindly Light." Church historians recognize him as the man who started the Oxford Movement (not to be confused with the Oxford Group Movement) in an attempt to revitalize the Anglican Church. He preached to great crowds at St. Mary's Church, Oxford, and his books influenced people who were serious about their faith. However, Newman felt it necessary to leave the Anglican Church and unite with the Roman Catholic Church.

Newman's sermons from his Anglican ministry show far more depth and excitement than those produced during his Roman days. At any rate, he was a gifted preacher and he left us many volumes of sermons. His philosophy of preaching calls the preacher to minister to an individual, not to a crowd; and to deal with one spiritual truth, not the whole spectrum of doctrine. His greatest gift was in recognizing and explaining the needs of the human heart. The weakest thing about his preaching is that he did not apply the medicine of the gospel.

If ye know these things, happy are
ye if ye do them. (John 13:17)

Every thing is plain and easy to the earnest; it is the double-minded who find difficulties. If you hate your own corruption in sincerity and truth, if you are really pierced to the heart that you do not do what you know you should do, if you *would* love God if you could, then the Gospel speaks to you words of peace and hope. It is a very different thing indolently to say, "I would I were a different man," and to close with God's offer to make you different, when it is put before you. Here is the test between earnestness and insincerity. You say you wish to be a different man; Christ takes you at your word, so to speak; He offers to make you different. He says, "I will take away from you the heart of stone, the love of this world and its pleasures, if you will submit to My discipline." Here a man draws back. No; he cannot bear to *lose* the love of the world, to part with his present desires and tastes; he cannot *consent* to be changed. After all he is well satisfied at the bottom of his heart to remain as he is, only he wants his conscience taken out of the way. Did Christ offer to do this for him, if He would but make bitter sweet and sweet bitter, darkness light and light darkness, *then* he would hail the glad tidings of peace;—till then he needs Him not.

But if a man is in earnest in wishing to get at the depths of his own heart, to expel the evil, to purify the good, and to gain power over himself, so as to do as well as know the Truth, what is the difficulty?—a matter of time indeed, but not of uncertainty is the recovery of such a man.

> Who can understand his errors?
> Cleanse thou me from secret faults.
> (Ps. 19:12)

Now reflect upon the *actual disclosures* of our hidden weakness, which accidents occasion. Peter followed Christ boldly, and suspected not his own heart, till it betrayed him in the hour of temptation, and led him to deny his Lord. David lived years of happy obedience while he was in private life. What calm, clear-sighted faith is manifested in his answer to Saul about Goliath:—"The Lord that delivered me out of the paw of the lion, and out of the paw of the bear, He will deliver me out of the hand of this Philistine."[1] Nay, not only in retired life, in severe trial, under ill usage from Saul, he continued faithful to his God; years and years did he go on, fortifying his heart, and learning the fear of the Lord; yet power and wealth weakened his faith, and for a season overcame him. There was a time when a prophet could retort upon him, "Thou art the man"[2] whom thou condemnest. He had kept his principles in words, but lost them in his heart. Hezekiah is another instance of a religious man bearing *trouble* well, but for a season falling back under the temptation of prosperity; and that, after extraordinary mercies had been vouchsafed to him.[3] And if these things be so in the case of the favored saints of God, what (may we suppose) is our own real spiritual state in His sight? It is a serious thought. The warning to be deduced from it is this:—Never to think we have a due knowledge of ourselves till we have been exposed to various kinds of temptations, and tried on every side. Integrity on one side of our character is no voucher for integrity on another. We cannot tell how we should act if brought under temptations different from those which we have hitherto experienced. This thought should keep us humble. We are sinners, but we do not know how great. He alone knows who died for our sins.

> Beware ye of the leaven of the
> Pharisees, which is hypocrisy.
> (Luke 12:1)

This then is hypocrisy;—not simply for a man to deceive others, knowing all the while that he *is* deceiving them, but to deceive himself *and* others at the same time, to aim at their praise by a religious profession, without perceiving that he loves their praise more than the praise of God, and that he is

1. 1 Samuel 17:37.
2. 2 Samuel 11:7.
3. 2 Kings 20:12–19.

professing far more than he practises. And if this be the true
Scripture meaning of the word, we have some insight (as it
appears) into the reasons which induced our Divine Teacher
to warn His disciples in so marked a way against hypocrisy.
An innumerable multitude was thronging Him, and His disciples were around Him. Twelve of them had been appointed
to minister to Him as His especial friends. Other seventy had
been sent out from Him with miraculous gifts; and, on their
return, had with triumph told of their own wonderful doings.
All of them had been addressed by Him as the salt of the
earth, the light of the world, the children of His kingdom.
*They* were mediators between Him and the people at large,
introducing to His notice the sick and heavy-laden. And now
they stood by Him, partaking in His popularity, perhaps
glorying in their connexion with the Christ, and pleased to be
gazed upon by the impatient crowd. Then it was that, instead
of addressing the multitude, He spoke first of all to His disciples, saying, "Beware of the leaven of the Pharisees, which is
hypocrisy;" as if He had said, "What is the chief sin of My
enemies and persecutors? not that they openly deny God, but
that they love a profession of religion for the sake of the praise
of men that follows it."

> Son, go work to day in my vineyard.
> He answered and said, I will not: but
> afterward he repented, and went.
> And he came to the second, and said
> likewise. And he answered and said,
> I go, sir: and went not.
> (Matt. 21:28–30)

We are in the dark about ourselves. When we act, we are
groping in the dark, and may meet with a fall any moment.
Here and there, perhaps, we see a little; or, in our attempts to
influence and move our minds, we are making experiments
(as it were) with some delicate and dangerous instrument,

which works we do not know how, and may produce unexpected and disastrous effects. The management of our hearts is quite above us. Under these circumstances it becomes our comfort to look up to God. "Thou, God, seest me!" Such was the consolation of the forlorn Hagar in the wilderness. He knoweth whereof we are made, and He alone can uphold us. He sees with most appalling distinctness all our sins, all the windings and recesses of evil within us; yet it is our only comfort to know this, and to trust Him for help against ourselves. To those who have a right notion of their weakness, the thought of their Almighty Sanctifier and Guide is continually present. They believe in the necessity of a spiritual influence to change and strengthen them, not as a mere abstract doctrine, but as a practical and most consolatory truth, daily to be fulfilled in their warfare with sin and Satan.

But he spake the more vehemently,
If I should die with thee, I will not
deny thee in any wise. (Mark 14:31)

Let us not promise much; let us not talk much of ourselves; let us not be high-minded, nor encourage ourselves in impetuous bold language in religion. Let us take warning, too, from that fickle multitude who cried, first Hosanna, then Crucify. A miracle startled them into a sudden adoration of their Saviour;—its effect upon them soon died away. And thus the especial mercies of God sometimes excite us for a season. We feel Christ speaking to us through our consciences and hearts; and we fancy He is assuring us to receive Him. Let us not be content with saying "Lord, Lord," without "doing the thing which He says." The husbandman's son who said, "I go, sir," yet went not to the vineyard, gained nothing by his fair words. One secret act of self-denial, one sacrifice of inclination to duty, is worth all the mere good thoughts, warm feelings, passionate prayers, in which idle people indulge themselves. It will give us more comfort on our deathbed to reflect on one deed of self-denying mercy, purity, or humility, than to recollect the shedding of many tears, and the recurrence of frequent transports, and much spiritual exultation. These latter feelings come and go; they may or may not accompany hearty obedience; they are never tests of it; but good actions are the fruits of faith, and assure us that we are Christ's; they comfort us as an evidence of the Spirit working in us. By them we shall be judged at the last day; and though they have no worth in themselves, by reason of that infection of sin which gives its character to everything we do, yet they will be accepted for His sake, who bore the agony in the garden, and suffered as a sinner on the cross.

> But thou, when thou prayest, enter into thy closet, and when thou hast shut the door, pray to thy Father which is in secret; and thy Father which seeth in secret shall reward thee openly. (Matt. 6:6)

Prayer *through* the day, is indeed the characteristic of a Christian spirit, but we may be sure that, in most cases, those who do not pray at stated times in a more solemn and direct manner, will never pray well at other times. We know in the common engagements of life, the importance of collecting and arranging our thoughts calmly and accurately before proceeding to any important business, in order to the right performance of it; and so in that one really needful occupation, the care of our eternal interests, if we would have our minds composed, our desires subdued, and our tempers heavenly through the day, we must, before commencing the day's employment, stand still awhile to look into ourselves, and commune with our hearts, by way of preparing ourselves for the trials and duties on which we are entering. A like reason may be assigned for evening prayer, viz. as affording us a time of looking back on the day past, and summing up (as it were) that account, which, if *we* do not reckon, at least God has reckoned, and written down in that book which will be produced at the Judgment; a time of confessing sin, and of praying for forgiveness, of giving thanks for what we have done well, and for mercies received, of making good resolutions in reliance on the help of God, and of sealing up and setting sure the day past, at least as a stepping-stone of good for the morrow.

> Serve the LORD with fear, and
> rejoice with trembling. (Ps. 2:11)

In heaven, love will absorb fear; but in this world, *fear and love must go together.* No one can love God aright without fearing Him; though many fear Him, and yet do not love Him. Self-confident men, who do not know their own hearts, or the reasons they have for being dissatisfied with themselves, do not fear God, and they think this bold freedom is to love Him. Deliberate sinners fear but cannot love Him. But devotion to Him consists in love and fear, as we may understand from our ordinary attachment to each other. No one really loves another, who does not feel a certain reverence towards him. When friends transgress this sobriety of affection, they may indeed continue associates for a time, but they have broken the bond of union. It is mutual respect which makes friendship lasting. So again, in the feelings of inferiors towards superiors. Fear must go before love. Till he who has authority shows he has it and can use it, his forbearance will not be valued duly; his kindness will look like weakness. We learn to contemn what we do not fear; and we cannot love what we contemn. So in religion also. We cannot understand Christ's mercies till we understand His power, His glory, His unspeakable holiness, and our demerits; that is, until we first fear Him. Not that fear comes first, and then love; for the most part they will proceed together. Fear is allayed by the love of Him, and our love sobered by our fear of Him.

# Robert S. Candlish
## (1806–1873)

Robert S. Candlish was one of the founders of the Free Church of Scotland and Alexander Whyte's predecessor at Free St. George's, Edinburgh. In 1862, he became principal of New College, Edinburgh.

Known primarily as a preacher of the Word, Candlish was an able scholar who could expound the Scriptures clearly and practically. His *First Epistle of John* is an example of exposition at its best. He wrote three volumes about Genesis and a number of theological studies, as well as devotional studies.

Woe is me! for I am undone;
because I am a man of unclean
lips. . . . (Isa. 6:5)

Ah! It is high time for me to place myself where Isaiah was, and to prostrate myself as Isaiah did. And let it not be as if this uncleanness of my own lips and tolerance of the uncleanness of the lips of the world were a casual infirmity, an outward excrescence upon my character and life. Ah, no! It is myself; my very self! I am a man of unclean lips! The unclean lips constitute my very manhood, my very nature. They are the sign and index of what I am. It is not that I have them, hanging as an uncongenial burden around me. But I am what they express. They proceed out of my heart. They are what my inner man, my whole inner man, truly is. It is my nature that I feel to be so deeply, thoroughly, hopelessly vitiated. Not only

are my lips unclean, I am myself a man of unclean lips! That is
my very nature. That is myself. Myself as I see myself, when
mine eyes see the King, the Lord of Hosts.

> Then said I, Here am I; send me.
> (Isa. 6:8)

It is a signal instance of grace on the part of the Lord that I
am allowed to be a volunteer. The Lord has a right, a dearly
purchased right, to deal with me very differently. He might
issue a peremptory command. He might utter his stern voice
of authority, and at once order me. But he knows what is in
man better than to treat thus the broken and relenting heart
of one whom he has smitten by the brightness of his glorious
holiness to the ground, and healed by the touch of his ever-
living sacrifice of blood. He is considerate. He is generous. His
servant is not coerced or constrained, as with bit and bridle.
He has the unspeakable privilege and happiness of giving
himself voluntarily, and, as it were, ultroneously, to the Lord,
who willingly gave himself for him. He simply hears, or over-
hears, a conversation in heaven; a question asked and waiting
to be answered.

> And being fully persuaded that,
> what he had promised, he was able
> also to perform. (Rom. 4:21)

I at least never dream of calling in question the omnipotence
of God. I perfectly well know, and am firmly convinced, that
what he has promised he is able also to perform. And yet I see
not how that knowledge and conviction will of itself make
me, or any man, strong in faith. Very true, O friend. To believe
that God is omnipotent, however strongly, with whatever full

persuasion, when that belief is the mere admission of a dogma in theology, a general truth or proposition, proved by reason and affirmed in Scripture; so to believe and be fully persuaded and assured that what God has promised he is able also to perform; will go but a little way towards strengthening or establishing you in that faith which glorifies God. But let me again remind you that the faith in question is believing God; not believing something about God, but believing God. It is a personal dealing of God with you, and of you with God. He and you come together; he to speak, you to hear; he to promise, you to believe; you to ask, he to give.

> Now it was not written for his sake
> alone . . . but for us also. . . .
> (Rom. 4:23–24)

Oh! Come, my brother, be confronted with thy God, face to face with him. Be alone with thy God; Jesus bringing thee near to him; the Spirit moving between thy God and thee. How canst thou then and there, here and now, best honor him and give him glory? How but by being fully persuaded, and in thy dealings with him proceeding on the full persuasion, that what he promises he is able also to perform? Remember that it is with none other than the Omnipotent that thou art invited to be at home; it is in none other than the Omnipotent that thou art called to confide. Take any promise of his within the range of this blessed book. Take it in its highest reach and widest sweep. Plead it for thyself and thine. Plead it for himself and his. Plead it, in the full persuasion that no difficulties such as sense might consider can stand in the way of its accomplishment; for what he has promised, what he promises, he is able to perform. Be strong in this faith, giving glory to God.

90

> Let the word of Christ dwell in you
> richly. . . . (Col. 3:16)

Let the word of Christ so dwell in you. Let it be Christ himself, dwelling in you; Christ himself, the living word. Let his word, or himself the word, dwell in you richly; moulding, fashioning, vivifying, regulating, your whole inner man; all its powers, faculties, affections; its susceptibilities and sensibilities; its movements of will. Let his word, let himself in his word, give his own tone and temper to all your emotions of joy and sorrow; of fear, or anxiety, or love, or hope. Let all within you be thus imbued, not stiffly and artificially, but spontaneously and gladly, with the word of Christ dwelling in you richly by the Spirit; and so becoming Christ himself dwelling in you as the word of life. Then, let there go forth from you, not stiffly and artificially, but spontaneously and gladly and lovingly, streams of overflowing benignity and benevolence; rich and gracious influences of holy zeal and love and joy; to the glory of God, celebrated in songs of praise; and the edifying of the church, in wise teaching and admonition.

> I am a stranger in the earth; hide not
> thy commandments from me.
> (Ps. 119:19)

The point and pith of this prayer would seem to lie in the continual need which one who is a stranger on the earth has of communion with him whose guest he is; with whom, as a stranger, he is a sojourner. In that character, as a stranger on the earth, I do not now desire to have more fellowship with the people of the land than is necessary for pious ends; for the comely burial of my dead, or for the discharge of my duty of love to the living. I would rather converse with him who says, "The land is mine." And the medium of conversation with him is his word, or his commandments. His commandments; his communications of whatever sort; precepts, promises, histories, prophecies, warnings, encouragements; all sayings of his, for they are all commandments; I desire to use as means of real personal converse with him. But I cannot do so unless he opens my eyes. Therefore, I pray, "Hide not thy commandments from me."

Esteeming the reproach of Christ
greater riches than the treasures in
Egypt; for he had respect unto the
recompence of the reward.
(Heb. 11:26)

In the service of God, if loyal and true, you must make up your mind to relinquish or forego not a few of those sources of pleasure and enjoyment which the world presents to you. And for whatever you may thus give up, he whom you serve may be expected, if he is to act worthily of himself, to provide some kind of equivalent. If you lose the favour of men, you have the favour of God. If you cease to have the peace which the world gives, when, with its refuges of lies, it soothes your conscience; you have the peace of God which passes understanding, the peace which Jesus gives, his own peace, which, when dying, he bequeaths and leaves to dying sinners. If you have to cut off a right hand, to pluck out a right eye; maimed as you are and wounded, you enter into life. If the good things of earth are to be your treasure no more; you have better treasure in heaven, where no moth corrupts, and no thief breaks through to steal. You are prevented now from giving full scope, in the line of the world's pursuits, to that principle of your nature which prompts you to acquire and to accumulate. But it is the glory of the gospel that it does not propose to suppress a principle so powerful, and, in its place, so useful. Rather it turns it to good account. For the work and labor of love assuredly affords ample room and scope for its exercise.

# Andrew A. Bonar

## (1810–1892)

Unlike his esteemed friend Robert Murray McCheyne, Andrew A. Bonar lived a long life. He was pastor of only two churches, remaining at the first for eighteen years, and the second from 1856 until his death. He was a friend of D. L. Moody and preached at Moody's Northfield conference in 1881. His brother, Horatius, was a hymnist as well as a minister.

In 1839, Bonar accompanied McCheyne on a visit to the Holy Land. Bonar was a confirmed premillennialist and often preached about the coming of the Lord. In addition to his book about McCheyne, Bonar wrote devotional commentaries on the Psalms and on Leviticus, as well as numerous evangelistic tracts and booklets. In 1894, Bonar's daughter Marjory edited and published her father's diary, a fascinating record of a long life of fruitful ministry.

Pray without ceasing. (I Thess. 5:17)

God has this week been impressing much upon me the way of redeeming time for prayer by learning to pray while walking or going from place to place. Also He has been showing me how to make more direct use of Scripture to my own case in daily reading. Tomorrow is the anniversary of my ordination day. I feel my unholiness, my prayerlessness, and my want of solemnity and sense of responsibility. I seem to have done nothing at all for this people, and I wonder much at my indifference of neighbouring clergymen. I feel also a great deal of envy at hearing of others' success.

> I pray thee, let a double portion of
> thy spirit be upon me. (II Kings 2:9)

O that his mantle would fall upon me! Evil days are begun. He was so reverent toward God, so full also in desire toward Him, whether in family prayer or at common ordinary meetings. He seemed never unprepared. His lamp was always burning, and his loins always girt. I never knew it otherwise, even when we were journeying in Palestine. Lord, grant me henceforth more holiness; may I work among my people with the deepest solemnity. Whether they feel God present or not, may I teach them I feel He is there. I have had joy also in this season through the sight of a living Saviour with whom I shall soon be, but especially in feeling how sweet it is to be near God, and drawn off from earth; the thought too of Christ coming again, it may be very soon. This terrible blow may be the answer to my prayers for holiness, for I used to pray that even if very awful, it were better that God should take the way that would make me holier, although I should suffer. [This was written shortly after the death of McCheyne.]

> The fruit of the Spirit is . . . joy. . . .
> (Gal. 5:22)

P reached with little freedom. Weariness of body is against me; but still more want of much prayer through the previous week. God will not let me preach with power when I am not much with Him. More than ever do I feel that I should be as much an intercessor as a preacher of the word. Also I have been taught that joy in the Spirit is the frame in which God blesses us to others. Joy arises from fellowship with Him—I find that whatever sorrow or humiliation of spirit presses on us, that should give way in some measure to a fresh taste of God's love when going forth to preach.

A sound heart is the life of the flesh:
but envy the rottenness of the
bones. (Prov. 14:30)

In my usual reading, in Genesis 37, I see how envy leads God to heap more blessing upon the envied one, and to withhold from the envier. Now, this has been my fault in regard to brethren who have been blessed. I have sought to find reasons why they *should* not; like the men in the parable, murmuring against the good man giving his money to them also. Lord, this day may I lay this aside for ever. Give more and more to those brethren whom I have despised or thought unworthy of revival work, and O that I could praise the Lord for His goodness in pouring out His Spirit! O that I could praise Him for His goodness to me and mine! Lord, why have I been made to share in this blessing? But, Lord, as yet we have had only drops; may we not this coming year have the Spirit among us working wonderfully as in those other places? One night when at Ferryden I found it very startling to myself to notice how coolly I spoke to people about faith and unbelief, how hard-hearted I was in telling the men at whose side I stood, 'if you now this moment receive Christ, you are for ever saved; if not, you perish.' The awful difference of the two sides of the line, the sin, and folly too, of not believing; why do I not feel deep, deep compassion for those that are deluded and perishing?

But seek ye first the kingdom of
God, and his righteousness. . . .
(Matt. 6:33)

Often I have wondered that I did not feel the temptations of Satan more frequently and plainly. But now I discover his plan. For a long time, indeed for years, I can see that he has contrived very many days to prevent my praying to any purpose. His temptations to me lie in the direction of putting half-lawful literature or literary work before me, which I am led on to read at once, without having first of all fully met with God. In short, he succeeds in reversing in my case, 'Seek *first* the kingdom of God.' Lord, give me power to resist. Lord, from this day give me many victories where formerly I fell under him.

> Deal bountifully with thy servant,
> that I may live, and keep thy word.
> (Ps. 119:17)

I have been thinking how one riding toward a city passes along, though vineyards with all their clusters (few of which he can reach after all) be on each side. This is the believer's way through earth, at its very best; but mine now is through the desert. I have been thinking too of the greatness of God. It is because He is so very great that He can and does attend to each one's smallest care and sorrow. Each one soul is to Him as much as a world, and he can bend down with the same love and loftiness of sympathy on that one as if that one were all. The very greatness of the ocean enables it to fill to the full every creek and bay. It is thus that my littleness helps to set forth God's exceeding greatness, and His sympathy in my sorrow, and His marking every tear, all sets forth the immensity of His grace and compassion. Therefore I can plead, 'For Thy name's sake, Lord, deal bountifully with Thy servant.'

> Most gladly therefore will I rather
> glory in my infirmities, that the
> power of Christ may rest upon me.
> (II Cor. 12:9)

I see distinctly that my Lord is teaching me to 'glory in my infirmities,' and to be willing to be set aside. My voice fails;

some of my people, specially the younger part, going else-where; my class melts away. Some very mortifying cases of ingratitude on the part of some; my influence with brethren manifestly declines—all this is saying, 'He must increase, but I must decrease;' and thus I am prepared by Him, whose 'way is perfect,' for finishing my ministry, and removing to the service within the veil. But I have some cases of peculiar blessing to set over against these discouragements. I have been trying to set down elsewhere some of these. I know 'He doeth all things well.'

# Robert Murray McCheyne
## (1813–1843)

Robert Murray McCheyne lived a brief life; but it was a full one and a blessed one. As young as he was, McCheyne was known throughout Scotland as a saintly person and a man burdened for souls.

In 1836, McCheyne became pastor of St. Peter's in Dundee. His pulpit ministry attracted crowds and many came to Christ. I can never forget visiting the church, where I had the privilege of handling McCheyne's Bible and reading his handwritten notations in the margins. He is buried next to the church. I stood by his grave and silently prayed, "Lord, send another man like him!"

McCheyne's dear friend was Andrew A. Bonar, whom you met elsewhere in this book. Bonar published *Memoir and Remains of Robert Murray McCheyne* in 1845, and it was an immediate success. Since that time, many editions have been published.

Consider the Apostle and High Priest
of our profession, Christ Jesus.
(Heb. 3:1)

Oh, brethren, could you and I pass this day through these heavens, and see what is now going on in the sanctuary above,—could you see what the child of God now sees who died last night,—could you see the Lamb with the scars of His five deep wounds in the very midst of the throne, surrounded by all the odors,—could you see the many angels round about the throne, whose number is ten thousand times ten thousand, and thousands of thousands, all singing, "Worthy is the Lamb that was slain,"—and were one of these angels to tell you, "This is He that undertook the cause of lost sinners; He undertook to be the second Adam,—the man in their stead; and lo! there He is upon the throne of heaven;— consider Him,—look long and earnestly upon His wounds— upon His glory,—and tell me, do you think it would be safe to trust Him? Do you think His sufferings and obedience will have been enough?—Yes, yes, every soul exclaims, Lord, it is enough! Lord, stay thy hand! Show me no more, for I can bear no more. Oh, rather let me ever stand and gaze upon the almighty, all-worthy, all-divine Saviour, till my soul drink in complete assurance that His work undertaken for sinners is a finished work! Yes, though the sins of all the world were on my one wicked head, still I could not doubt that His work is complete, and that I am quite safe when I believe in Him.

These are they which came out of
great tribulation, and have washed
their robes, and made them white in
the blood of the Lamb. (Rev. 7:14)

Every one that gets to the throne must put their foot upon the thorn. The way to the crown is by the cross. We must taste the gall if we are to taste the glory. When justified by faith, God brought Israel through the Red Sea, He led them into the wilderness; so, when God saves a soul, He tries it. He never gives faith without trying it. The way to Zion is through the valley of Baca. You must go through the wilderness of Jordan if you are to come to the Land of Promise. Some believers are much surprised when they are called to suffer. They thought they would do some great thing for God; but all that God permits them to do is to *suffer*.

Go round every one in glory,—every one has a different story, yet every one has a tale of suffering. One was persecuted in his family,—by his friends and companions; another was visited by sore pains and humbling disease,—neglected by the world; another was bereaved of children; another had all these afflictions meeting in one,—deep called unto deep. Mark, all are *brought out of them.* It was a dark cloud, but it passed away; the water was deep, but they have reached the other side. Not one of them blames God for the road He led them: "Salvation" is their only cry. Is there any of you, dear children, murmuring at your lot? Do not sin against God. This is the way God leads all His redeemed ones. You must have a palm as well as a white robe. No pain, no palm; no cross, no crown; no thorn, no throne; no gall, no glory. Learn to glory in tribulations also. "I reckon that the sufferings of this present time are not worthy to be compared with the glory that shall be revealed in us."

There is no fear in love; but perfect
love casteth out fear. (I John 4:18)

Twice God spake from heaven, and said, "This is My beloved Son, in whom I am well pleased." God perfectly loves His own Son. He sees infinite beauty in His person. God sees Himself manifested. He is infinitely pleased with His finished work. The infinite heart of the infinite God flows out in love towards our Lord Jesus Christ. And there is no fear in the bosom of Christ. All His fears are past. Once He said, "While I suffer thy terrors I am distressed;" but now He is in perfect love, and perfect love casteth out fear. *Hearken, trembling souls!* Here you may find rest to your souls. You do not need to live another hour under your tormenting fears. Jesus Christ has borne the wrath of which you are afraid. He now stands a refuge for the oppressed—a refuge in the time of trouble. Look to Christ, and your fear will be cast out. Come to the feet of Christ, and you will find rest. Call upon the name of the Lord, and you will be delivered.

You say you cannot look, nor come, nor cry, for you are

helpless. Hear, then, and your soul shall live. Jesus is a Saviour to the helpless. Christ is not only a Saviour to those who are naked and empty, and have not goodness to recommend themselves, but He is a Saviour to those who are unable to give themselves to Him. You cannot be in too desperate a condition for Christ. As long as you remain un-believing, you are under His perfect wrath—wrath without any mixture. The wrath of God will be as amazing as His love. It comes out of the same bosom. But the moment you look to Christ, you will come under His perfect love—love without any coldness—light without any shade—love without any cloud or mountain between. God's love will cast out all your fears.

> But we have the mind of Christ.
> (I Cor. 2:16)

Now, every believer has the mind of Christ formed in him. He thinks as Christ does: "This is the spirit of a sound mind" (2 Tim. 1:7). This is being of the same mind in the Lord. I do not mean that a believer has the same all-seeing mind, the same infallible judgment concerning everything, as Christ has; but up to his light he sees things as Christ does.

He sees *sin* as Christ does. Christ sees sin to be evil and bitter. He sees it to be filthy and abominable—its pleasures all a delusion. He sees it to be awfully dangerous. He sees the inseparable connection between sin and suffering. So does a believer.

He sees the *gospel* as Christ does. Christ sees amazing glory in the gospel, the way of salvation which He Himself has wrought out. It appears a most complete salvation to Him—most free—most glorifying to God and happy for man. So does the believer.

He sees the *world* as Christ does. Christ knows what is in man. He looked on this world as vanity compared with the smile of His Father. Its riches, its honours, its pleasures, appeared not worth a sigh. He saw it passing away. So does the believer.

He sees *time* as Christ did. "I must work the work of Him that sent Me while it is day; the night cometh"—"I come quickly." So does a believer look at time.

He sees *eternity* as Christ does. Christ looked at everything in the light of eternity. "In my Father's house are many mansions." Everything is valuable in Christ's eyes, only as it bears on eternity. So with believers.

> Father, I will that they also, whom
> thou hast given me, be with me
> where I am. . . . (John 17:24)

He does not mean that we should be presently taken out of this world. Some of you that have come to Christ may, this day, be favoured with so much of His presence, and of the love of the Father, so much of the joy of heaven, and such a dread of going back to betray Christ in the world, that you may be wishing that this house were indeed the gate of heaven; you may desire that you might be translated from the table below at once to the table above. "I am in a strait betwixt two, having a desire to depart and be with Christ." Still Christ does not wish that. "I pray not that Thou shouldest take them out of the world, but that Thou shouldst keep them from the evil." "Whither I go, thou canst not follow Me now." (Like that woman in Brainerd's *Journal*—"O blessed Lord, do come! Oh, do take me away! Do let me die and go to Jesus Christ. I am afraid, if I live, I shall sin again.")

He means, that when our journey is done, we should come to be with Him. Every one that comes to Christ has a journey to perform in this world. Some have a long, and some a short one. It is through a wilderness. Still Christ prays that at the end you may be with Him. Every one that comes to Christ hath his twelve hours to fill up for Christ. "I must work the works of Him that sent me, while it is day." But when that is done, Christ prays that you may be with Him. He means that you shall come to *His Father's house* with Him. "In My Father's house are many mansions." You shall dwell in the same house with Christ. You are never very intimate with a person till you see them in their own house—till you know them at home. This is what Christ wants with us—that we shall come to be with Him, at His own home. He wants us to come to the same Father's bosom with Him. "I ascend to My Father and your Father." He wants us to be in the same smile with Him, to sit on the same throne with Him, to swim in the same ocean of love with Him.

. . . who loved me and gave himself
for me. (Gal. 2:20)

The wounds of Christ were the greatest outlets of His glory that ever were. The divine glory shone more out of His wounds than out of all His life before. The veil was then rent in twain, and the full heart of God allowed to stream through. It was a human body that writhed, pale and racked, upon the accursed tree; they were human hands that were pierced so rudely by the nails; it was human flesh that bore that deadly gash upon the side; it was human blood that streamed from hands, and feet, and side; the eye that meekly turned to His Father was a human eye; the soul that yearned over His mother was a human soul. But oh, there was divine glory streaming through all! Every wound was a mouth to speak of the grace and love of God! *Divine holiness* shone through. What infinite hatred of sin was there when He thus offered Himself a sacrifice without spot unto God! *Divine wisdom* shone through: all created intelligences could not have devised a plan whereby God would have been just, and yet the justifier. *Divine love;* every drop of blood that fell came as a messenger of love from His heart to tell the love of the fountain. This was the love of God. He that hath seen a crucified Christ hath seen the Father. Oh, look on the broken bread, and you will see this glory still streaming through! Here is the heart of God laid bare,—God is manifest in flesh. Some of you are poring over your own heart,—examining your feelings,—watching your disease. Avert the eye from all within. Behold Me,—behold Me! Christ cries. Look to Me, and be ye saved. Behold the glory of Christ! There is much difficulty about your own heart, but no darkness about the heart of Christ. Look in through His wounds; believe what you see in Him.

> Blessed are the dead which die in
> the Lord from henceforth: Yea, saith
> the Spirit, that they may rest from
> their labours; and their works do
> follow them. (Rev. 14:13)

That which makes everything laborious here is sin—the opposition of Satan and the world, and the drag of our old nature. Some believers have a constant struggle with Satan. He is standing at their right hand to resist them; he is constantly distracting them in prayer, hurling fiery darts at their soul, tempting to the most horrid sin. Their whole life is labor. But when we die in the Lord, we shall rest from this labor. Satan's work will be clean done. The accuser of the brethren will no more annoy. No lion shall be there, neither shall any ravenous beast go up thereon, but the redeemed shall walk there. But, above all, the wicked heart, the old man, the body of sin, makes this life a dreadful labor. When we wake in the morning, it lies like a weight upon us. When we would run in the way of God's commandments, it drags us back. When we would fly, it weighs us down. "O wretched man that I am!"

But to depart and be with Christ, is to be free from this. We shall drop this body of sin altogether. No more any flesh—all spirit, all new man; no more any weight or drag—we shall rest from our labors. Oh, it is this makes death in the Lord blessed! We shall not rest from all work; we shall be as the angels of

God—we shall serve Him day and night in His temple. We shall not rest from our work, but from our labors. There will be no toil, no pain, in our work. We shall rest in our work. Oh, let this make you willing to depart, and make death look pleasant, and heaven a home. "We shall rest from our labors." It is the world of holy love, where we shall give free, full, unfettered, unwearied expression to our love for ever.

# Frederick William Faber
## (1814–1863)

Most of us know Frederick William Faber as a hymnist. "My God, How Wonderful Thou Art," "Faith of Our Fathers," and "There's A Wideness in God's Mercy" are all sung by evangelical Protestants, many of whom would not believe you if you told them the composer was a Roman Catholic.

Faber had a Protestant upbringing, but John Henry Newman and the Oxford Movement won him over. Faber ended up in London, supervising the Brompton oratory and having occasional disagreements with Newman. Faber wrote many poems, hymns, and devotional books, most of which have perished with time. A. W. Tozer thought highly of Faber's hymns and included many of them in his *Christian's Book of Mystical Verse*.

Put on therefore, as the elect of
God . . . kindness, humbleness of
mind, meekness, longsuffering. . . .
(Col. 3:12)

We must first ask ourselves what kindness is. Words, which we are using constantly, soon cease to have much distinct meaning in our minds. They become symbols and figures rather than words, and we content ourselves with the general impression they make upon us. Now let us be a little particular about kindness, and describe it as accurately as we can. Kindness is the overflowing of self upon others. We put others in the place of self. We treat them as we would wish to be treated ourselves. We change places with them. For the time self is another, and others are self. Our self love takes the shape of complacence in unselfishness.

We cannot speak of the virtues without thinking of God. What would the overflow of self upon others be in Him the Ever-blessed and Eternal? It was the act of creation. Creation was divine kindness. From it as from a fountain, flow the possibilities, the powers, the blessings of all created kindness. This is an honourable genealogy for kindness. Then, again, kindness is the coming to the rescue of others, when they need it and it is in our power to supply what they need; and this is the work of the Attributes of God towards His creatures. His omnipotence is for ever making up our deficiency of power. His justice is continually correcting our erroneous judgments. His mercy is always consoling our fellow-creatures under our hardheartedness. His truth is perpetually hindering the consequences of our falsehood. His omniscience makes our ignorance succeed as if it were knowledge. His perfections are incessantly coming to the rescue of our imperfections. This is the definition of Providence; and kindness is our imitation of this divine action.

. . . and is a discerner of the
thoughts and intents of the heart.
(Heb. 4:12)

It seems to me that our thoughts are a more true measure of ourselves than our actions are. They are not under the control of human respect. It is not easy for them to be ashamed of themselves. They have no witnesses but God. They are not bound to keep within certain limits or observe certain proprieties. Religious motives alone can claim jurisdiction over them. The struggle, which so often ensues within us before we can bring ourselves to do our duty, goes on entirely within our thoughts. It is our own secret, and men cannot put us to the blush because of it. The contradiction, which too often exists between our outward actions and our inward intentions, is only to be detected in the realm of our thoughts, whither none but God can penetrate, except by guesses, which are not the less offences against charity because they happen to be correct. In like manner, as an impulse will sometimes show more of our real character, than what we do after deliberation, our first thoughts will often reveal to us faults of disposition which outward restraints will hinder from issuing in action. Actions have their external hindrances, while our thoughts better disclose to us our possibilities of good and evil. Of course there is a most true sense in which the conscientious effort to cure a fault is a better indication of our character than the fault we have not yet succeeded in curing. Nevertheless we may die at any moment; and when we die, we die as we are. Thus our thoughts tell us, better than our actions can do, what we shall be like the moment after death. Lastly, it is in the world of thought that we most often meet with God, walking as in the shades of ancient Eden. It is there we hear His whispers. It is there we perceive the fragrance of His recent presence. It is thence that the first vibrations of grace proceed.

> To hear the groaning of the prisoner;
> to loose them that are appointed to
> death. (Ps. 102:20)

There is also a grace of kind listening, as well as a grace of kind speaking. Some men listen with an abstracted air, which shows that their thoughts are elsewhere. Or they seem to listen, but by wide answers and irrelevant questions show that they have been occupied with their own thoughts, as being more interesting, at least in their own estimation, than what you have been saying. Some listen with a kind of importunate ferocity, which makes you feel that you are being put upon your trial, and that your auditor expects beforehand that you are going to tell him a lie, or to be inaccurate, or to say something which he will disapprove, and that you must mind your expressions. Some interrupt, and will not hear you to the end. Some hear you to the end, and then forthwith begin to talk to you about a similar experience which has befallen themselves, making your case only an illustration of their own. Some, meaning to be kind, listen with such a determined, lively, violent attention, that you are at once made uncomfortable, and the charm of conversation is at an end. Many persons, whose manners will stand the test of speaking, break down under the trial of listening. But all these things should be brought under the sweet influences of religion. Kind listening is often an act of the most delicate interior mortification, and is a great assistance towards kind speaking. Those who govern others must take care to be kind listeners, or else they will soon offend God, and fall into secret sins.

... then came Jesus, the doors being
shut, and stood in the midst, and
said, Peace be unto you. (John 20:26)

There is hardly a man or woman in the world, who has not got some corner of self into which he or she fears to venture with a light. The reasons for this may be various, as various as the individual souls. Nevertheless, in spite of the variety of reasons, the fact is universal. For the most part we hardly know our own reasons. It is an instinct, one of the quick instincts of corrupt nature. We prophesy to ourselves that, if we penetrate into that corner of self, something will have to be done which either our laziness or our immortification would shrink from doing. If we enter that sanctuary, some charm of easy devotion or smooth living will be broken. We shall find ourselves face to face with something unpleasant, something which will perhaps constrain us to all the trouble and annoyance of a complete interior revolution, or else leave us very uncomfortable in conscience. We may perhaps be committed to something higher than our present way of life, and that is out of the question. Religion is yoke enough as it is.

So we leave this corner of self curtained off, locked up like a room in a house with disagreeable associations attached to it, unvisited like a lumber closet where we are conscious that disorder and dirt are accumulating, which we have not just now the vigour to grapple with. But do we think that God cannot enter there, except by our unlocking the door, or see anything when He is there, unless we hold Him a light?

> If we say that we have no sin, we
> deceive ourselves, and the truth is
> not in us. (I John 1:8)

Self-deceit increases with our age. This is another of its characteristics. Some weeds grow in our souls by what appears a chance. Others die, if peculiar circumstances do not nurture them. Some are planted there by a single act of sin, an act which had neither parents or children, neither antecedents or consequences, so far as we can see; and they remain hardly green, barely not dead, and never grow at all. But self-deceit is an inevitable growth. The broadening of life is the widening of our faculties for deceiving ourselves. Simplicity is the only thing which is fatal to self-deceit. If we could be perfectly simple, we could inflict a mortal wound upon the monster.

But life multiplies things. It entangles our motives. It distracts our attention. It complicates our daily conduct. It bewilders us by its rapidity, its versatility, its contradictoriness, its imperiousness, its fertility. All these things are prolific of new possibilities for self-deceit; and self-deceit fills them as air fills a vacuum, silently if allowed its own way and time, with a report if compelled to act suddenly and under distress. Only of this we may be sure, that the fountain flows more copiously each succeeding year, and that unless grace is evaporating the waters as they spring, life is but a match between grace and self-deceit, in which the latter will be victorious; and all that grace can do is to delay the hour of its own defeat. It is one of those operations of grace which must be a complete one in order to be decisively triumphant.

> Cast not away therefore your confidence, which hath great recompence of reward. (Heb. 10:35)

All our spiritual exercises, of whatever nature they may be, are so many means of acquiring confidence in God. They all let us deeper down into Him. They all unfold more and more of the nature of grace, and of the poverty of our own nature. They all bring experiences of Jesus in the soul; and each of these experiences is a new ground of confidence in Him. Our simple perseverance in anything good is a process of augmentation of our confidence. Outward temptations help us. They frighten us away from self-trust. They make us better acquainted with our possibilities of sin. They reveal to us in an alarming manner the vigour and the unweariedness of the spiritual powers, which are arrayed against us. They lead us to try all methods of keeping right, and we exhaust them, and find, that only confidence in God wears, endures, and succeeds. Inward trials lead to the same result, only still more swiftly and more infallibly. God's arms are more closely folded round us in interior trials, than in the sensible sweetnesses of His consoling visitations. A much tried man is always a man of unbounded faith, and of a confidence in God which looks, to us of lower faith, superstitious in little things, and presumptuous in great ones.

Be ye therefore perfect, even as
your Father which is in heaven is
perfect. (Matt. 5:48)

In what does perfection consist? In a childlike, short-sighted charity which believes all things; in a grand supernatural conviction that every one is better than ourselves; in estimating far too low the amount of evil in the world; in looking far too exclusively on what is good; in the ingenuity of kind constructions; in an inattention, hardly intelligible, to the faults of others; in a graceful perversity of incredulousness about scandals, which sometimes in the saints runs close upon being a scandal of itself. This is perfection, this is the temper and genius of saints and saintlike men. It is a life of desire, oblivious of earthly things. It is a radiant energetic faith, that man's slowness and coldness will not interfere with the success of God's glory. Yet all the while it is instinctively fighting, by prayer and reparation, against evils, which it will not allow itself consciously to believe. No shadow of moroseness ever falls over the bright mind of a saint. It is not possible that it should do so.

# Frederick W. Robertson

## (1816–1853)

F. W. Robertson wanted to be a soldier but his commission was delayed so long that he followed his father's counsel and entered Oxford to study for the ministry. Five days later, the commission arrived. I bless the army clerk who delayed that commission and gave us a truly great preacher of the Word.

Robertson had a hard life and a difficult ministry. He was too evangelical to please the liberals in the Anglican Church, and too liberal to satisfy the ultraconservatives. An ultraconservative, partisan newspaper, *The Rock,* used to print lies about Robertson—and not bother to correct the stories. During his six years at Trinity Chapel, Brighton, Robertson preached penetrating sermons (usually with two points each) that can be read and reread with great profit. He was probably the first of the "psychological" preachers. Although his talents were not fully recognized during his lifetime, the publication of his sermons after his death enhanced his reputation. Today he is recognized as one of England's greatest preachers.

These selections reveal the courage of Robertson as he proclaimed truth. Perhaps he became a soldier after all!

Sanctify them through thy truth: thy
word is truth. (John 17:17)

He is sanctified by the self-devotion of his Master from the world, who has a life in himself independent of the maxims and customs which sweep along with them other men. In his

113

Master's words, "A well of water *in* him, springing up into everlasting life," keeping his life on the whole pure, and his heart fresh. His true life is hid with Christ in God. His motives, the aims and objects of his life, however inconsistent they may be with each other, however irregularly or feebly carried out, are yet on the whole above, not here. His citizenship is in heaven. He may be tempted—he may err—he may fall—but still in his darkest aberrations, there will be a something that keeps before him still the dreams and aspirations of his best days—a thought of the Cross of Christ, and the self-consecration that it typifies—a conviction that that is the Highest, and that alone the true Life. And that—if it were only that—would make him essentially different from other men, even when he mixes with them and seems to catch their tone, among them but not one of them. And that Life within him is Christ's pledge that he shall be yet what he longs to be—a something severing him, separating him, consecrating him. For him and for such as him the consecration prayer of Christ was made. "They are not of the world, even as I am not of the world: Sanctify them through thy Truth: Thy Word is Truth."

> But none of these things move
> me. . . . (Acts 20:24)

This is self-reliance—to repose calmly on the thought which is deepest in our bosoms, and be unmoved if the world will not accept it yet. To live on your own convictions against the world, is to overcome the world—to believe that what is truest in you is true for all: to abide by that, and not be over-anxious to be heard or understood, or sympathised with, certain that at last all must acknowledge the same, and that while you stand firm, the world will come round to you: that is independence. It is not difficult to get away into retirement, and there live upon your own convictions: nor is it difficult to mix with men, and follow their convictions: but to enter into the world, and there live out firmly and fearlessly according to your own conscience, that is Christian greatness.

There is a cowardice in this age which is not Christian. We shrink from the consequences of truth. We look round and cling dependently. We ask what men will think—what others will say—whether they will not stare in astonishment. Perhaps they will; but he who is calculating that, will accomplish nothing in this life. The Father—the Father who is with us and in us—what does He think? God's work cannot be done without a spirit of independence. A man is got some way in the Christian life when he has learned to say humbly and yet majestically, "I dare to be alone."

And ye shall know the truth, and the
truth shall make you free.
(John 8:32)

There is a tendency in the masses always to think—not what is true, but—what is respectable, correct, orthodox: we ask is that authorized? It comes partly from cowardice, partly from indolence: from habit: from imitation: from the uncertainty and darkness of all moral truths, and the dread of timid minds to plunge into the investigation of them. Now, truth known and believed respecting God and man, frees from this, by warning of individual responsibility. But responsibility is personal. It cannot be delegated to another, and thrown off upon a church. Before God, face to face, each soul must stand, to give account.

Do not, however, confound mental independence with mental pride. It may, it ought to co-exist with the deepest humility. For that mind alone is free which, conscious ever of its own feebleness, feeling hourly its own liability to err, turning thankfully to light from whatever side it may come, does yet refuse to give up that right, with which God has invested it of judging, or to abrogate its own responsibility, and so humbly, and even awfully, resolves to have an opinion, a judgment, a decision of its own.

Fear enslaves, courage liberates—and that always. Whatever a man intensely dreads, that brings him into bondage, if it be above the fear of God, and the reverence of duty. The apprehension of pain, the fear of death, the dread of the world's laugh, of poverty, or the loss of reputation, enslave alike.

From such fear Christ frees, and through the power of the truths I have spoken of. He who lives in the habitual contemplation of immortality cannot be in bondage to time, or enslaved by transitory temptations. I do not say he will not, "he cannot sin," saith the Scripture, while that faith is living. He who feels his soul's dignity, knowing what he is and who, redeemed by God the Son, and freed by God the Spirit, cannot cringe, nor pollute himself, nor be mean. He who aspires to gaze undazzled on the intolerable brightness of that One before whom Israel veiled their faces, will scarcely quail before any earthly fear.

> But as for me, I will walk in mine
> integrity. . . . (Ps. 26:11)

The next qualification is integrity. But by integrity I do not mean simply sincerity or honesty; integrity rather according to the meaning of the word as its derivation interprets it— entireness—wholeness—soundness: that which Christ means when He says, "If thine eye be single or sound, thy whole body shall be full of light."

This integrity extends through the entireness or wholeness of the character. It is found in small matters as well as great; for the allegiance of the soul to truth is tested by small things rather than by those which are more important. There is many a man who would lose his life rather than perjure himself in a court of justice, whose life is yet a tissue of small insincerities. We think that we hate falsehood when we are

116

only hating the consequences of falsehood. We resent hypocrisy, and treachery, and calumny, not because they are untrue, but because they harm us. We hate the false calumny, but we are half pleased with the false praise. It is evidently not the element of untruth here that is displeasing, but the element of harmfulness. Now he is a man of integrity who hates untruth as untruth: who resents the smooth and polished falsehood of society which does no harm: who turns in indignation from the glittering whitened lie of sepulchral Pharisaism which injures no one. Integrity recoils from deceptions which men would almost smile to hear called deception.

> If any man will do his will, he shall
> know of the doctrine. . . . (John 7:17)

This universe is governed by laws. At the bottom of everything here there is a law. Things are in this way and not that: we call that a law or condition. All departments have their own laws. Obey the laws of the body: such laws as say, Fix the attention: strengthen by exercise: and then their prizes are yours—health, strength, pliability of muscle, tenaciousness of memory, nimbleness of imagination, etc.

Obey the laws of your spiritual being, and it has its prizes too. For instance, the condition or law of a peaceful life is submission to the law of meekness: "Blessed are the meek, for they shall inherit the earth." The condition of the Beatific vision is a pure heart and life: "Blessed are the pure in heart, for they shall see God." To the impure, God is simply invisible. The condition annexed to a sense of God's presence—in other words, that without which a sense of God's presence cannot be—is obedience to the laws of love: "If we love one another, God dwelleth in us, and His love is perfected in us." The condition of spiritual wisdom, and certainty in truth is obedience to the will of God, surrender of private will: "If any man will do His will, he shall know of the doctrine, whether it be of God, or whether I speak of myself."

117

Commit thy way unto the LORD;
trust also in him; and he shall bring
it to pass. (Ps. 37:5)

There are times when a dense cloud veils the sunlight: you cannot see the sun, nor feel him. Sensitive temperaments feel depression: and that unaccountably and irresistibly. No effort can make you *feel.* Then you hope. Behind the cloud the sun is: from thence he will come: the day drags through, the darkest and longest night ends at last. Thus we bear the darkness and the otherwise intolerable cold, and many a sleepless night. It does not shine now—but it will.

So too, spiritually. There are hours in which physical derangement darkens the windows of the soul; days in which shattered nerves make life simply endurance; months and years in which intellectual difficulties, pressing for solution, shut out God. Then faith must be replaced by hope. "What I do thou knowest not now; but thou shalt know hereafter." Clouds and darkness are round about Him: *but* Righteousness and Truth are the habitation of His throne. "My soul, hope thou in God: for I shall yet praise Him, who is the health of my countenance and my God."

Love not the world, neither the
things that are in the world.
(I John 2:15)

Worldliness then consists in these three things:—Attachment to the Outward—attachment to the Transitory—attachment to the Unreal: in opposition to love for the Inward, the Eternal, the True: and the one of these affections is necessarily expelled by the other. If a man love the world, the love of the Father is not in him. But let a man once feel the power of the kingdom that is within, and then the love fades of that emotion whose life consists only in the thrill of a nerve, or the vivid sensation of a feeling: he loses his happiness and wins his blessedness. Let a man get but one glimpse of the King in His beauty, and then the forms and shapes of things here, are to him but the types of an invisible loveliness: types which he is content should break and fade. Let but a man feel truth—that goodness is greatness—that there is no other greatness—and then the degrading reverence with which the titled of this world bow before wealth, and the ostentation with which the rich of this world profess their familiarity with title: all the pride of life, what is it to him? The love of the Inward— Everlasting, Real—the love, that is, of the Father, annihilates the love of the world.

# John Charles Ryle
## (1816–1900)

The Liverpool Cathedral is one of the most beautiful in England. The first bishop of Liverpool, J. C. Ryle, is buried in this cathedral where he preached for twenty years.

Ryle was the leader of the evangelical party in the Church of England. His policy was to encourage the conservative men to remain in the church rather than to abandon ship and leave the liberals to pursue their program unhindered. For this position, he was severely criticized by ultraconservative evangelicals. *The Rock,* the same newspaper that attacked F. W. Robertson, called Ryle a neoevangelical. He was probably the first man to receive that designation, even though today the term is used quite freely.

Pastors know Ryle for his helpful *Expository Thoughts on The Gospels.* He also wrote numerous gospel tracts.

The fruit of the righteous is a tree of
life; and he that winneth souls is
wise. (Prov. 11:30)

I want all converted people to be missionaries. I do not want them all to go out to foreign lands, and preach to the heathen; but I do want all to be of a missionary spirit, and to strive to do good at home. I want them to testify to all around them that the strait gate is the way to happiness, and to persuade them to enter in by it.

When Andrew was converted he found his brother Peter, and said to him, "We have found the Messias, which is, being interpreted, the Christ. And he brought him to Jesus." (John 1:41, 42.) When Philip was converted he found Nathaniel, and said to him, "We have found Him, of whom Moses in the law, and the prophets did write, Jesus of Nazareth, the son of Joseph. And Nathaniel said unto him, Can there any good thing come out of Nazareth? Philip said unto him, Come and see." (John 1:45, 46.) When the Samaritan woman was converted, she "left her waterpot, and went into the city, and said to the men, Come, see a man which told me all things that ever I did: is not this the Christ?" (John 4:28, 29.) When Saul the Pharisee was converted, "Straightway he preached Christ in the synagogues, that He is the son of God." (Acts 9:20.)

I long to see this kind of spirit among Christians in the present day. I long to see more zeal to commend the strait gate to all who are yet outside, and more desire to persuade them to enter in and be saved. Happy indeed is that Church whose members not only desire to reach heaven themselves, but desire also to take others with them!

> . . . and these have no root, which
> for a while believe, and in time of
> temptation fall away. (Luke 8:13)

How much Evangelical religion is completely unreal? You will sometimes see men professing great affection for the pure "Gospel," while they are practically inflicting on it the greatest injury. They will talk loudly of soundness in the faith, and have a keen nose for heresy. They will run eagerly after popular preachers, and applaud Protestant speakers at public meetings to the very echo. They are familiar with all the phrases of evangelical religion, and can converse fluently about its leading doctrines. To see their faces at public meetings, or in church, you would think them eminently godly. . . . And yet these people in private will sometimes do things of which even some heathens would be ashamed. They are neither truthful, nor straightforward, nor honest, nor manly, nor just, nor good-tempered, nor unselfish, nor merciful, nor humble, nor kind! And is such Christianity as this real? It is not. It is a miserable imposture, a base cheat and caricature.

How much Revivalist religion in the present day is utterly unreal! You will find a crowd of false professors bringing discredit on the work of God wherever the Holy Spirit is poured out. You will see a mixed multitude of Egyptians accompanying the Israel of God, and doing it harm, whenever Israel goes out of Egypt. How many now-a-days will profess to be suddenly convinced of sin,—to find peace in Jesus,—to be overwhelmed with joys and ecstacies of soul,—while in reality they have no grace at all. Like the stony-ground hearers, they endure but for a season. "In the time of temptation they fall away." (Luke 8:13) As soon as the first excitement is passed off, they return to their old ways, and resume their former sins. Their religion is like Jonah's gourd, which came up in a night and perished in a night. They have neither root nor vitality. They only injure God's cause and give occasion to God's enemies to blaspheme. And is Christianity like this real? It is nothing of the kind. It is base metal from the devil's mint, and is worthless in God's sight.

> The backslider in heart shall be
> filled with his own ways. . . .
> (Prov. 14:14)

It is a miserable thing to be a backslider. Of all unhappy things that can befall a man, I suppose it is the worst. A stranded ship, a broken-winged eagle, a garden overrun with weeds, a harp without strings, a church in ruins,—all these are sad sights; but a backslider is a sadder sight still. That true grace shall never be extinguished, and true union with Christ never be broken off, I feel no doubt. But I do believe that a man may fall away so far that he shall lose sight of his own grace, and despair of his own salvation. And if this is not hell, it is certainly the next thing to it! A wounded conscience, a mind sick of itself, a memory full of self-reproach, a heart pierced through with the Lord's arrows, a spirit broken with a load of inward accusation,—all this is a *taste of hell.* It is a hell on earth. Truly that saying of the wise man is solemn and weighty,—"The backslider in heart shall be filled with his own ways." (Prov. 14:14.)

Now, what is the cause of most backsliding? I believe, as a general rule, one of the chief causes is neglect of private prayer. Of course the secret history of falls will not be known till the last day. I can only give my opinion as a minister of Christ and a student of the heart. That opinion is, I repeat distinctly, that backsliding generally first begins with *neglect of private prayer.*

Bibles read without prayer, sermons heard without prayer, marriages contracted without prayer, journeys undertaken without prayer, residences chosen without prayer, friendships formed without prayer, the daily act of private prayer itself hurried over or gone through without heart,—these are the kind of downward steps by which many a Christian descends to a condition of spiritual palsy, or reaches the point where God allows him to have a tremendous fall.

> Man shall not live by bread alone,
> but by every word that proceedeth
> out of the mouth of God. (Matt. 4:4)

Every living thing which God creates requires food. The life that God imparts needs sustaining and nourishing. It is so with animal and vegetable life,—with birds, beasts, fishes, reptiles, insects, and plants. It is equally so with spiritual life. When the Holy Ghost raises a man from the death of sin and makes him a new creature in Christ Jesus, the new principle in that man's heart requires food, and the only food which will sustain it is the Word of God. . . .

Love to the Word is one of the characteristics we see in Job.

Little as we know of this Patriarch and his age, this at least stands out clearly. He says, "I have esteemed the words of His mouth more than my necessary food." (Job 23:12.)

Love to the Word is a shining feature in the character of David. Mark how it appers all through that wonderful part of Scripture, the 119th Psalm. He might well say, "Oh, how I love thy law!" (Psalm 119:97.)

Love to the Word is a striking point in the character of St. Paul. What were he and his companions but men "mighty in the Scriptures?" What were his sermons but expositions and applications of the Word?

Love to the Word appears pre-eminently in our Lord and Saviour Jesus Christ. He read it publicly. He quoted it continually. He expounded it frequently. He advised the Jews to "search" it. He used it as His weapon to resist the devil. He said repeatedly, "The Scripture must be fulfilled."—Almost the last thing He did was to "open the understanding of His disciples, that they might understand the Scriptures." (Luke 24:45.) I am afraid that man can be no true servant of Christ, who has not something of his Master's mind and feeling towards the Bible.

> It is fine to be zealous, provided the
> purpose is good. . . . (Gal. 4:18, NIV)

There is such a thing as zeal from *party spirit*. It is quite possible for a man to be unwearied in promoting the interests of his own Church or denomination, and yet to have no grace in his own heart,—to be ready to die for the peculiar opinions of his own section of Christians, and yet to have no real love to Christ. Such was the zeal of the Pharisees. They "compassed sea and land to make one proselyte, and when he was made, they made him two-fold more the child of hell than themselves." (Matt. 23:15.) This zeal is not true.

There is such a thing as zeal from mere *selfishness*. There are times when it is men's interest to be zealous in religion. Power and patronage are sometimes given to godly men. The good things of the world are sometimes to be attained by wearing a cloak of religion. And whenever this is the case there is no lack of false zeal. Such was the zeal of Joab, when he served David. Such was the zeal of only too many Englishmen in the days of the Commonwealth, when the Puritans were in power.

There is such a thing as zeal from the *love of praise*. Such was the zeal of Jehu, when he was putting down the worship of Baal. Remember how he met Jonadab the son of Rechab, and said, "Come with me, and see my zeal for the Lord." (2 Kings 10:16.) Such is the zeal that Bunyan refers to in "Pilgrim's Progress," when he speaks of some who went "for praise" to mount Zion. Some people feed on the praise of their fellow-creatures. They would rather have it from Christians than have none at all.

> Which say, Stand by thyself, come
> not near to me; for I am holier than
> thou. (Isa. 65:5)

When St. Paul said, "Come out and be separate," he did not mean that Christians should be singular, eccentric, and peculiar in their dress, manners, demeanour, and voice. Anything which attracts notice in these matters is most objectionable, and ought to be carefully avoided. To wear clothes of such a color, or made in such a fashion, that when you go into company every eye is fixed on you, and you are the object of general observation, is an enormous mistake. It gives occasion to the wicked to ridicule religion, and looks self-righteous and affected. There is not the slightest proof that our Lord and His apostles, and Priscilla, and Persis, and their companions, did not dress and behave just like others in their own ranks of life. On the other hand, one of the many charges our Lord brings against the Pharisees was that of "making broad their phylacteries, and enlarging the borders of their garments," so as to be "seen of men." (Matt. 23:5.) True sanctity and sanctimoniousness are entirely different things. Those who try to show their unworldliness by wearing conspicuously ugly clothes, or by speaking in a whining, snuffling voice, or by affecting an unnatural slavishness, humility, and gravity of manner, miss their mark altogether, and only give occasion to the enemies of the Lord to blaspheme.

When St. Paul said, "Come out and be separate," he did not mean that Christians ought to retire from the company of mankind, and shut themselves up in solitude. It is one of the crying errors of the Church of Rome to suppose that eminent holiness is to be attained by such practices. . . . Separation of this kind is not according to the mind of Christ. He says distinctly in His last prayer, "I pray not that Thou shouldest take them out of the world, but that Thou shouldest keep them from the evil." (John 17:15.) There is not a word in the Acts or Epistles to recommend such a separation. True believers are always represented as mixing in the world, doing their duty in it, and glorifying God by patience, meekness, purity, and courage in their several positions, and not by cowardly desertion of them. Moreover, it is foolish to suppose that we can keep the world and the devil out of our hearts by going into holes and corners. True religion and unworldliness are best seen, not in timidly forsaking the post which God has allotted to us, but in manfully standing our ground, and showing the power of grace to overcome evil.

> Henceforth I call you not servants;
> for the servant knoweth not what
> his lord doeth: but I have called you
> friends. . . . (John 15:15)

**M**an's friendship is sadly blind. He often injures those he loves by injudicious kindness: he often errs in the counsel he gives; he often leads his friends into trouble by bad advice, even when he means to help them. He sometimes keeps them back from the way of life, and entangles them in the vanities of the world, when they have well nigh escaped. The friendship of the Lord Jesus is not so: it always does us good, and never evil.

The Lord Jesus *never spoils* His friends by extravagant indulgence. He gives them everything that is really for their benefit; He withholds nothing from them that is really good; but He requires them to take up their cross daily and follow Him. He bids them endure hardships as good soldiers: He calls on them to fight the good fight against the world, the flesh, and the devil. His people often dislike it at the time, and think it hard; but when they reach heaven they will see it was all well done.

The Lord Jesus *makes no mistakes* in managing His friends' affairs. He orders all their concerns with perfect wisdom: all things happen to them as much of sickness and as much of health, as much of poverty and as much of riches, as much of sorrow and as much of joy, as He sees their souls require. He leads them by the right way to bring them to the city of habitation. He mixes their bitterest cups like a wise physician, and takes care that they have not a drop too little or too much. His people often misunderstand His dealings; they are silly enough to fancy their course of life might have been better ordered: but in the resurrection-day they will thank God that not their will, but Christ's was done.

# *John Ker*
## (1819–1886)

One glorious June day, a friend was showing four of us American tourists the beauties of "Covenanter country" several miles outside Edinburgh. We stopped to look at an old church and graveyard where there were monuments to the Covenanters who were martyred. There in the church was a memorial window dedicated to John Ker. Across the street stood the house in which he was born. What a bonnie day it turned out to be!

Ker (pronounced either "car" or "care") was a noted preacher in his day and a gifted teacher of preachers at the United Free Church seminary. He was one of George Morrison's favorite preachers, and he is also one of mine. Besides several volumes of sermons, he wrote *The Psalms in History and Biography, Lectures on Preaching* (a definitive work), and *Thoughts for Heart and Life,* a collection of insights, any of which Ker could have expanded into a sermon. They are brief—but they will make you think!

. . . from faith to faith: as it is
written. The just shall live by faith.
(Rom. 1:17)

Those Christians are blessed who need to leave their simple views of childhood's faith no more than the field-lark does her nest—rising right over it to look at God's morning sun, and his wide, beautiful world, singing a clear, happy song, and then sinking straight down again to their heart's home. But those

128

are not less blessed who, like the dove, lose their ark for a while, and return to it, having found no rest for the sole of their foot save there. They have a deeper experience within, and carry a higher and wider message to the world. The olive leaf in the mouth, plucked from the passing flood, is more than the song at coming daylight. It is as Paul's "Thanks be to God who giveth us the victory," compared with the children's "Hosannah."

> My house shall be called the house
> of prayer; but ye have made it a den
> of thieves. (Matt. 21:13)

One is struck in reading the account of the purifying of the temple by Christ (Matt. 21:12), that He should have bestowed so much thought on what was so soon to become obsolete by His own word, "It is finished!" We do not read elsewhere of the indignation of our Lord rising to such a height, and taking the form of outward compulsion. It is the seal of Christ set on the sacredness of the Old Testament worship, all the more needed that He is about to remove it; but still more it is a vivid warning beforehand against the union between covetousness and religion, or rather the form of religion. That evil reached a visible height when the sale of indulgences and the building of St. Peter's went hand in hand. But it has appeared so often, and in all sections of the Church, that the entrance of the money-changers into the temple may be called the normal danger of Christianity. Drunkenness and sensuality, which had their shrines in the old pagan Pantheon, have still a place in the hearts of many professed worshippers in the house of God, but it is Mammon who still sets up his tables in the open court.

> And when they saw him, they wor-
> shipped him: but some doubted.
> (Matt. 28:17)

Is doubt a sin? Not always. We should not, to begin with, say that doubt is the proper state for any mind; for if things were right, belief in the great spiritual realities would be as natural as seeing the light: therefore doubt is unnatural, something that should not be, and from which we ought to seek escape.

But doubt may be called at first a temptation rather than a sin—a temptation ready to recur from outward events and inward states of mind, and infections of thought from other spirits. These are not necessarily sinful. It is wrong not to seek deliverance from doubt—it is wrong to cherish it as an excuse for sin, to inquire captiously, to press frivolous objections, to seek evidence which is impossible or which we do not require in similar cases for practical action in life, to scatter doubt where we have no hope or wish for a solution of our own, and it is wrong not to feel for ever the pressure and misery of it.

> Unto the upright there ariseth light
> in the darkness. . . . (Ps. 112:4)

How shall we seek deliverance [from doubt]? By calm, reverential inquiry in the depths of the nature God has given us, and of that Word which professes to be the revelation of it and of Him—by humble, hopeful prayer to the Father of lights, whose will cannot be that any soul He has made should walk in darkness; by holding to the nearest, clearest truth, whatever it may be, and acting upon it, assured that every truth leads up; by an effort to be true ourselves and thoroughly genuine,—"Unto the upright there ariseth light in the darkness;" and if we think we have found great truths, but are troubled with difficulties on the edges, then by a constant recurrence to the center and soul of things, where we feel we can repose,—the great assured character of God as a God of justice, love, and mercy, who will bring all right, and enable the soul to realise that prophecy which shall yet come to the world, "But there the glorious Lord will be unto us a place of broad rivers and streams."

> . . . how unsearchable are his judg-
> ments, and his ways past finding
> out! (Rom. 11:33)

There will be nothing grander in the revelation of the future than the way in which God will reconcile the material and spiritual world's fixed law with perfect liberty, and show how, in the midst of, and through the first, the second grows up to full stature. The pity is that the two are so often set in opposition, the men of law doubting spirit and denying freedom, the men of spirit looking suspiciously on the discoveries of law. To a Christian man both are united in the holiest, inmost shrine of his religion, the Incarnation. Believing in the harmony of those two natures there, we believe also in the other, though unable to combine them in the system of thought; and when we stand before the shrine—God manifest—we shall have the key to the union of the two worlds, in all the temple, to its utmost walls and deepest base, in all space, through all time.

So shall be solved those questions of the supernatural in the natural, of miracle, of prayer and its answer, that vex many; the breathings and heavings of the inner life that start up through the body of nature.

He is the great, the happy man, who can have his heart of faith at the centre of life, and pursue the search into law with his mind, feeling that life and light agree. "With Thee is the fountain of life, in Thy light shall we see light."

> . . . work out your own salvation
> with fear and trembling. (Phil. 2:12)

The Pharisees were rebuked for making their religion public. Daniel would have sinned had he made his private. So different is duty when religion is popular or unpopular. Sometimes a man has no religion if he does not show it; sometimes very little if he obtrudes it. One thing we must always show—the fruits in the life.

There are things in religion not for common talk, which a delicate mind will no more thrust in than it will its heart's deepest affections. David says, "Come near all ye that fear God: I will tell what He hath done for my soul." Those that "fear God" are invited, and they must "come near." . . .

Our Saviour was thirty years in the world before He said much in it, as far as we know. Then He spoke "as one having authority." He bade some of the healed speak, others to be silent, as suited character and circumstance. He kept silence on occasions—when the Syro-Phoenician woman cried after Him, when His accusers testified against Him. There are many seasons for silence as well as for speech.

> For we can do nothing against the
> truth, but for the truth. (II Cor. 13:8)

Great thoughts and books sometimes disappear for generations, and turn up again unexpectedly, like messages dropped in the sea, and carried to far-off shores. The ocean of time has its hidden currents, as well as that of space; and a curious history might be written of these reappearances. They help us to believe that no true word or deed is finally lost, and that a time is coming when, in this sense also, the sea shall give up the dead which are in it.

# Charles Henry Mackintosh ("C. H. M.")

## (1820–1896)

I cannot forget the day when a small box containing *Notes on the Pentateuch,* by "C. H. M.," arrived at my home. I was a young believer planning to enter the ministry, and I had read that D. L. Moody had recommended that everybody read these six small volumes. I sent away for them on the strength of that recommendation, and I was not disappointed. In these intervening years I found I disagreed with some of the author's interpretations, but I hope I never fail to share his love for the Word and his deep desire to magnify Jesus Christ in all things.

Mackintosh was born in Ireland and was converted to Christ through the witness of his sister. The writings of John Nelson Darby, founder of the Plymouth Brethren movement, were very helpful to him, and Mackintosh became a spiritual leader in that fellowship. He was principal of a school for about ten years, but then began to devote his full time to the spoken and written ministry of the Word.

In the beginning God created the
heaven and the earth. (Gen. 1:1)

The first sentence in the divine canon sets us in the presence of Him who is the infinite source of all true blessedness. There is no elaborate argument in proof of the existence of God. The Holy Ghost could not enter upon anything of the kind. God reveals Himself. He makes Himself known by His works. "The heavens declare the glory of God, and the firmament showeth His handiwork." "All Thy works shall praise Thee, O Lord." "Great and marvelous are Thy works, Lord God Almighty." None but an infidel or an atheist would seek an argument in proof of the Being of One who, by the word of His mouth, called worlds into existence, and declared Himself the All-wise, the Almighty, and the everlasting God. Who but "God" could "create" anything? "Lift up your eyes on high, and behold who hath created these things, that bringeth out their host by number; He calleth them all by names, by the greatness of His might, for that He is strong in power; not one faileth." (Is. 40:26) "The gods of the heathen are idols, but the Lord made the heavens." In the Book of Job (chap. 38–41) we have an appeal of the very grandest description, on the part of Jehovah Himself, to the work of creation, as an unanswerable argument in proof of His infinite superiority; and this appeal, while it sets before the understanding the most vivid and convincing demonstration of God's omnipotence, touches the heart also by its amazing condescension. The majesty and the love, the power and the tenderness, are all divine.

> By faith Noah, being warned of God
> of things not seen. . . . (Heb. 11:7)

Nature is governed by what it sees,—it is governed by its senses. Faith is governed by the pure Word of God; (inestimable treasure in this dark world!) this gives stability, let outward appearances be what they may. When God spoke to Noah of judgment impending, there was no sign of it,—it was "not seen as yet"; but the Word of God made it a present reality to the heart that was enabled to mix that Word with faith. Faith does not wait to *see* a thing ere it believes, for "faith cometh by hearing and hearing by the Word of God."

All that the man of faith needs, is to know that God has spoken; this imparts perfect certainty to his soul. "Thus saith the Lord," settles everything. A single line of sacred Scripture is an abundant answer to all the reasonings and all the imaginations of the human mind; and when one has the Word of God as the basis of his convictions, he may calmly stand against the full tide of human opinion and prejudice. It was the Word of God which sustained the heart of Noah during his long course of service; and the same Word has sustained the millions of God's saints from that day to this, in the face of the world's contradiction. Hence, we cannot set too high a value upon the Word of God. Without it, all is dark uncertainty; with it, all is light and peace. Where it shines, it marks out for the man of God a sure and a blessed path; where it shines not, one is left to wander amid the bewildering mazes of human tradition.

> But God forbid that I should glory, save in the cross of our Lord Jesus Christ, by whom the world is crucified unto me, and I unto the world.
> (Gal. 6:14)

The same cross which connects me with God, has separated me from the world. A dead man is, evidently, done with the world; and hence, the believer, having died in Christ, is done with the world; and, having risen with Christ, is connected with God, in the power of a new life—a new nature. Being thus inseparably linked with Christ, he, of necessity, participates in His acceptance with God, and in His rejection by the world. The two things go together. The former makes him a worshiper and a citizen in heaven, the latter makes him a witness and a stranger on earth. That brings him inside the veil: this puts him outside the camp. The one is as perfect as the other. If the cross has come between me and my sins, it has just as really come between me and the world. In the former case, it puts me into the place of peace with God; in the latter, it puts me into the place of hostility with the world, *i.e.*, in a moral point of view; though, in another sense, it makes me the patient, humble witness of that precious, unfathomable, eternal grace which is set forth in the cross.

> . . . he that doeth the will of God
> abideth for ever. (I John 2:17)

Nothing will endure but that which is of God. I must realize the link between me and the living God: I must know myself as one called of Him into the position which I occupy, else I shall have no stability, and exhibit no consistency therein. It will not do to follow in the track of other people merely because it is their track. God will graciously give each a path to walk in, a sphere to move in, and a responsibility to fulfill; and we are bound to know our calling and the functions thereof, that, by His grace ministered to our souls daily, we may work therein effectually, to His glory. It matters not what our measure may be, provided it be what God hath dealt to us. We may have "five talents," or we may have but "one;" still, if we use the "one," with our eye fixed on the Master, we shall just be as sure to hear from his gracious lips the words, "Well done," as if we had used the "five." This is encouraging. Paul, Peter, James, and John had each his peculiar measure—his specific ministry; and so with all: none needs to interfere with another. A carpenter has a saw and a plane, a hammer and a chisel, and he uses each as he needs it. Nothing can be more worthless than imitation. If, in the natural world, we look at the various orders of creation, we see no imitation. All have their proper sphere, their proper functions. And if it be thus in the natural world, how much more in the spiritual. The field is wide enough for all. In every house there are vessels of various sizes and various shapes: the master wants them all.

And he gave them their request; but
sent leanness into their soul.
(Ps. 106:15)

$A$braham was called of God from Ur to Canaan, and hence God led him forth on the way. When Abraham tarried at Charran, God waited for him; when he went down into Egypt, He restored him; when he needed guidance, He guided him; when there was a strife and a separation, He took care of him; so that Abraham had only to say, "Oh, how great is Thy goodness which *Thou hast laid up* for them that fear Thee, which Thou hast wrought for them that trust in Thee, before the sons of men!" He lost nothing by the strife. He had his tent and his altar before, and he had his tent and his altar afterwards. "Then Abram removed *his tent,* and came and dwelt in the plain of Mamre, which is in Hebron, and built there *an altar* unto the Lord." Lot might choose Sodom but as for Abraham, he sought and found his all in God. There was no altar in Sodom. Alas! all who travel in that direction are in quest of something quite different from that. It is never the worship of God, but the love of the world, that leads them thither. And even though they should attain their object, what is it?—how does it end? Just thus: "He gave them their request, but sent leanness into their souls."

When the LORD turned again the
captivity of Zion, we were like them
that dream. Then was our mouth
filled with laughter, and our tongue
with singing. . . . (Ps. 126:1–2)

$T$here are two kinds of laughter spoken of in Scripture. There is, first, the laughter with which the Lord fills our mouth, when, at some trying crisis, He appears in a signal manner for our relief.

"When the Lord turned again the captivity of Zion, we were

137

like them that dream. Then was our mouth filled with *laughter*, and our tongue with singing: then said they among the heathen, the Lord hath done great things for us, whereof we are glad." (Psalm 126:1, 2) Again, there is the laughter with which unbelief fills our mouths, when God's promises are too magnificent for our narrow hearts to take in, or the visible agency too small in our judgment, for the accomplishment of His grand designs. The first of these we are never ashamed or afraid to avow.—Zion's sons are not ashamed to say, "Then was our mouth filled with laughter." (Psalm 126:2) When Jehovah makes us to laugh, we may laugh heartily. "But Sarah denied, saying, 'I laughed not;' for she was afraid." Unbelief makes us cowards and liars: faith makes us bold and truthful,—it enables us to "come boldly," and to "draw near with true hearts."

> Accounting that God was able to
> raise him up, even from the
> dead. . . . (Heb. 11:19)

It is one thing to rest in God's blessings, and another thing to rest in Himself: it is one thing to trust God when I have before my eyes the channel through which the blessing is to flow, and quite another thing to trust Him when that channel is entirely stopped up. This was what proved the excellency of Abraham's faith. He showed that he could not merely trust God for an innumerable seed while Isaac stood before him in health and vigor, but just as fully if he were a smoking victim on the altar. This was a high order of confidence in God,—it was unalloyed confidence; it was not a confidence propped up in part by the Creator and in part by the creature. No; it rested on one solid pedestal, viz., God Himself. "He accounted that God was able." He never accounted that Isaac was able. Isaac, without God, was nothing: God, without Isaac, was everything. This is a principle of the very last importance, and one eminently calculated to test the heart most keenly. Does it make any difference to me to see the apparent channel of all my blessings dried up? Am I dwelling sufficiently near the fountain-head to be able, with a worshipping spirit, to behold all the creature streams dried up? This I do feel to be a searching question. Have I such a simple view of God's sufficiency as to be able, as it were, to "stretch forth my hand and take the knife to slay my son"? Abraham was enabled to do this, because his eye rested on the God of resurrection,—"he accounted that God was able to raise him up even from the dead."

# George MacDonald

## (1824–1905)

The popularity of C. S. Lewis has led to the "resurrection" of George MacDonald, the Scottish preacher, poet, and novelist whose writings first awakened Lewis to spiritual vision. MacDonald's children's books probably gave Lewis the idea for his *Chronicles of Narnia*.

A congregational preacher, MacDonald had a difficult time in his first pastorate. He had rather liberal views of final judgment, and his sermons were not the traditional Scottish exposition. The church decreased his salary and tried to starve him into complying with its traditions. He resigned and turned to writing and preaching (without remuneration) in various churches.

I find then a law, that, when I would
do good, evil is present with me.
(Rom. 7:21)

Foolish is the man, and there are many such men, who would rid himself or his fellows of discomfort by setting the world right, by waging war on the evils around him, while he neglects that integral part of the world where lies his business, his first business—namely, his own character and conduct.

There is no way of making three men right but by making right each one of the three; but a cure in one man who repents and turns is a beginning of the cure of the whole human race.

Rightness alone is cure. The return of the organism to its true self is its only possible ease. To free a man from suffering, he must be set right, put in health; and the health at the root of man's being, his rightness, is to be free from wrongness, that is, from sin. A man is right when there is no wrong in him. The wrong, the evil is in him; he must be set free from it.

> Order my steps in thy word: and let
> not any iniquity have dominion over
> me. (Ps. 119:133)

It is the indwelling badness, ready to produce bad actions, that we need to be delivered from. Against this badness if a man will not strive, he is left to commit evil and reap the consequences. To be saved from these consequences would be no deliverance; it would be an immediate, ever deepening damnation. It is the evil in our being—no essential part of it, thank God—the miserable fact that the very child of God does not care for his Father and will not obey Him, causing us to desire wrongly, yet making it impossible for us not to feel wrongly—this is what He came to deliver us from—not the things we have done, but the possibility of doing such things any more.

> Surely I have behaved and quieted
> myself, as a child that is weaned of
> his mother: my soul is even as a
> weaned child. (Ps. 131:2)

As the love of Him who is love transcends ours as the heavens are higher than the earth, so must He desire in His child infinitely more than the most jealous love of the best mother can desire in hers. He would have him rid of all discontent, all fear, all grudging, all bitterness in word or thought, all gauging and measuring of his own with a differ-

141

ent rod from that he would apply to another's. He will have no curling of the lip; no indifference in him to the man whose service in any form he uses; no desire to excel another, no contentment at gaining by his loss. He will not have him receive the smallest service without gratitude; would not hear from him a tone to har the heart of another, a word to make it ache, be the ache ever so transient. From such, as from all other sins, Jesus was born to deliver us; not, primarily, or by itself, from the punishment of any of them. When all are gone, the holy punishment will have departed also. He came to make us good, and therein blessed children.

> Jesus knowing that the Father had
> given all things into his hands, and
> that he was come from God, and
> went to God. (John 13:3)

The world was for Him no chamber of terror. He walks to the door of the sepulcher, the sealed cellar of His Father's house, and calls forth its four-days dead. He rebukes the mourners, He stays the funeral, and gives back the departed children to their parents' arms. The roughest of its servants do not make Him wince; none of them are so arrogant as to disobey His word; He falls asleep in the midst of the storm that threatens to swallow His boat. Hear how, on that same occasion, He rebukes his disciples! The children to tremble at a gust of wind in the house! God's little ones afraid of the storm! Hear Him tell the watery floor to be still.

All His life He was among His Father's things, either in heaven or in the World . . . He claimed none of them as His own, would not have had one of them His except through His Father. Did He ever say, "This is mine, not yours"? Did He not say, "All things are mine, therefore they are yours"? That the things were His Father's made them precious things to Him. Oh, for His liberty among the things of the Father! Only by knowing them the things of our Father can we escape enslaving ourselves to them.

> And all they in the synagogue, when
> they heard these things, were filled
> with wrath. (Luke 4:28)

The Nazarenes heard with indignation. Their wonder at His gracious words was changed to bitterest wrath. The very beams of their ugly religion were party-spirit, exclusiveness, and pride in the fancied favor of God for them only of all the nations: to hint at the possibility of a revelation of the glory of God to a stranger; far more, to hint that a stranger might be fitter to receive such a revelation than a Jew, was an offense reaching to the worst insult; and it was cast in their teeth by a common man of their own city! "Thou art but a well-known carpenter's son, and dost thou teach *us!* Darest thou imply a divine preference for Capernaum over Nazareth?"

> But the meek shall inherit the earth;
> and shall delight themselves in the
> abundance of peace. (Ps. 37:11)

To inherit the earth is to grow ever more alive to the presence, in it and in all its parts, of Him who is the life of men. How far one may advance in such inheritance while yet in the body will simply depend on the meekness he attains while yet in the body; but it may be . . . that the new heavens and the new earth are the same in which we now live, righteously inhabited by the meek, with their deeper-opened eyes.

Which is more the possessor of the world—he who has a thousand houses, or he who, without one house to call his own, has ten in which his knock at the door would rouse instant jubilation? Which is the richer—the man who, his large money spent, would have no refuge; or he for whose necessity a hundred would sacrifice comfort? Which of the two possessed the earth—king Agrippa or tent-maker Paul?

I thank thee, O Father, Lord of heaven and earth, because thou hast hid these things from the wise and prudent, and hast revealed them unto babes. (Matt. 11:25)

These wise and prudent, careful to make the words of His messengers rime with their conclusions, interpret the great heart of God, not by their own hearts, but by their miserable intellects; and, postponing the obedience which alone can give power to the understanding, press upon men's minds their wretched interpretations of the will of the Father, instead of the doing of that will upon their hearts. They call their philosophy the truth of God, and say men must hold it, or stand outside. They are the slaves of the letter in all its weakness and imperfection—and will be until the spirit of the Word, the spirit of obedience, shall set them free.

The babes must beware lest the wise and prudent come between them and the Father. They must yield no claim to authority over their belief, made by man or community, by church any more than by synagogue. That alone is for them to believe which the Lord reveals to their souls as true; that alone is it possible for them to believe with what He counts belief. The divine object for which teacher or church exists is the persuasion of the individual heart to come to Jesus, the Spirit, to be taught what He alone can teach.

Terribly has His gospel suffered in the mouths of the wise and prudent: how would it be faring now, had its first messages been committed to persons of repute, instead of those simple fishermen? It would be nowhere, or, if anywhere, unrecognizable. From the first we should have had a system founded on a human interpretation of the divine gospel, instead of the gospel itself, which would have disappeared. As it is, we have had one dull, miserable human system after another usurping its place; but, thank God, the gospel remains!

# Alexander Maclaren

## (1826–1910)

Alexander Maclaren prepared his sermons directly from the Hebrew and Greek. He did very little pastoral work and rarely participated in civic or denominational activities. Yet he built a great church on the power of expository preaching, and his *Expositions of Holy Scripture* is still a gold mine for preachers who love the Word of God.

Maclaren was pastor of the Union Chapel, Manchester, for forty-five years. For another six years (1903–1909) he preached only occasionally at Union Chapel. He was a masterful preacher, yet he suffered from stage fright before each service. He was often depressed by his preaching (he had such high ideals), but would say, "Well, I can't help it. I did my best, and there I leave it." He was a man of God whose ministry flowed from his own life of faith. "The first, second, and third requisite for our work is personal godliness," he often reminded pastors and ministerial students.

> . . . he leadeth me in the paths of
> righteousness for his name's sake.
> (Ps. 23:3)

The quiet mercies of the preceding verse are not in themselves the end of our Shepherd's guidance; they are means to an end, and that is—work. Life is not a fold for the sheep to lie down in, but a road for them to walk on. All our blessings of every sort are indeed given us for our delight. They will never fit us for the duties for which they are intended to prepare us, unless they first be thoroughly enjoyed. The highest good they yield is only reached through the lower one. But, then, when joy fills the heart, and life is bounding in the veins, we have to learn that these are granted, not for pleasure only, but for pleasure in order to power. We get them, not to let them pass away like waste steam puffed into empty air, but that we may use them to drive the wheels of life. The waters of happiness are not for a luxurious bath where a man may lie, till, like flax steeped too long, the very fibre be rotted out of him; a quick plunge will brace him, and he will come out refreshed for work. Rest is to fit for work, work is to sweeten rest.

All this is emphatically true of the spiritual life. Its seasons of communion, its hours on the mount, are to prepare for the sore sad work in the plain; and he is not the wisest disciple who tries to make the Mount of Transfiguration the abiding place for himself and his Lord.

The angel of the LORD encampeth
round about them that fear him,
and delivereth them. (Ps. 34:7)

The vision of the divine presence ever takes the form which our circumstances most require. David's then need was safety and protection. Therefore he saw the Encamping Angel; even as to Joshua the leader He appeared as the Captain of the Lord's host; and as to Isaiah, in the year that the throne of Judah was emptied by the death of the earthly king, was given the vision of the Lord sitting on a throne, the King Eternal and Immortal. So to us all His grace shapes its expression according to our wants, and the same gift is Protean in its power of transformation; being to one man wisdom, to another strength, to the solitary companionship, to the sorrowful consolation, to the glad sobering, to the thinker truth, to the worker practical force—to each his heart's desire, if the heart's delight be God. So manifold are the aspects of God's infinite sufficiency, that every soul, in every possible variety of circumstance, will find there just what will suit it. That armour fits every man who puts it on. That deep fountain is like some of those fabled springs which give forth whatsoever precious draught any thirsty lip asked. He takes the shape that our circumstances most need. Let us see that we, on our parts, use our circumstances to help us in anticipating the shapes in which God will draw near for our help.

> My soul thirsteth for God, for the
> living God. (Ps. 42:2)

No man is made to be satisfied from himself. For the stilling of our own hearts, for the satisfying of our own nature, for the strengthening and joy of our being, we need to go beyond ourselves, and to fix upon something external to ourselves. We are not independent. None of us can stand by himself. No man carries within him the fountain from which he can draw. If a heart is to be blessed, it must go out of the narrow circle of its own individuality; and if a man's life is to be strong and happy, he must get the foundation of his strength somewhere else than in his own soul. . . .

We are made, next, to need, not *things*, but *living beings.* 'My soul thirsteth'—for what? An abstraction, a possession, riches, a thing? No! 'my soul thirsteth for God, for *the living God.*'Yes, hearts want hearts. The converse of Christ's saying is equally true; He said, 'God is a Spirit, and they that worship Him must worship Him in spirit'; man has a spirit, and man must have Spirit to worship, to lean upon, to live by, or all will be inefficient and unsatisfactory. Oh, lay this to heart, my brother!—no *things* can satisfy a living soul.

Thou art fairer than the children of
men; grace is poured into thy
lips. . . . (Ps. 45:2)

'T hou art fairer than the children of men.' Put side by side
with that, words which possibly refer to, and seem to contra-
dict it. A later prophet, speaking of the same Person, said: 'His
visage was so marred, more than any man, and His form than
the sons of men. . . . There is no form nor comeliness, and
when we shall see Him there is no beauty that we should
desire Him.' We have to think, not of the outward form,
howsoever lovely with the loveliness of meekness and transfigured with the refining patience of suffering it may have
been, but of the beauty of a soul that was all radiant with a
lustre of loveliness that shames the fragmentary and marred
virtues of the best of us, and stands before the world for ever
as the supreme type and high-water mark of the grace that is
possible to a human spirit. God has lodged in men's nature the
apprehension of Himself, and of all that flows from Him, as
true, as good, as beautiful; and to these three there corre-
spond wisdom, morality, and art. The latter, divorced from the
other two, becomes earthly and devilish. This generation
needs the lesson that beauty wrenched from truth and
goodness, and pursued for its own sake, by artist or by poet or
by *dilettante*, leads by a straight descent to ugliness and to
evil, and that the only true satisfying of the deep longing for
'whatsoever things are lovely' is to be found when we turn to
Christ and find in Him, not only wisdom that enlightens the
understanding, and righteousness that fills the conscience,
but beauty that satisfies the heart. He is 'altogether lovely.'

That they might set their hope in
God, and not forget the works of
God, but keep his commandments.
(Ps. 78:7)

I f my memory weaken me for present work, either because
it depresses my hope of success, or because it saddens me

with the remembrance of departed blessings, then it is a curse and not a good. And if I dream myself away in any future, and forget the exigencies of the imperative and swiftly-passing moment, then the faculty of hope, too, is a curse and a weakening. But both are delivered from their possible abuses, if both are made into means of helping us to fill the present with loving obedience. These two faculties are like the two wings that may lift us to God, like the two paddles, one on either side of the ship, that may drive us steadily forward, through all the surges and the tempest. They find their highest field in fitting us for the grinding tasks and the heavy burdens that the moment lays upon us.

So, dear friends! We are very different in our circumstances and positions. For some of us Hope's basket is nearly empty, and Memory's sack is very full. For us older men the past is long, the earthly future is short. For you younger people the converse is the case. It is Hope whose hands are laden with treasures for you, Memory carries but a little store. Your past is brief; your future is probably long. The grains of sand in some of our hour-glasses are very heaped and high in the lower half, and running very low in the upper. But whichever category we stand in, one thing remains the same for us all, and that is duty, keeping God's commandments. That is permanent, and that is the one thing worth living for. 'Whether we live we live unto the Lord; or whether we die we die unto the Lord.'

So let us front this New Year, with all its hidden possibilities, with quiet, brave hearts, resolved on present duty, as those ought who have such a past to remember and such a future to hope for.

> Bow down thine ear, O LORD, hear
> me: for I am poor and needy.
> (Ps. 86:1)

Nothing in our prayers is often more hollow and unreal than the formal repetitions of the syllables of that divine name, often but to fill a pause in our thoughts. But to 'call upon the Name of the Lord' means, first and foremost, to bring before our minds the aspects of His great and infinite character, which are gathered together into the Name by which we address Him. So when we say 'Jehovah!' 'Lord!' what we ought to mean is this, that we are gazing upon the majestic, glorious thought of Being, self-derived, self-motived, self-ruled, the being of Him whose Name can only be, 'I am that I am.' Of all other creatures the name is, 'I am that I have been made,' or 'I am that I became,' but of Him the Name is, 'I am that I am.' Nowhere outside of Himself is the reason for His being, nor the law that shapes it, nor the aim to which it tends. And this infinite, changeless Rock is laid for our confidence, Jehovah the Eternal, the Self-subsisting, Self-sufficing One.

There is more than that thought in this wondrous Name, for it not only expresses the timeless, unlimited, and changeless being of God, but also the truth that He has entered into what He deigns to call a Covenant with us men. The name Jehovah is the seal of that ancient Covenant, of which, though the form has vanished, the essence abides for ever, and God has thereby bound Himself to us by promises that cannot be abrogated. So that when we say, 'O Lord!' we summon up before ourselves, and grasp as the grounds of our confidence, and we humbly present before Him as the motives, if we may so call them, for His action, His own infinite being and His covenanted grace.

> Let the beauty of the LORD our God
> be upon us: and establish thou the
> work of our hands upon us. . . .
> (Ps. 90:17)

This prayer expresses a deep longing, natural to all men, and which yet seems incompatible with the stern facts of mortality and decay. We should all like to have our work exempted from the common lot. What pathetically futile attempts to secure this are pyramids, and rock-inscriptions, and storied tombs, and posthumous memoirs, and rich men's wills! Why should any of us expect that the laws of nature should be suspended for our benefit, and our work made lasting while everything beside changes like the shadows of the clouds? Is there any way by which such exceptional permanence can be secured for our poor deeds? Yes, certainly. Let us commit them to God, praying this prayer, 'Establish Thou the work of our hands upon us.'

Our work will be established if it is His work. This prayer in our text follows another prayer (verse 16)—namely, 'Let *Thy* work appear unto Thy servants.' That is to say, My work will be perpetual when the work of my hands is God's work done through me. When you bring your wills into harmony with God's will, and so all your effort, even about the little things of daily life, is in consonance with His will, and in the line of His purpose, then your work will stand. If otherwise, it will be like some slow-moving and frail carriage going in the one direction and meeting an express train thundering in the other. When the crash comes, the opposing motion of the weaker will be stopped, reversed, and the frail thing will be smashed to atoms. So, all work which is man's and not God's will sooner or later be reduced to impotence and either annihilated or reversed, and made to run in the opposite direction. But if our work runs parallel with God's, then the rushing impetus of His work will catch up our little deeds into the swiftness of its own motion, and will carry them along with itself, as a railway train will lift straws and bits of paper that are lying by the rails, and give them motion for a while. If my will runs in the line of His, and if the work of my hands is 'Thy work,' it is not in vain that we shall cry 'Establish it upon us,' for it will last as long as He does.

# Andrew Murray
## (1828–1917)

Andrew Murray was a Dutch Reformed pastor who ministered in South Africa. His emphasis was on prayer and the
deeper life, but he also had a burden for missions. He was in
great demand as a conference speaker.

Murray wrote many books; perhaps the most famous is
*Abide in Christ*. In my early years as a believer, *With Christ in
the School of Prayer* meant much to me. I also appreciate his
commentary on Hebrews, *The Holiest of All*. Each of his
books makes it apparent that the author had been in communion with the Lord.

Thou art worthy, O Lord, to receive
glory and honour and power: for
thou hast created all things, and for
thy pleasure they are and were
created. (Rev. 4:11)

The call to humility has been too little regarded in the
Church, because its true nature and importance has been too
little apprehended. It is not a something which we bring to
God, or He bestows; it is simply *the sense of entire nothing-
ness, which comes when we see how truly God is all, and in
which we make way for God to be all.* When the creature
realises that this is the true nobility, and consents to be with
his will, his mind, and his affections, the form, the vessel in
which the life and glory of God are to work and manifest

themselves, he sees that humility is simply acknowledging the truth of his position as creature, and yielding to God His place.

> Let this mind be in you, which was
> also in Christ Jesus. (Phil. 2:5)

In this view it is of inconceivable importance that we should have right thoughts of what Christ is, of what really constitutes Him the Christ, and specially of what may be counted His chief characteristic, the root and essence of all His character as our Redeemer. There can be but one answer: it is His humility. What is the incarnation but His heavenly humility, His emptying Himself and becoming man? What is His life on earth but humility; His taking the form of a servant? And what is His atonement but humility? 'He humbled Himself and became obedient unto death.' And what is His ascension and His glory, but humility exalted to the throne and crowned with glory? 'He humbled Himself, therefore God highly exalted Him.' In heaven, where He was with the Father, in His birth, in His life, in His death, in His sitting on the throne, it is all, it is nothing but humility. Christ is the humility of God embodied in human nature; the Eternal Love humbling itself, clothing itself in the garb of meekness and gentleness, to win and serve and save us. As the love and condescension of God makes Him the benefactor and helper and servant of all, so Jesus of necessity was the Incarnate Humility. And so He is still in the midst of the throne, the meek and lowly Lamb of God.

> ... learn of me; for I am meek and
> lowly in heart. ... (Matt. 11:29)

We must learn of Jesus, how He is meek and lowly of heart. He teaches us where true humility takes its rise and

154

finds its strength—in the knowledge that it is God who worketh all in all, that our place is to yield to Him in perfect resignation and dependence, in full consent to be and to do nothing of ourselves. This is the life Christ came to reveal and to impart—a life to God that came through death to sin and self. If we feel that this life is too high for us and beyond our reach, it must but the more urge us to seek it in Him; it is the indwelling Christ who will live in us this life, meek and lowly. If we long for this, let us, meantime, above everything, seek the holy secret of the knowledge of the nature of God, as He every moment works all in all; the secret, of which all nature and every creature, and above all, every child of God, is to be the witness,—that it is nothing but a vessel, a channel, through which the living God can manifest the riches of His wisdom, power, and goodness. The root of all virtue and grace, of all faith and acceptable worship, is that we know that we have nothing but what we receive, and bow in deepest humility to wait upon God for it.

> ... he that is greatest among you, let
> him be as the younger; and he that
> is chief, as he that doth serve.
> (Luke 22:26)

*H*ow much there may be of earnest and active religion while humility is still sadly wanting.

See it in the disciples. There was in them fervent attachment to Jesus. They had forsaken all for Him. The Father had revealed to them that He was the Christ of God. They believed in Him, they loved Him, they obeyed His commandments. They had forsaken all to follow Him. When others went back, they clave to Him. They were ready to die with Him. But deeper down than all this there was a dark power, of the existence and the hideousness of which they were hardly conscious, which had to be slain and cast out, ere they could be the witnesses of the power of Jesus to save. It is even so still. We may find professors and ministers, evangelists and workers, missionaries and teachers, in whom the gifts of the Spirit are many and manifest, and who are the channels of blessing to multitudes, but of whom, when the testing time comes, or closer intercourse gives fuller knowledge, it is only too painfully manifest that the grace of humility, as an abiding characteristic, is scarce to be seen. All tends to confirm the lesson that humility is one of the chief and the highest graces; one of the most difficult of attainment; one to which our first and chiefest efforts ought to be directed; one that only comes in power, when the fulness of the Spirit makes us partakers of the indwelling Christ, and He lives within us.

> . . . he that loveth not his brother
> whom he hath seen, how can he
> love God whom he hath not seen?
> (I John 4:20)

What a solemn thought, that our love to God will be measured by our everyday intercourse with men and the love it displays; and that our love to God will be found to be a delusion, except as its truth is proved in standing the test of daily life with our fellow-men. It is even so with our humility. It is easy to think we humble ourselves before God: humility towards men will be the only sufficient proof that our humility before God is real; that humility has taken up its abode in us, and become our very nature; that we actually, like Christ, have made ourselves of no reputation. When in the presence of God lowliness of heart has become, not a posture we assume for a time, when we think of Him, or pray to Him, but the very spirit of our life, it will manifest itself in all our bearing towards our brethren. The lesson is one of deep import: the only humility that is really ours is not that which we try to show before God in prayer, but that which we carry with us, and carry out, in our ordinary conduct; the insignificances of daily life are the importances and the tests of eternity, because they prove what really is the spirit that possesses us. It is in our most unguarded moments that we really show and see what we are. To know the humble man, to know how the humble man behaves, you must follow him in the common course of daily life.

> God, I thank thee, that I am not as
> other men are. . . . (Luke 18:11)

The chief mark of counterfeit holiness is its lack of humility. Every seeker after holiness needs to be on his guard, lest unconsciously what was begun in the spirit be perfected in the flesh, and pride creep in where its presence is least expected. Two men went up into the temple to pray: the one a Pharisee, the other a publican. There is no place or position so sacred but the Pharisee can enter there. Pride can lift its head in the very temple of God, and make His worship the scene of its self-exaltation. Since the time Christ so exposed his pride, the Pharisee has put on the garb of the publican, and the confessor of deep sinfulness equally with the professor of the highest holiness, must be on the watch. Just when we are most anxious to have our heart the temple of God, we shall find the two men coming up to pray. And the publican will find that his danger is not from the Pharisee beside him, who despises him, but the Pharisee within who commends and exalts. In God's temple, when we think we are in the holiest of all, in the presence of His holiness, let us beware of pride. 'Now there was a day when the sons of God came to present themselves before the Lord, and Satan came also among them.'

> How many hired servants of my
> father's have bread enough and to
> spare, and I perish with hunger! I
> will arise and go to my father. . . .
> (Luke 15:17–18)

'Where sin abounded, grace did abound more exceedingly.' This reveals how the very essence of grace is to deal with and take away sin, and how it must ever be: the more abundant the experience of grace, the more intense the consciousness of being a sinner. It is not sin, but God's grace showing a man and ever reminding him what a sinner he was, that will keep him truly humble. It is not sin, but grace, that will make me indeed know myself a sinner, and make the sinner's place of deepest self-abasement the place I never leave.

I fear that there are not a few who, by strong expressions of self-condemnation and self-denunciation, have sought to humble themselves, and have to confess with sorrow that a humble spirit, a 'heart of humility,' with its accompaniments of kindness and compassion, of meekness and forbearance, is still as far off as ever. Being occupied with self, even amid the deepest self-abhorrence, can never free us from self. It is the revelation of God, not only by the law condemning sin, but by His grace delivering from it, that will make us humble. The law may break the heart with fear; it is only grace that works that sweet humility which becomes a joy to the soul as its second nature. It was the revelation of God in His holiness, drawing nigh to make Himself known in His grace, that made Abraham and Jacob, Job and Isaiah, bow so low.

# Robert William Dale

## (1829–1895)

R. W. Dale was one of the leading Congregational pastors in Britain and was pastor of the great Carr's Lane Church in Birmingham for more than forty years. He was a respected theologian, and yet he had a concern for the social problems of his day. His preaching was biblical and doctrinal. He told a friend one day, "I am starting a series on Bible doctrine." His friend replied, "Your people will not take it." Dale replied, "They will *have* to take it!" And they did.

Dale believed in conditional immortality, but he co-operated enthusiastically with the Moody-Sankey meetings. He once told G. Campbell Morgan that Moody was the only preacher he ever heard who had the right to preach about hell. "I never heard Moody refer to hell without tears in his voice," Dale explained.

Blessed is the man that endureth temptation: for when he is tried, he shall receive the crown of life, which the Lord hath promised to them that love him. (James 1:12)

The *'crown of life,'* the victor's wreath, is for those who have endured temptation. The perfect life itself, which God will give, is the crown which we hope for. Just as the flowers are the crown, when we speak of a crown of flowers, or the laurel, when we speak of a crown of laurel. Life—life with clearer vision than is possible to us in this world; life sensitive to more

159

subtle and more ravishing harmonies; life with diviner buoyancy and vigour; life with more intense affections; life with wider horizons of thought; life with new and unhoped-for possibilities of righteousness; life with the capacity for closer friendships with the saintly spirits of the city of God; life with loftier raptures of adoration; life with profounder awe in the presence of God's majesty; life with the blessedness of a more intimate communion with the peace and love of God—life is what we hope for.

Not the shining palaces of the heavenly city, but the regal spirit; not the golden harps of the blessed, but the perfect music of the moral and spiritual harmony which comes from being filled with God; not the white robes, but the stainless spiritual purity; not the wreath of honor, but the Divine approval of our righteousness, of which the wreath is but the gracious symbol. The higher, larger, purer life is what we hope for; and this is what God has promised us. He promises it to those who love Him and who have endured temptation; for it is by the endurance of temptation in the power of love for Christ that the capacity for receiving that life in its amplest measure and noblest perfection is enlarged and perfected.

> Every good gift and every perfect
> gift is from above, and cometh
> down from the Father of lights, with
> whom is no variableness, neither
> shadow of turning. (James 1:17)

*The Father of lights:* that is a striking description of God. God is like the sun who is the center and chief of all the glories of the visible universe. The sun among the stars is like a father among his children, a prince among his subjects. But the sun of the visible heavens holds no constant place; he rises in the morning and only gradually reaches his meridian splendour, and then he gradually declines and sinks in the west. With God there can be no variation; His splendour is always the splendour of noonday. As the result of what the ancients regarded as the revolution of the spheres, the sun of the visible heavens is sometimes obscured; a shadow is cast upon him; he is eclipsed. But as there is no change in God's own glory, neither can that glory be dimmed by change in His creation; no shadow is cast upon him by any turning. All His gifts are good: He cannot tempt us, for His goodness is unchangeable.

> If any man offend not in word, the
> same is a perfect man, and able also
> to bridle the whole body. (James 3:2)

But how wonderful a faculty speech is! It makes human society possible. Apart from words—visible or audible signs expressing inward thought and feeling—the inner life of every man would be an island surrounded by an impassable ocean. There could be no commerce, no politics, no church. One great school of philosophy has maintained that apart from language—definite signs for ideas—there could even be no thought. How wonderful again, I say, is this faculty of speech! The words of a mother to her child, of a child to a mother—the words of lovers—the words of friends—the words of dying men—how these remain in the memory of those to whom they were spoken, a light, a joy, a power, through all succeeding years. What palaces of beauty the poets have built for us with words! What treasures of wisdom the wise of all countries and of all ages have laid up for us in words! The words of great political orators have changed the temper and the thoughts of nations, have provoked war, have compelled peace. The words of great preachers have shaken the hearts of men with fear, inspired them with immortal hope, made real the invisible and eternal kingdom of God. The words of prophets, of apostles, have wrought miracles in the moral life of men, in many centuries, in many lands. The words of Christ!—the accent of God is in them, and we listen with wonder and awe and immeasurable joy. And to describe the eternal glory of Christ Himself, we speak of Him as the *Word* of God.

Yes—speech is capable of great and noble uses. But it is also capable of uses most base, most malignant, and most foul. And James warns us that to govern the tongue, to restrain it from great and flagrant sins, is a task beyond human strength.

> This wisdom descendeth not from above, but is earthly, sensual, devilish. (James 3:15)

This is a dreary and depressing passage. It reminds us that the joy and strength of the Churches of Apostolic times were impaired by the very spirit and temper which have desolated the religious life of so many Churches in later generations. Even in those early days, there were men who had a measureless self-conceit, a bitter jealousy of those whom their brethren regarded with affection and trust, an arrogant confidence in their own opinion and their own judgment; men in whom there was very little of the spirit of Christ, but who were quite certain that they, and they alone, had the mind of Christ; men who were resolved, whatever might come of it, to force upon the Church their own beliefs, either with regard to doctrine or practice; who made parties in the Church to carry out their purposes, held secret meetings, flattered those who stood by them as being faithful to conscience and to Christ, and disparaged the fidelity of all who differed from them. Even then such men broke up the peace of Churches, and in the confusion which they created many wicked things were said, and many wicked things were done. These men had power, real power of a kind; but it was not a wisdom that came *from above.'* They showed the same kind of faculty that is possessed by men whose ambition is wholly earthly and unspiritual; they practised the same arts. Their power was a real power; but it was *'earthly, sensual, devilish.'* The passage stands on the pages of this Epistle as an awful warning to the Church of every generation.

> But the wisdom that is from above
> is first pure . . . without partiality,
> and without hypocrisy. (James 3:17)

The man whose conduct is governed by worldly wisdom is apt to be shifty—what he himself would call politic. He sets his sails to the prevailing wind; speaks well of men today of whom he spoke ill yesterday—not because the men themselves are better than they were, but because yesterday he could get nothing by speaking well of them, and today he can. His very judgment of men is determined by his interests or his passions; and since with changing circumstances his interests and his passions vary, his judgment varies too. You can never count upon him. But the man who is governed by divine wisdom has his fixed principles, and by these both his judgment and his conduct are ruled. He looks upon human affairs from divine heights. The compass which guides his course is not deflected from its true meridian by the attraction of self-interest, or by the varying currents of prevailing opinion. He judges men today as he judged them yesterday,—unless indeed he has learnt new facts about them which require him to modify his judgment. He does not think better of them simply because they have become rich and powerful and able to help him, or worse of them because they have become poor, and have lost their riches and are unable to help him any longer. He does not treat them differently for any such reasons as these. He maintains that true consistency which comes not from an obstinate adherence to his own opinions, but from persistent loyalty to the high and eternal principles by which human conviction and human conduct should be governed. This, I think, suggests that quality of divine wisdom which is described by the word represented by the phrase 'without variance.'

> So then each one of us shall give
> account of himself to God.
> (Rom. 14:12)

We are free, and we know it. And if to this freedom there are mysterious limitations,—if achievement hesitates, and falters, and follows far behind purpose, the Christian Gospel has its word of power and of grace for us in this great trouble. Yes, we are free; and yet how conscious at times we are of chains—chains some of which we have forged ourselves by evil-doing in years gone by. We choose the right, and for more than two thousand years moralists have said we are unable to stand to our choice. Yes, free—free, and yet in chains. To be conscious that we are bound is to be conscious that we are free, that in our own inner life there is a spontaneous self-asserting force which claims the right, even though it may not have the power, to work out its own destiny. Christ came to 'preach deliverance to the captive, and the opening of the prison to them that are bound,' and in age after age, in our own time as in times gone by, men have listened to His voice, have believed His promise, hoping it might be true, and in response to hope rather than to faith Christ has come—has come as the angel came to Peter sleeping in his chains between the two soldiers, and at the touch of an invisible hand the chains have fallen away and the man has become free.

We have to give account of ourselves to God. How is it, my brother, between you and Him? You can tell. Deal with yourself honestly, and you can discover how it stands between you and Him.

> It is high time to awake out of sleep:
> for now is our salvation nearer than
> when we believed. (Rom. 13:11)

The golden age of the Church lies, not in the past, but in the future. We may be humiliated by the passionate devotion to

Christ which glowed in the hearts of the apostles and of many of their immediate converts; we may wonder at the courage and fortitude which during the early Christian generations confronted fearlessly all that was mightiest and most venerable in the ancient civilisation, and endured imprisonment, torture, and death in the power of an exulting hope and a triumphant faith; but it is apparent, both from the apostolic epistles and from later Christian writings, that even in those heroic times there were vast numbers of Christian men and women who fell far short of the saintly life. The glory of God which dwells in the Church of every age was clouded then, as it is clouded now, by human infirmity and sin.

Nor do we look back with regret upon the brief years during which our Lord Himself was visibly present in the world: it was expedient for us that He should go away. The great hour is yet to come: we move forwards to it day by day, year by year. *'Now is salvation nearer to us than when we first believed.'*

# Joseph Parker
## (1830–1902)

Joseph Parker was a man's man and a man's preacher, and yet he had the tender heart of a child. He was a self-made preacher, having little advantage in life for getting formal education; yet he taught other men how to preach. When he accepted the pastorate at Poultry Chapel, London, the church was old and declining, so he relocated it, built a huge auditorium, and filled it every Sunday with three thousand eager listeners. Added to that, he addressed more than one thousand men and women at the Thursday noon meeting.

Parker was a consecrated autocrat; he ran the church. He made a lasting impact on thousands of lives, particularly the young men who attended the Thursday meeting. He wrote many books, but his most famous contribution is *The People's Bible,* a twenty-five volume set that contains his remarkable series of sermons from Genesis to Revelation. It took him seven years to complete this series, and he preached three sermons a week.

But he that is spiritual judgeth all
things. (I Cor. 2:15)

Many men also suffer from looking for the wrong thing. They are looking for argument, demonstration, long and elaborate statement of *pros* and *cons.* They will be disappointed with Christ. He will have nothing but pureness of soul, love of heart, a desire after the very spirit and genius of childhood; where he sees these things there he abides, and he makes the heart burn with new love, and gives the eyes the delight of continually changing and brightening vision. Lord, make us little children; enable us to look for the right things, namely, the revelation of thy heart, thy love, thy purpose of redemption; deliver us from this satanic temptation of wanting to understand miracles, signs, and wonders, and impossibilities; lead us up the green gentle slopes of loving prayer and desire; and then when we get near the top we shall be able to look down and see the miracles as very little things; help us, Lord, and give us vision of soul.

Spiritual insight can only come with spiritual life; in other words, if you have not the life, you cannot have the insight. Unless we live and move and have our being in God we cannot read the Bible aright. We must be in the Spirit. This is the day of the Holy Ghost, this the Pentecostal era. Yet men are fooling away their time in asking wrong questions about wrong subjects; they are busy at the wrong door; they will agitate themselves about things that need not come within purview just now.

> In these [porches] lay a great multi-
> tude of impotent folk, of blind, halt,
> withered, waiting. . . . (John 5:3)

The world is a hospital, the whole earth is an asylum. Understand, that the man who is, popularly speaking, in the robustest health today may be smitten before the setting of the sun with a fatal disease. In the midst of life we are in death; our breath at best is in our nostrils. Man respires and cannot get his breath again, and he is gone—we call him dead. Life is a perpetual crisis. We are always walking on the cobweb string; it is snapped at any moment. "Whatsoever thy hand findeth to do, do it with thy might." Blessed is that servant who shall be found when his Lord cometh, waiting and watching and working. Great God, we are all waiting, doing nothing! There they were waiting, groaning, sighing. That was a prayer meeting, if you please. A sigh was a prayer, a groan was an entreaty, a cry of distress was a supplication. All the people in the porches were waiting. Are we not all doing the same thing?

The thing we want most seems not to have come yet—it never does come. We shall have it tomorrow, and in the inspiration of this hope we are comparatively strong and joyful today. "Man never is, but always to be blessed." We are waiting for help, waiting till we get a little round, waiting till the ship comes in, waiting for sympathy, waiting for a friend without whose presence there seems to be nobody on the face of the earth, waiting: The method which means patience, hope, content, assurance that God will in his own due course and time redeem his promises and make the heart strong; the other method of waiting is a method of fretfulness, and vexation, and impatience, and distrust, and complaining,— and that kind of thing wears the soul out.

> Therefore they gathered them
> together, and filled twelve baskets
> with the fragments of the five barley
> loaves, which remained over and
> above unto them that had eaten.
> (John 6:13)

It was like Jesus Christ to give ten thousand times more than the people really needed. At the wedding feast they said there was no wine, and he gave them firkin after firkin of wine, a whole Niagara of the wine of the kingdom of heaven, that never made the judgment dark, or the knees tremble in weakness, or the mind play the tricks of the fool. He began well—"This beginning of miracles did Jesus in Cana of Galilee." There never was so much wine in the little town before. When does Jesus do just enough to save the sinner? He saves the sinner with an eternal salvation, with an everlasting redemption; his Cross is not able simply and only to lift the world a little, it can lift the world to heaven.

168

What a different meaning is this! We began by seeing the disciples sweeping up the crumbs, gathering up the little pieces that had been left over, and putting them into baskets; whereas Jesus Christ did not call them to this kind of work, he said, "Gather up the broken portions," he took the bread and brake it, and there was ten thousand times more than the universe could eat: and he said, Take care of the broken portions, my finger prints are upon them; these may be unto you some day as my broken body. Whatever Christ did he did sacramentally; he never uttered a word in any language without sanctifying that word, making it the gem of speech, the diamond of eloquence.

> When Jesus therefore perceived that
> they would come and take him by
> force, to make him a king, he
> departed again into a mountain
> himself alone. (John 6:15)

The Church should be like the Master: it should not rule by force. I would never compel even a child to go to church; much less would I attempt to compel anyone who was momentarily in my power. I would not bribe a man to go to church—certainly I would in no way inflict upon him loss or humiliation for not going. I would try to make the church itself the attraction. No child should be punished for not learning its Bible. Punish a child if you please for not learning the spelling-book or the geography, but do not associate penal suffering with biblical learning.

The Church should be like the Master: it should seek to rule by love. Not one penny would I take from any man by the law to support any form of religion, either my own or yours. Whatever is done must be done of a willing mind, and everything that is given must have this written upon it—"The love of Christ constraineth us." And in proportion as Jesus Christ will not force you, ought you to love him. If it were a contest of force, then you might rejoice in the apparent victory which you win for a moment; but when he says to you, "It is not a contest of hand against hand or sword against sword, but of your obstinacy against my love;" when he says, "I could by mere omnipotence crush you between my fingers, but that would only be a triumph of physical power. No; I will teach you, preach to you, love you, die for you, show you my hands and my feet," the very stripping of himself of his physical almightiness should constitute his supreme power as One who wants to captivate your love, and sit down on the throne of your confidence forever.

> The Jews marvelled, saying, How knoweth this man letters, having never learned? (John 7:15)

Now above all things it is preeminently true that religion is not learned by letters; it is a divine action in the soul; it is a divine communion; it is the claiming of a kinship long ignored or long misunderstood; it is the look of friend to friend; it is the recognition which comes into the eyes of the wandering child when through all his sin and sorrow and disablement he begins to trace the outline of a pursuing and loving father. Then grammar would be out of place; only one eloquence is possible—the eloquence of sobbing, the eloquence that chokes the throat when it would talk, for talk in such circumstances approaches profanity.

Yet there are those who can give you all their reasons for being religious. It would be harsh to condemn them. There is a piety that goes by the calendar: there is a prayer appointed for today which must not be said tomorrow, and which would have been out of place yesterday; there is a mechanical, formal, and even disciplinary way of living, but there is a religion that cannot give any reasons for itself beyond the reasons which childhood suggests, which love breathes, which an ineffable confidence clings to. We must make room for all these varieties. Make room for all and every kind of learning. Christianity is not a controversy; it is peace, it is a sacred gladness of the heart that dare sometimes scarcely allow itself to hear its own voice, lest it should lose a charm, a possession infinite. There is a silence that is eloquent. Being justified by faith through our Lord Jesus Christ, we have peace with God—a peace that passeth understanding, a joy unspeakable and full of glory.

> And as Jesus passed by, he saw a
> man which was blind from his birth.
> (John 9:1)

Why did he pass that way? Could he not have gone by some other path? The answer is, No. Grace has its necessities; love has its predestinations. Jesus Christ always looked out for opportunities of doing good. He knew which road to take; he said, The blind man is down this road, therefore this is the road along which I am about to travel. This is how he came to find so many opportunities for doing good: how can we? We do not look for them. Jesus Christ made it his business to find out who wanted him. He even stands at the door sometimes, and knocks. In a sense, does he not thrust himself upon men who need him? So graciously and quietly that it has no appearance of obtrusiveness or aggression; still he makes himself felt by events, by appeals, by sudden recollections, by suggestions from friends, by Church service and sacrament,— yea, a thousand ways he sends us hints that he is there, and has with him all the resources which are needed for our redemption, purification, and final coronation in heaven.

When you felt inclined to pray it was Jesus Christ who moved you in that direction. When you said, I think I see more clearly today; truth seems to be enlarging,—it was Christ who was performing a miracle upon you. Trace all happy impulse, all sacred inspiration, all ennobling influence, to the touch, the glance, the benediction of Christ.

> For I have given you an example,
> that ye should do as I have done to
> you. (John 13:15)

What will he do in the moment of supreme consciousness? He will show his diadem now; with his right hand he will take away the cloud which veiled it, and the shining of that diadem shall put out the sun. What will he do in this summer time?

We have analogous times in our own consciousness, when we feel what we are, when the divinity stirs within us, when we feel the blood of a hundred kings burning in our veins. What is our wish under the pressure of such heroic and tempting consciousness? Surely to do some great thing; surely to vindicate our right to be called by brilliant names.

What did Jesus Christ do? Mark the time: the whole pith of this part of the discourse is in the point of time—"Jesus knowing"—in modern words, the consciousness of Jesus urged to its highest point, realising its utmost sensitiveness, receiving into itself the full revelation of the divine meaning. "Jesus knowing"—that his right hand was full, and his left hand—yea, "that the Father had given all things into his hands"—what did he do? He arose from supper, he laid aside his garments, he took a towel and girded himself, he poured water into a basin, "and began to wash the disciples' feet."

# James Hudson Taylor
## (1832–1905)

Converted when a teen-ager, largely through his mother's prayers, Hudson Taylor early determined that God wanted him to be a missionary doctor in China. He studied medicine and theology in England and learned how to trust God for each need a day at a time. He argued, "If I cannot trust Him at home, how can I ever trust Him in China?"

Hudson Taylor arrived in Shanghai in 1854 under the auspices of the London Missionary Society. In 1860 he felt led to become an independent worker, and in 1866 the China Inland Mission was organized. Today it is known as the Overseas Missionary Fellowship. He and his workers pioneered missions in inland China and saw many come to Christ. Traditional missionaries wondered at Taylor's adoption of native dress and habits of life, but his policy paid off.

*Hudson Taylor's Spiritual Secret,* by Dr. and Mrs. Howard Taylor, came to my life at a time when I desperately needed it. I have read Taylor's biography and autobiography many times and always have been helped.

Wherefore in all things it behoved
him to be made like unto His
brethren. (Heb. 2:17)

Had our Lord appeared on earth as an angel of light, He would doubtless have inspired far more awe and reverence, and would have collected together even larger multitudes to attend His ministry. But to save man He became Man, not merely like man, but *very* man. In language, in costume, in everything unsinful, He made Himself one with those He sought to benefit. Had He been born a noble Roman, rather than a Jew, He would, perhaps, if less loved, have commanded more of a certain kind of respect; and He would assuredly thereby have been spared much indignity to which He was subjected. This, however, was not His aim; He emptied Himself. Surely no follower of the meek and lowly Jesus will be likely to conclude that it is "beneath the dignity of a Christian missionary" to seek identification with this poor people, in the hope that he may see them washed, sanctified, and justified in the name of the Lord Jesus, and by the Spirit of our God! Let us rather be followers of Him who "knowing that the Father had given all things into His hands, and that He was come from God, and went to God, He riseth from supper, and laid aside His garments, and took a towel, and girded Himself. After that He poured water into a basin, and began to wash the disciples' feet, and to wipe them with the towel wherewith He was girded."

> God hath spoken once; twice have I
> heard this, that power belongeth
> unto God. (Ps. 62:11)

God Himself is the great source of power. It is His possession. "Power belongeth unto God", and He manifests it according to His sovereign will. Yet, not in an erratic or arbitrary manner, but according to His declared purpose and promises. True, our opponents and hindrances are many and mighty, but our God, the living God, is Almighty.

Further, God's power is available power. We are supernatural people, born again by a supernatural birth, kept by a supernatural power, sustained on supernatural food, taught by a supernatural Teacher from a supernatural Book. We are led by a supernatural Captain in right paths to assured victories. The risen Saviour, ere He ascended on high, said: "All power is given unto Me. Go ye therefore".

Again, He said to His disciples: "Ye shall receive power when the Holy Spirit is come upon you". Not many days after this, in answer to united and continued prayer, the Holy Spirit did come upon them, and they were all filled. Praise God, He remains with us still. The power given is not a gift from the Holy Spirit. He Himself is the power. Today He is as truly available, and as mighty in power, as He was on the day of Pentecost. But since the days before Pentecost, has the whole Church ever put aside every other work, and waited upon God for ten days, that that power might be manifested? We have given too much attention to method, and to machinery, and to resources, and too little to the source of power.

> Then Jesus answered and said unto her, O woman, great is thy faith: be it unto thee even as thou wilt.
> (Matt. 15:28)

By faith the walls of Jericho fell down—yet what more unlikely! We walk by faith. Do we? What record is there on high of things that by faith we have obtained? Is each step each day an act of faith? Do we, as children of God, really believe the Bible? Are we ready to take the place of even a worm, as our Master did—"But I am a worm and no man"? Or if we realize our powerlessness and our insignificance, do we believe that it is possible—that it is God's will for us—that we should thresh mountains? "Fear not," said the Lord by the prophet of old, "fear not, thou worm Jacob, . . . behold I will make thee a sharp threshing instrument having teeth: thou shalt thresh the mountains and beat them small, and shalt make the hills as chaff. Thou shalt fan them, and the wind shall carry them away, and the whirlwind shall scatter them: and thou shalt rejoice in the Lord, and shalt glory in the Holy One of Israel".

How then, do we ask, are we to thresh mountains? Let us listen to our Master: "Have faith in God. For verily I say unto you, That whosoever shall say unto this mountain, Be thou removed, and be thou cast into the sea; and shall not doubt in his heart, but shall believe that those things which he saith shall come to pass, he shall have whatsoever he saith." Do we ask when this shall be? The Lord continues: "What thing soever ye desire *when ye pray,* believe that ye receive them, and ye shall have them". Let us therefore "be careful for nothing; but in everything by prayer and supplication with thanksgiving, let our requests be made known unto God".

> And Jesus answering saith unto
> them, Have faith in God.
> (Mark 11:22)

Hold God's faithfulness. Abraham held God's faith, and offered up Isaac, accounting that God was able to raise him up. Moses held God's faith, and led the millions of Israel into the waste howling wilderness. Joshua knew Israel well, and was ignorant neither of the fortifications of the Canaanites, nor of their martial prowess: but he held God's faithfulness, and led Israel across Jordan. The Apostles held God's faith, and were not daunted by the hatred of the Jews, nor by the hostility of the heathen. And what shall I saw more, for the time would fail me to tell "of those who, holding God's faithfulness, had faith, and by it subdued kingdoms, wrought righteousness, obtained promises, stopped the mouths of lions, quenched the violence of fire, escaped the edge of the sword, out of weakness were made strong, waxed valiant in fight, turned to flight the armies of aliens."

All God's giants have been weak men, who did great things for God because they reckoned on God being with them. See the cases of David, of Jonathan and his armour-bearer, of Asa, Jehoshaphat, and many others. Oh! beloved friends, if there is a living God, faithful and true, let us hold His faithfulness. Holding His faithfulness, we may go into every province of China. Holding His faithfulness, we may face, with calm and sober but confident assurance of victory, every difficulty and danger. We may count on grace for the work, on pecuniary aid, on needful facilities, and on ultimate success. Let us not give Him a partial trust, but daily, hourly, serve Him, "holding God's faithfulness".

> ... bid them that they make them fringes in the borders of their garments ... and that they put upon the fringe of the borders a ribband of blue ... that ye may look upon it, and remember all the commandments of the Lord. (Num. 15:38–39)

God would have all His people wear a badge. They were to make them fringes in the borders of their garments, and to put upon the fringes a ribband of blue, that they might look upon it and remember all the commandments of the Lord, and do them, and might be a holy people. Blue is the color of heaven. When the clouds come between, then, and only then, is the deep blue lost. It is the will of God that there should never be a cloud between His people and Himself, and that as the Israelite of old, wherever he went, carried the ribband of blue, so His people today should manifest a heavenly spirit and temper wherever they go, and should, like Moses, in their very countenances bear witness to the glory and beauty of the God whom they love and serve.

How interesting it must have been to see that ribband of blue carried by the farmer into the field, by the merchant to his place of business, by the maid-servant into the inner most parts of the dwelling, when performing her daily duties. Is it less important the Christian of today, called to be a witness for Christ, should be manifestly characterised by His spirit? Should we not all be "imitators of God, as dear children," and "walk in love, as Christ also hath loved us, and given Himself for us"? And should not this spirit of Godlikeness be carried into the smallest details of life, and not be merely reserved for special occasions?

> . . . the LORD gave, and the LORD
> hath taken away; blessed be the
> name of the LORD. (Job 1:21)

The great accuser having no fault to find with Job's character or life, insinuates that it is all the result of selfishness. "Doth Job fear God for nought?" Indeed he did not, as Satan well knew! Nor has anyone, before or since. There is no service which pays so well as the service of our Heavenly Master: there is none so royally rewarded. Satan was making a true assertion, but the insinuation—that it was for the sake of the reward that Job served God, was not true. And to vindicate the character of Job himself, Satan is permitted to test Job.

And soon Satan shows the malignity of his character by bringing disaster after disaster upon the devoted man. But God who sent the trial gave also the needful grace, and Job replied: "The Lord gave, and the Lord hath taken away; blessed be the Name of the Lord".

Was not Job mistaken? Should he not have said: "The Lord gave, and Satan hath taken away"? No, there was no mistake. He was enabled to discern the hand of God in all these calamities. Satan himself did not presume to ask God to be allowed *himself* to afflict Job. He says to God: "Put forth *Thine* hand now, and touch all that he hath, and he will curse Thee to Thy face". And again: "Put forth *Thine* hand now, and touch his flesh and bone, and he will curse Thee to Thy face". Satan knew that none but God could touch Job, and Job was quite right in recognising the Lord Himself as the doer. Oftentimes shall we be helped and blessed if we bear this in mind—that Satan is *servant*, and not *master*, and that he, and wicked men incited by him, are only permitted to do that which God by His determined counsel and foreknowledge had before

178

determined should be done. Come joy or come sorrow, we may always take it from the hand of God.

> . . . the joy of the LORD is your strength. (Neh. 8:10)

What is the joy of the Lord? Is it joy that there *is* such a Lord? For we cannot *realize* His existence without joy. Or, is it joy that He is *our* Lord? For possession is a fruitful source of joy. Or, again, is it joy that He has *imparted* to us, and shed abroad in our hearts by His Spirit? Or, lastly, is it His *own* joy which is our strength? We feel no doubt that, while all these sources of joy are ours, it is to the last of them that this passage specifically refers.

John 15:11 refers to our Saviour's *joy in fruit-bearing* through His branches. It was *His* will that His joy might remain in them; and that consequently *their* joy might be full. Here we see the joy of the Lord distinguished from the joy of His people.

In Hebrews 12:2, we have the joy of the Lord in the redemption of His people—joy to despise the shame and endure the cross. It was strength for self-sacrifice.

In Zephaniah 3:17, we have the joy of the Lord in the possession of His purchased inheritance. Oh, how wonderful is this joy! "He will rejoice over thee with joy, He will rest in His love, He will joy over thee with singing."

It is the consciousness of the threefold joy of the Lord—His joy in ransoming us—His joy in dwelling within us as our Saviour and Power for fruitbearing—and His joy in possessing us, as His Bride and His delight; it is the consciousness of this joy which is our real strength. Our joy in Him may be a fluctuating thing: His joy in us knows no change.

# Charles Haddon Spurgeon
## (1834–1892)

C. H. Spurgeon was certainly one of the greatest preachers of the gospel of all times, and perhaps the greatest Baptist preacher of modern times. He became pastor of a small church in Waterbeach, near Cambridge, when he was only seventeen years old. God blessed the work, and in 1854 he was called to New Park Street Church, London. When the invitation to preach there came to him, Spurgeon was sure it was a mistake.

The rest is glorious history. A breath of revival touched the dying congregation. Souls came to Christ; the work grew, the congregation had to seek larger facilities. The Metropolitan Tabernacle was opened in 1861, one of the largest Nonconformist houses of worship in Europe. It seated 6,000 persons, and during Spurgeon's ministry, it was filled twice each Sunday. It is estimated that more than 100 million copies of his individual sermons have been distributed around the world. The sermons of Spurgeon have been published in 50 large volumes, and they are read and studied with profit by many people who love Christ and the gospel.

My selections are taken not from Spurgeon's sermons but from a selection of his Sunday morning prayers. Spurgeon's pastoral prayers are as rich as his sermons.

Nevertheless I have somewhat
against thee, because thou hast left
thy first love. (Rev. 2:4)

But, Lord, we have yet another burden—it is that we ourselves do not love Thee as we should, that oftentimes we grow

180

lukewarm and chill, and doubt creeps over us, and unbelief mars our confidence, and we sin and forget our God. O Lord help us! Pardon is not enough, we want sanctification. We beseech Thee let the weeds that grow in the seed plot of our soul be cut up by the roots. We do want to serve Thee. We long that every thought we think, and word we say or write, should be all for Thee. We would lead consecrated lives, for we are persuaded that we only live as we live unto God, that aught else is but trifling. Oh, to be taken up as offerings wholly to be consumed upon the altar of the Lord, joyfully ascending to Him in every outgoing of our life. Now this morning be pleased to refresh us. Draw nigh unto us, Thou gracious God; it is only Thy presence that can make us happy, holy, devout or strong. Shadow us now with Thy wings, cover us with Thy feathers, and under Thy wings may we trust. May we follow very near unto Thee, and so feel the quickening warmth, the joy which only Thy nearness can bring.

> Nevertheless not my will, but thine, be done. (Luke 22:42)

And now do we hoist sail and draw up anchor to sail into another year. O Thou blessed Pilot of the future as of the past, we are so happy to leave all to Thee; but in leaving all to Thee we have one wish, and it is that Thou wouldst in the next year glorify the Father's name in us more than in any other year of our lives. Perhaps this may involve deeper trial, but let it be if we can glorify God. Perhaps this may involve the being cast aside from the service that we love; but we would prefer to be laid aside if we could glorify Thee the better. Perhaps this may involve the ending of all life's pleasant work and the being taken home—well, Thy children make no sort of stipulations with their God, but this one prayer ascends from all true hearts this morning, "Father, glorify Thy name." Wilt Thou glorify Thyself, great Father, by making us more holy. Purge us every day, we beseech Thee, from the selfishness that clings to us. Deliver us also from the fear of man, from the love of approbation so far as these might lead us astray. Help us to be resolute and self-contained to do, and think, and speak the right at all times. Give us great love to our fellow men. May we love them so that we could die for them if need be.

But he knoweth the way that I take:
when he hath tried me, I shall come
forth as gold. (Job 23:10)

Lord, we desire this morning to contemplate with admiration Thy ways toward us. Thou hast put some of us into the furnace. There is no child of Thine but knows something of the heat of the furnace, and we perceive that Thou art as a refiner unto us, and that the fire is meant to consume our dross and tin, therefore do we thank Thee for it. For all the acts of discipline to which we are subject we would praise the wisdom and the love of our divine Father. Thou wouldst not have us live in sin; sin is much worse than furnace work. All the trial in the world is not so hard to carry as a sense of sin. Lord, if Thou dost give us choice to keep our sins and to live in pleasure, or to have them burnt away with trial, we will say to Thee, Lord, give us the sanctified affliction, but deliver us from all the influences of sin, from every evil habit, from all the accretions of former sin, all the ore that is mixed with the precious metal, everything that diminishes the brightness of Thy grace in us, everything that keeps Thee from taking delight in us, take it away, we beseech Thee: and if this life is to be to Thy people the crucible and the burning heat, even to a white heat, so let it be, so long as Thou dost sit at the furnace mouth to watch the ore that nothing should be lost. Oh, blessed God, help any of Thy children that are in the midst of the heat now. Let them see the Lord sitting near and watching, and let them feel perfectly at ease, because in His hands all things must be well.

> . . . bind the sacrifice with cords,
> even unto the horns of the altar.
> (Ps. 118:27)

O Lord, we would cling to Thee more firmly than ever we have done: we would say, "Return unto Thy rest, O my soul, for the Lord hath dealt bountifully with thee, for Thou hast delivered my soul from death, mine eyes from tears and my feet from falling." We would this morning "take the cup of salvation and call upon the name of the Lord." We would "pay our vows unto the Lord now, in the courts of the Lord's house, in the midst of all His people." Blessed be the name of the Lord, we have been brought low, but the Lord hath helped us; we have oftentimes wandered, but He has restored us; we have been tried, but He has preserved us; yea, we have found His paths to be "paths of pleasantness" and all the ways of His wisdom to be "ways of peace." We bear our willing witness to the testimony of the Lord, we set our seal that "He is true" and we cry again "Bind the sacrifice with cords, even with cords unto the horns of the altar." From henceforth let no man trouble us, for we "bear in our body the marks of the Lord Jesus." We are His branded servants henceforth and forever. Our ear is nailed to our Master's door-post, to go no more out forever.

> Jesus saith unto them, Loose him,
> and let him go. (John 11:44)

And now hear Thou us again while we cry unto Thee. Our chief desire is for Thy cause in the earth. We are often very heavy about it. The days seem to us to be neither dark nor light, but mingled; oh that the element of light might overcome the darkness! We do pray Thee, raise up in these days a race of men that shall know the gospel and hold it fast. We do feel that we have so much superficial religion, so much profession without true possession to back it up. Oh, Lord, may our churches be built with precious stones, and not with wood, hay, and stubble. May we ourselves so know the gospel that no one can beat us out of it; may we so hold it that our faces shall be like flints against the errors of the age; so practice it that our lives shall be an argument that none can answer, for the power of the gospel of Jesus. And with this be pleased to grant to Thy churches more power over the sons of men. Oh, Lord, make Thy ministers throughout all the world to be more fruitful in soul winning. Let us not rest without sowing the good seed beside all waters. Forgive us our coldness and indifference; forgive us that we sleep as do others, for it is high time for us to awake out of sleep. Oh, Lord, do help us to live while we live; shake us clear of these cerements, these grave clothes, which cling to us; say to us, most blessed Jesus, what Thou saidst concerning Lazarus of old, "Loose him, and let him go." May we get right away from the old death and the old lethargy, and live under the best conditions of life, diligently serving God. Convert the nations, we pray Thee! Help our dear brethren who stand far out in the thick heathen darkness, like lone sentinels; let them bear their witness well, and may the day come when the Christian church shall become a missionary church, when all over the world those that love Christ shall be determined that He shall conquer. Thou hast not yet made the church "terrible as an army with banners:" would God she were. May those days of Christian earnestness come to us, and then shall we look for the latter day of glory.

> All nations whom thou hast made
> shall come and worship before thee,
> O Lord; and shall glorify thy name.
> (Ps. 86:9)

Hallowed be Thy Name." Oh, that all the earth would ever reverence it. As for ourselves, enable us by Thy grace to use it with awe and trembling; and may a consideration of the glorious character which is intended by Thy gracious name, ever lay us in the very dust before Thee, and yet lift us up with holy joy and with an unwavering confidence. We come before Thee this morning through Christ Jesus to express our entire confidence in Thee. We believe that Thou art, and that Thou art the rewarder of them that diligently seek Thee.

Glorious Jehovah, the God of Abraham, of Isaac, and of Jacob, Thou hast not changed: Thou art still a covenant God, and Thou keepest that covenant to all Thy people; neither dost Thou permit a single word of it to fall to the ground. All Thy promises are yea and amen in Christ Jesus to Thy glory by us, and we believe those promises will be fulfilled in every jot and tittle: not one of them shall want its mate, not one of them shall fall to the ground like the frivolous words of men. Hast Thou said and wilt Thou not do it? Hast Thou commanded and shall it not come to pass? We are utterly ashamed and full of confusion, because we have to confess that we have doubted Thee. Many of our actions have been atheistic. We have lived at times as if there were no God.

Wash me thoroughly from mine iniquity, and cleanse me from my sin. (Ps. 51:2)

W e would each one of us ask this morning that we may be washed as to our feet: we trust Thou hast bathed us once for all in the sin-removing fountain. Thou hast also washed us in the waters of regeneration, and given us the renewing of our minds through Jesus Christ. But oh, for daily cleansing! Dost Thou see any fault in us?—oh, we know that Thou dost—wash us that we may be clean. Are we deficient in any virtue? Oh, supply it, that we may exhibit a perfect character, to the glory of Him who hast made us anew in Christ Jesus. Or, is there something that would be good, carried to excess? Be pleased to modify it lest one virtue should slaughter another, and we should not be the image of Christ completely. Oh, Lord and

Master, Thou who didst wash Thy disciples' feet of old, still be very patient toward us, very condescending towards our provoking faults, and go on with us, we pray Thee, till Thy great work shall be completed, and we shall be brethren of the First-born, like unto Him.

> And the God of peace shall bruise
> Satan under your feet shortly.
> (Rom. 16:20)

Thou knowest, Lord, for Thou searchest the heart and Thou triest the reins of the children of men—Thou knowest we can truly say, unless indeed we be under a very deep delusion, that we do wish to promote Thy glory among the sons of men; and that we count nothing to be riches, but that which makes us rich towards God; nothing to be health, but that which is sanity before the most High—holiness in Thy sight; and we reckon nothing to be pure, but what Thou hast cleansed; and nothing to be good, but that upon which Thy blessing rests. Yet Lord, though it be so, though our mind has been by Thy Spirit set towards holiness, there is a death within us; the old nature which strives against our life, and the members of the body often join with the corrupt nature within, to lead us astray. We swing towards holiness and then we seem like the pendulum, to swing the other way. We are wretched, because of this, and we cry out to Thee to deliver us. Oh, that Thou wouldst deliver us!

We do thank Thee that Jesus gives us the victory; but we long to have that victory in ourselves more constantly realised—more perfectly enjoyed. We would lie in the very dust before Thee because of sin; and yet, at the same time, rejoice in the great Sinbearer, that the sin is not imputed to us, that it is put away by His precious blood, that we are accepted in the Beloved. But even this does not content us; we are crying after the work of the Holy Ghost within, till Satan shall be bruised under our feet, and sin shall be utterly destroyed.

# Marcus Dods
## (1834–1909)

Can you imagine waiting six years for a church to call you as pastor? At the beginning of his ministry, the great Scottish biblical scholar Marcus Dods was a "probationer" from 1858 to 1864, but he patiently waited for God's leading. He was pastor of Renfield Free Church, Glasgow, until 1889, at which time he became professor of New Testament at New College, Edinburgh.

Dods is best known for his books of biblical studies. He was more sympathetic to "modern views" than some of his associates, and in 1891 was tried for heresy by the General Assembly of the church. He was acquitted. I think that Dods had a weak view of inerrancy, but I appreciate his written ministry nonetheless.

Dods contributed the commentaries on Genesis, John, and I Corinthians to the *Expositor's Bible.*

He was in the world, and the world
was made by him, and the world
knew him not. (John 1:10)

When our Lord came to earth the heathen world was mainly represented by the Roman Empire, and one of the earliest events of His life on earth was His enrolment as a subject of that empire. If we had been invited before His coming to imagine what would be the result upon this empire of His appearance, we should probably have expected something very different from that which actually happened. The real Sovereign is to appear; the Being who made all that is is to come and visit His possessions. Will not a thrill of glad expectancy run through the world? Will not men eagerly cover up whatever may offend Him, and eagerly attempt, with such scant materials as existed, to make preparations for His worthy reception? The one Being who can make no mistakes, and who can rectify the mistakes of a worn-out, entangled world, is to come for the express purpose of delivering it from all ill: will not men gladly yield the reins to Him, gladly second Him in all His enterprise? Will it not be a time of universal concord and brotherhood, all men joining to pay homage to their common God? "He was in the world, and the world was made by Him"—that is the true, bare, unvarnished statement of the fact. There He was, the Creator Himself, that mysterious Being who had hitherto kept Himself so hidden and remote while yet so influential and supreme; the wonderful and unsearchable Source and Fountain out of which had proceeded all that men saw, themselves included,—there at last He was *in* the world" Himself had made, apparent to the eyes of men, and intelligible to their understandings; a real person whom they could know as an individual, whom they could love, who could receive and return their expressions of affection and trust. He was in the world, and the world knew Him not.

There was a man sent from God,
whose name was John. (John 1:6)

Going from the comfortable home and well-provided life and fair prospects of a priest's family, he went to the houseless wilderness, and adopted the meagre, comfortless life of an ascetic; not from any necessity, but because he felt that to entangle himself with the affairs of the world would be to blind him to its vices, and to silence his remonstrance, if not to implicate him in its guilt. Like thousands besides in all ages of the world's history, he felt compelled to seek solitude, to subdue the flesh, to meditate undisturbed on things Divine, and discover for himself and for others some better way than religious routine and the "good wine of Mosaic morality turned to the vinegar of Pharisaism." Like the Nazarites of the earlier times of his country, like the old prophets, with whose indignation and deep regret at the national vices he was in perfect sympathy, he left the world, gave up all the usual prospects and ways of life, and betook himself to a life of prayer, and thought, and self-discipline in the wilderness. When first he went there, he could only dimly know what lay before him; but he gathered a few friends of like disposition around him, and, as we learn "taught them to pray." He formed in the wilderness a new Israel, a little company of praying souls, who spent their time in considering the needs of their fellow-countrymen, and in interceding with God for them, and who were content to let the pleasures and excitements of the world pass by while they longed for and prepared themselves to meet the great Deliverer.

> And when Jesus beheld him, he said,
> Thou art Simon the son of Jona:
> thou shalt be called Cephas, which is
> by interpretation, A stone. (John 1:42)

Coming in this mood, he is greeted with words which seem to say to him, I know the character identified with the name "Simon, son of John;" I know all you fear, all the remorseful thoughts that possess you; I know how you wish now you were a man like Andrew, and could offer yourself as a serviceable subject of this new kingdom. But no! thou art Simon; nothing can change that, and such as you are you are welcome; but "thou shalt be called Rock," Peter. The men standing round, and knowing Simon well, might turn away to hide a smile; but Simon knew the Lord had found him, and uttered the very word which could bind him for ever to Him. And the event showed how true this appellation was. Simon became Peter,—bold to stand for the rest, and beard the Sanhedrim. By believing that this new King had a place for him in His kingdom, and could give him a new character which should fit him for service, he became a new man, strong where he had been weak, helpful and no longer dangerous to the cause he loved.

Such are the encouragements with which the King of men welcomes the diffident. He gives men the consciousness that they are known; He begets the consciousness that it is not with sin in the abstract He undertakes to do, but with sinners He can name, and whose weaknesses are known to Him. But He begets this consciousness that we may trust Him when He gives us assurance that a new character awaits us and a serviceable place in His kingdom. He assures the most despondent that for them also a useful life is possible.

> Lord, to whom shall we go? thou
> hast the words of eternal life.
> (John 6:68)

When Christ sifts His followers those remain who have spiritual tastes and wants. The spiritual man, the man who would rather be like God than be rich, whose efforts after worldly advancement are not half as earnest and sustained as his efforts after spiritual health; the man, in short, who seeks first the kingdom of God and His righteousness, and lets other things be added or not to this prime requisite, cleaves to Christ because there is that in Christ which satisfies his taste and gives him the life he chiefly desires. There is in Christ a suitableness to the wants of men who live in view of God and eternity, and who seek to adjust themselves, not only to the world around them so as to be comfortable and successful in it, but also to the things unseen, to the permanent laws which are to govern human beings and human affairs throughout eternity. Such men find in Christ that which enables them to adjust themselves to things eternal. They find in Christ just that revelation of God, and that reconcilement to Him, and that help to abiding in Him, which they need. They cannot imagine a time, they cannot picture to themselves a state of society, in which the words and teaching of Jesus would not be the safest guide and the highest law. Life eternal, life for men as men, is taught by Him; not professional life, not the life of a religious rule that must pass away, not life for this world only, but life eternal, life such as men everywhere and always ought to live—this is apprehended by Him and explained by Him; and power and desire to live it are quickened within men by His words. Coming into His presence we recognise the assuredness of perfect truth. That which outrides all such critical times as the disciples were now passing through is true spirituality of mind. The man who is bent on nourishing his spirit to life everlasting simply cannot dispense with what he finds in Christ.

Except a grain of wheat fall into the ground and die, it abideth alone: but if it die, it bringeth forth much fruit. (John 12:24)

As with the grain, so is it with each human life. One of two things you can do with your life; both you cannot do, and no third thing is possible. You may consume your life for your own present gratification and profit, to satisfy your present cravings and tastes and to secure the largest amount of immediate enjoyment to yourself—you may eat your life; or you may be content to put aside present enjoyment and profits of a selfish kind and devote your life to the uses of God and men. In the one case you make an end of your life, you consume it as it goes; no good results, no enlarging influence, no deepening of character, no fuller life, follows from such an expenditure of life—spent on yourself and on the present. But in the other case you find that you have entered into a more abundant life; by living for others your interests are widened, your desire for life increased, the results and ends of life enriched. "He that loveth his life shall lose it; and he that hateth his life in this world shall keep it unto life eternal." It is a law we cannot evade. He that consumes his life now, spending it on himself—he who cannot bear to let his life out of his own hand, but cherishes and pampers it and gathers all good around it, and will have the fullest present enjoyment out of it,—this man is losing his life; it comes to an end as certainly as the seed that is eaten. But he who devotes his life to other uses than his own gratification, who does not so prize self that everything must minister to its comfort and advancement, but who can truly yield himself to God and put himself at God's disposal for the general good,—this man, though he may often seem to lose his life, and often does lose it so far as present advantage goes, keeps it to life everlasting.

> I go to prepare a place for you.
> (John 14:2)

This of itself is enough to give us hopeful thoughts of the future state. Christ is busied in preparing for us what will give us satisfaction and joy. When we expect a guest we love and have written for, we take pleasure in preparing for his reception,—we hang in his room the picture he likes; if he is infirm, we wheel in the easiest chair; we gather the flowers he admires and set them on his table; we go back and back to see if nothing else will suggest itself to us so that when he comes he may have entire satisfaction. This is enough for us to know—that Christ is similarly occupied. He knows our tastes, our capabilities, our attainments, and he has identified a place as ours and holds it for us. What the joys and the activities and occupations of the future shall be we do not know. With the body we shall lay aside many of our appetites and tastes and proclivities, and what has here seemed necessary to our comfort will at once become indifferent. We shall not be able to desire the pleasures that now allure and draw us. The need of shelter, of retirement, of food, of comfort, will disappear with the body; and what the joys and the requirements of a spiritual body will be we do not know. But we do know that at home with God the fullest life that man can live will certainly be ours.

> And whatsoever ye shall ask in my
> name, that will I do, that the Father
> may be glorified in the Son.
> (John 14:13)

It means that we pray for such things as will promote Christ's kingdom. When we do anything in another's name, it is for him we do it. When we take possession of a property or a legacy in the name of some society, it is not for our own private advantage, but for the society, we take possession. When an officer arrests any one in the Queen's name, it is not to satisfy his private malice he does so; and when he collects money in the name of government, it is not to fill his own pocket. Yet how constantly do we overlook this obvious condition of acceptable prayer! To pray in Christ's name is to seek what He seeks, to ask aid in promoting what He has at heart. To come in Christ's name and plead selfish and worldly desires is absurd. To pray in Christ's name is to pray in the spirit in which He Himself prayed and for objects He desires. When we measure our prayers by this rule, we cease to wonder that so few seem to be answered. Is God to answer prayers that positively lead men away from Him? Is He to build them up in the presumption that happiness can be found in the pursuit of selfish objects and worldly comfort? It is when a man stands, as these disciples stood, detached from worldly hopes and finding all in Christ, so clearly apprehending the sweep and benignity of Christ's will as to see that it comprehends all good to man, and that life can serve no purpose if it do not help to fulfil that will—it is then a man prays with assurance and finds his prayer answered. Christ had won the love of these men and knew that their chief desire would be to serve Him, that their prayers would always be that they might fulfil His purposes. Their fear was, not that He would summon them to live wholly for the ends for which He had lived, but that when He was gone they should find themselves unfit to contend with the world.

# Phillips Brooks

## (1835–1893)

Most people know Phillips Brooks only as the composer of "O Little Town of Bethlehem." He was much more, for he was a mighty preacher and a man whose ministry encouraged Christian morality and spiritual unity among God's people.

Brooks was a big man in every way—physically (he stood six feet, four inches, and weighed nearly three hundred pounds); intellectually; spiritually. He preached rapidly and always aimed to communicate God's truth. A bachelor, he loved children, indulged the ones he knew, and poured out his love on needy souls and hungry saints. He was not an expositor or a doctrinal preacher. He knew how to preach, and his twenty-two years of ministry at Trinity Church, Boston, were so successful that he was elected bishop of Boston. Unfortunately, he died fifteen months after his consecration.

I appreciate his sermons, and his *Lectures on Preaching,* delivered at Yale in 1877, is certainly one of the best books about preaching ever published in America. In fact, I am convinced that most of our homiletics books are but footnotes to these marvelous lectures.

For thy mercy is great above the
heavens: and thy truth reacheth
unto the clouds. (Ps. 108:4)

For I think that the first condition of any permanent hold on any truth is this, that the truth itself should be live enough and large enough to open constantly and bring to every new condition through which we pass some new experience of itself. The truth that is narrow and partial we outgrow; only the truth that is broad and complete grows up with us and can be kept. The one is like the clothes of childhood that are cast aside; the other is like the live body that grows up with the growing soul, and at each stage offers it a fit instrument for its work and a fit medium through which to receive its education.

The true faith which a man has kept up to the end of his life must be one that has opened with his growth and constantly won new reality and colour from his changing experience. The old man does believe what the child believed; but how different it is, though still the same. It is the field that once held the seed, now waving and rustling under the autumn wind with the harvest that it holds, yet all the time it has kept the corn. The joy of his life has richened his belief. His sorrow has deepened it. His doubts have sobered it. His enthusiasms have fired it. His labour has purified it.

> Behold, thou desirest truth in the
> inward parts. (Ps. 51:6)

The great purpose of life—the shaping of character by truth—is to be sought in all the life. There are no wasted hours. It must begin in the life's morning and run on till the nightfall comes. With the first opening of conscious existence—nay, who can say how long before existence becomes conscious—this process, the shaping of character by truth, begins. In each period of the changing life it may change its methods and yet be the same process still. In the early life the channel through which truth enters for its work is obedient trust. Later it is individual conviction; but he mangles the life, and loses its symmetry and unity, who breaks off either half or dishonours either channel; who either thinks there can be no religion till the mind can understand its grounds, or tries to keep the mature mind under the power of traditional ideas of which it has received no personal conviction.

> Howbeit in vain do they worship me,
> teaching for doctrines the com-
> mandments of men. (Mark 7:7)

And the second characteristic of the faith that can be kept will be its evidence, its proved truth. It will not be a mere aggregation of chance opinions. The reason why a great many people seem to be always changing their faith is that they never really have any faith. They have indeed what they call a faith, and are often very positive about it. They have gathered together a number of opinions and fancies, often very ill-considered, which they say that they believe, using the deep and sacred word for a very superficial and frivolous action of their wills. They no more have a faith than the city vagrant has a home who sleeps upon a different doorstep every night. And yet he does sleep somewhere every night; and so these wanderers among the creeds at each given moment are believing something, although that something is for ever altering. We do not properly believe what we only think. A thousand speculations come into our heads, and our minds dwell upon them, which are not to be therefore put into our creed, however plausible they seem. Our creed, our *credo*, anything which we call by such a sacred name, is not what we have thought, but what our Lord has told us.

> . . . as the servants of Christ, doing
> the will of God from the heart.
> (Eph. 6:6)

And then the third quality of a creed that a man may keep up to the end is that it is a creed capable of being turned into action. A mere speculation, however true it be, I think you never can be sure that the mind will hold. The faith which you keep must be a faith that demands obedience, and you can keep it only by obeying it. Are not both of these true? Those parts of religion which are purely speculative, if indeed such mere speculation is part of religion at all, are the parts in which men most often and most easily change. A hundred men change their views of abstract truth for one who alters his conviction of practical duty. The one may be changed and nothing suffers; a change in the other alters the whole life.

Look at two men holding the same truth—the truth of the Trinity, for instance. To one it presents itself always as a doctrine to be learned, to the other as a law to be obeyed. One's view of it is always theoretical, the other's always practical. They both believe it, but one asserts it, demonstrates it, reasons about it. The other lives by it. Which is the true believer? I can conceive of the first man losing his belief and yet going on much the same. Convince him with a specious argument and he will let it drop, and, except that he talks of it no longer, nobody will know the difference. But take the truth of the Divine Father, the Divine Saviour, the Divine Comforter, out of the other's life, and all is gone. Duty no longer has a zest, nor prayer an object, nor grief a consolation. The whole life falls to pieces when its truth is gone. Is not this last the man who will keep the faith?

> Look not every man on his own
> things, but every man also on the
> things of others. (Phil. 2:4)

The truth is, that we are our best when we try to be it not for ourselves alone, but for our brethren; and that we take God's gifts most completely for ourselves when we realize that He sends them to us for the benefit of other men, who stand beyond us needing them. I have spoken very feebly, unless you have felt something of the difference which it would make to all of us if this truth really took possession of us. It would make our struggles after a higher life so much more intense as they become more noble. "For their sakes I sanctify myself," said Jesus; and He hardly ever said words more wonderful than those. There was the power by which He was holy; the world was to be made holy, was to be sanctified through Him. I am sure that you or I could indeed be strengthened to meet some great experience of pain if we really believed that by our suffering we were to be made luminous with help to other men. They are to get from us painlessly what we have got most painfully from God. There is the power of the bravest martyrdom and the hardest work that the world has ever seen.

And I was afraid, and went and hid
thy talent in the earth. . . .
(Matt. 25:25)

It seems very certain that the world is to grow better and richer in the future, however it has been in the past, not by the magnificent achievements of the highly-gifted few, but by the patient faithfulness of the one-talented many. If we could draw back the curtains of the millennium and look in, we should see not a Hercules here and there standing on the world-wasting monsters he had killed, but a world full of men, each with an arm of moderate muscle, but each triumphant over his own little piece of the obstinacy of earth or the ferocity of the brutes. It seems as if the heroes had done almost all for the world that they can do, and not much more can come till common men awake and take their common tasks.

I do believe the common man's task is the hardest. The hero has the hero's aspiration that lifts him to his labour. All great duties are easier than the little ones, though they cost far more blood and agony. That is a truth we all find out. And this is part of the reason why we make allowance for our poor friend in the parable. But if we look at it in a higher way, surely we may come to feel that the very certainty that the world must be saved by the faithfulness of commonplace people is what is needed to rescue such people from commonplaceness in their own eyes, and clothe their lives with the dignity which they seem so woefully to lack, and which, if any man does not see somewhere shining through the rusty texture of his life, he cannot live it well.

> My meat is to do the will of him that
> sent me, and to finish his work.
> (John 4:34)

And the world of God includes two notions, one of revelation and one of commandment. Whenever God speaks by any of His voices, it is first to tell us some truth which we did not know before, and second to bid us do something which we have not been doing. Every word of God includes these two. Truth and duty are always wedded. There is no truth which has not its corresponding duty. And there is no duty which has not its corresponding truth. We are always separating them. We are always trying to learn truths, as if there were no duties belonging to them, as if the knowing of them would make no difference in the way we lived. That is the reason why our hold on the truths we learn is so weak.

He who takes any new word of God completely gets both a new truth and a new duty. He, then, who lives by every word of God, is a man who is continually seeing new truth and accepting the duties that arise out of it. And it is for this, for the pleasure of seeing truth and doing its attendant duty, that he is willing to give up the pleasures of sense, and even, if need be, to give up the bodily life to which the pleasures of sense belong.

200

# Alexander Whyte
## (1836–1921)

When Alexander Whyte was seven years old, Robert Murray McCheyne visited his town, Kirriemuir, and gave the boy a tract. Little did either of them know that one day Whyte would be Scotland's leading preacher with a ministry reaching around the world.

Whyte has been called "the last of the Puritans." He preached surgical sermons that penetrated the heart and pierced the conscience. He was a hard worker, both as a preacher and a pastor, for he loved and cared for his people. "I would have all lazy students drummed out of the college," he said, "and all lazy ministers out of the Assembly!" His books of sermons, especially his biographical studies, still speak to our hearts. Whyte knew the human heart—and what Christ can do for the heart.

Comfort ye, comfort ye my people,
saith your God. (Isa. 40:1)

No man living in any known sin is ever comforted of God. The Holy Ghost never yet spake one word of all His abounding consolations to any man so long as he lived in any actual sin, or in any neglect of known duty. You have that much-needed caution bound up into the very heart of God's great name, when He proclaimed His great Name to Moses. "The Lord God, merciful and gracious, long-suffering, and abundant in goodness and truth, keeping mercy for thousands, forgiving iniquity and transgression and sin—*but*"—and here comes this great correction and caution—"will by no means clear the guilty." That is to say, as long as you are living in any *guilt*, as long as your conscience accuses you, He will by no means clear or comfort you. "He that forsaketh his sin shall find mercy"—but he only. You do not really care for God's mercy or His comfort either, so long as you live in any sin. And it is well that you do not; for you can have neither. Your peace will be like a river, when you put away your sin; but not one word of true peace, not one drop of true comfort, can you have till then. You will have to put out God's eyes, and pervert His judgment, and turn His Throne upside down, before you can have His comfort with your sin. Choose which you will have: "If a man love Me, he will keep My words: and My Father will love him, and We will come unto him, and make Our abode with him." Are *you* that man? Are you intending to be that man? And when and in what are you to begin? Are you from this day to keep that word of His, which up to this day you know you have not kept? Then, from this day Jesus and His Father will come to your good and honest, if broken and contrite heart, and will make Their abode with you. And from this memorable day it will be said over you from heaven, what was said from heaven in Israel over all the men in Israel like you: "To this man will I look, saith the Lord, even to him that is poor and of a contrite spirit, and who trembleth at My word."

Who hath believed our report?
(Isa. 53:1)

Among the amazing things of which this amazing chapter is full, there is nothing that arrests us, and overawes us, and, indeed, staggers us more than this—that it "pleased the Lord to bruise" His Messiah-Son. But the simple truth of God in this matter is this. God was so set, from everlasting, on the salvation of sinners that the most awful steps that had to be taken in order to work out that salvation are here said to have absolutely pleased Him. It is somewhat like our Lord's own words—"I delight to do Thy will": even when His Father's will led Him to the garden of Gethsemane and the Cross of Calvary. God so loved the world that He gave up His only-begotten Son to die for the sin of the world. God could not be pleased with the death of His Son—in itself. No. But nothing has ever pleased Him more than that His Son should lay down His life in atonement for those sinners whom the Father had chosen and ordained to everlasting life. Paul has everything. And he has the Father's indebtedness to His Son and His good pleasure in His death in this great passage: "God hath set forth Christ Jesus to be a propitiation through faith in His blood: to declare His righteousness, that He might be just and the justifier of him which believeth in Jesus." It pleased the Lord to bruise Him, because in this way alone could God's full hatred of sin be declared to men and angels, and at the same time God's justice might be manifested in the salvation of sinners.

> . . . to give his life a ransom for many. (Matt. 20:28)

You have heard sometimes about hell being let loose. Yes, but hear this. Come to Caiaphas' palace on the passover night, and look at this. "Then did they spit in His face, and buffeted Him: they blindfolded Him and then they smote Him with the palms of their hands, saying: Prophesy to us, Thou Christ, who is it that smote Thee? And they stripped Him, and put on Him a scarlet robe. And when they had platted a crown of thorns"—I wonder in what sluggard's garden it grew!—"they put it upon His head, and a reed in His right hand; and they bowed the knee before Him and mocked Him, saying: Hail! King of the Jews! And they spit upon Him again, and took the reed out of His hand, and smote Him upon the head. Then Pilate took Jesus and scourged Him. After which they brought Jesus forth wearing the crown of thorns and the purple robe. And when the Chief Priests saw Jesus, they cried out, Crucify Him! crucify Him! Then Pilate delivered Him to them to be crucified." My brethren,—these are dreadful, most dreadful, things. And all the time, God Almighty, the God and Father of Jesus Christ, restrained Himself; He held Himself in, and sat as still as a stone, seeing and hearing all that. The arrest, the trial, the buffeting, the spitting, the jesting and the jeering, the bloody scourging, the crown of thorns, the reed, and the purple robe—Why? In the name of amazement, why did the Judge of all the earth sit still and see all that said and done? Do you know what made Him sit still? Did you ever think about it? And would you like to be told how it could be? God Almighty, my brethren, not only sat still, but He ordained it all; and His Son *endured* it all,—*in order to take away sin.*

> We give thanks to God and the
> Father of our Lord Jesus Christ,
> praying always for you. (Col. 1:3)

I am as certain as I am standing here, that the secret of much mischief to our own souls, and to the souls of others, lies in the way that we stint, and starve, and scamp our prayers, by hurrying over them. Prayer worth calling prayer: prayer that God will call true prayer and will treat as true prayer, takes far more time, by the clock, than one man in a thousand thinks. After all that the Holy Ghost has done to make true prayer independent of times, and of places, and of all kinds of instruments and assistances,—as long as we remain in this unspiritual and undevotional world, we shall not succeed, to be called success, in prayer, without time, and times, and places, and other assistances in prayer. Take good care that you are not spiritual overmuch in the matter of prayer. Take good care lest you take your salvation far too softly, and far too cheaply. If you find your life of prayer to be always so short, and so easy, and so spiritual, as to be without cost and strain and sweat to you, you may depend upon it, you are not yet begun to pray. As sure as you sit there, and I stand here, it is just in this matter of *time* in prayer that so many of us are making shipwreck of our own souls, and of the souls of others.

Unto me, who am less than the least
of all saints. . . . (Eph. 3:8)

You must not idolise Paul. You must not totally misread and persistently misunderstand Paul, as if Paul had not been a man of like passions with yourselves. Paul was a far better believer than you or I are. But as to sin there is no difference. And the very greatness of Paul's faith; the very unparalleled concentration and identifying power of his faith; all that only made the sudden blasts that struck at his faith all the more terrible to bear. Oh, yes! You may depend upon it Paul had a thousand things behind him that swept down guilt and shame and sorrow upon his head to the day of his death. The men and the women and the children he had haled to prison; the holy homes he had desolated with his temple hordes; the martyrdoms he had instigated, the blood of which would never in this world be washed off his hands; in these, and in a thousand other things, Paul was a child of wrath even as others. And that wrath of God would awaken in his conscience, and would assault his faith, just as that same wrath of God assaults your faith and mine every day we live: if, that is to say, we live at all. No, there is no difference. The only difference is that Paul always met that rising wrath with a faith in Christ crucified that has never been equalled. 'I, through the law,' he said, or tried to say, every time the law clutched at him as its prisoner—'I through the law am dead to the law. For I am crucified with Christ.'

> Ye are not under the law, but under
> grace. (Rom. 6:14)

Ａnd then, what is grace? Grace is love. But grace is not love simply, and purely, and alone. Grace and love are, in their innermost essence, one and the same thing. Only, grace is love adapting itself to certain special circumstances. As, for instance, love may exist between equals, or it may rise to those who are above it, or it may flow down to those who are beneath it. But grace has only one direction that it can take. Grace always flows down. And thus it is that sovereigns are said to be gracious to their subjects. But though a subject may loyally and truly and devotedly love his sovereign, yet the most loving of subjects is never said to be gracious to his sovereign. Because grace always flows down. Now, among many other relations that God holds to us, He is our Sovereign, and therefore His love to us is always called His sovereign grace. It is called mercy also, because we are in misery on account of our sin. But it is called grace above all, because we are not only in an estate of sin and misery, but because we are so infinitely beneath God, and are in that and in every other way so utterly unworthy of His love. And thus it is that with its infinite condescension toward us, grace has the most absolute freeness in all its outgoings and down-flowings also. And as grace is free, so is it sure. Nothing can change, or alter, or turn away, sovereign grace. And, with all that, it is unconditional. That is to say, as no merit of mortal man ever drew down on him the grace of God, so no demerit and no ill-desert of any man on whom it has once rested, will ever cause that grace to be withdrawn. It is not of works, lest any man should boast. Therefore it is of faith, that it might be by grace; to the end the promise might be sure to all the seed. If by grace, then it is no more of works; otherwise grace is no more grace. Grace, then, is grace,—that is to say, it is sovereign, it is free, it is sure, it is unconditional, and it is everlasting.

But without faith it is impossible to
please him. . . . (Heb. 11:6)

This is my beloved Son, in whom I
am well pleased. (Matt. 3:17)

First in His believing study and believing appropriation of
the Messianic Scriptures, and then in His life of unceasing
and believing prayer, our Lord stands at our head as the
author and finisher of faith. And not more in His believing
reading of the word than in His believing prayer and intercession continually. 'Who, in the days of His flesh, when He had
offered up prayers and supplications, with strong crying and
tears unto Him that was able to save Him from death, and
was heard in that He feared.' Day and night, early and late, our
Lord lived and moved and had His being in believing prayer.
He could never have entered on His great work, far less could
He ever have finished it, but for His faith in His father as the
Hearer of prayer. At every successive step in the process of
our redemption, He took that step after a season of prayer, till
He had fulfilled in His own experience what He preaches with
such point to us concerning believing prayer. Preaching
clearly and undeniably from His own experience in prayer,
He says to us in one great place—concerning prayer: 'What
things soever ye desire, when ye pray, believe that ye receive
them, and ye shall have them.' There is a window opened into
our Lord's secret life of prayer in these wonderful words—
words much too wonderful for the best believer among us,
but true to the letter of Him and of His faith in His Father. 'I
know,' He said to His Father, at the grave of Lazarus, 'I know
that Thou hearest me always. But because of the people that
stand by I said it, that they might believe that Thou hast heard
Me.' Such close communion of faith, and such strong assurance of faith, was there between the Father and the Son in the
Son's life of believing reading and believing praying.

# Dwight Lyman Moody
## (1837–1899)

D. L. Moody was born in Northfield, Massachusetts, into a very poor family. At seventeen, he went to Boston to work in his uncle's shoestore; and it was in Boston that Edward Kimball led him to Christ. It took him a year to join Mount Vernon Congregational Church.

Moody arrived in Chicago in 1856, the same year that Marshall Field came to that city. Moody prospered as a shoe salesman, but more and more of his time was devoted to Christian work, particularly the Sunday school and the YMCA. Finally, in 1861, he went into full-time ministry. His trip to England in 1873 was the beginning of an evangelistic ministry that would influence both Britain and America. During his ministry, Moody traveled more than a million miles and preached (it is estimated) to more than one hundred million persons. (That was before the day of public-address systems, radio, and television.) It is claimed that he personally dealt with seven hundred and fifty thousand individuals.

Whatsoever is born of God over-cometh the world: and this is the victory that overcometh the world, even our faith. (I John 5:4)

Notice that everything human in this world fails. Every man the moment he takes his eye off God, has failed. Every man has been a failure at some period of his life. Abraham failed. Moses failed. Elijah failed. Take the men that have become so famous and that were so mighty—the moment they got their eye off God, they were weak like other men; and it is a very singular thing that those men failed on the strongest point in their character. I suppose it was because they were not on the watch. Abraham was noted for his faith, and he failed right there—he denied his wife. Moses was noted for his meekness and humility, and he failed right there—he got angry. God kept him out of the promised land because he lost his temper. I know he was called "the servant of God," and that he was a mighty man, and had power with God, but humanly speaking, he failed, and was kept out of the promised land. Elijah was noted for his power in prayer and for his courage, yet he became a coward. He was the boldest man of his day, and stood before Ahab, and the royal court, and all the prophets of Baal; yet when he heard that Jezebel had threatened his life, he ran away to the desert, and under a juniper tree prayed that he might die. Peter was noted for his boldness, and a little maid scared him nearly out of his wits. As soon as she spoke to him, he began to tremble, and he swore that he didn't know Christ. I have often said to myself that I'd like to have been there on the day of Pentecost alongside of that maid when she saw Peter preaching.

"Why," I suppose she said, "what has come over that man? He was afraid of *me* only a few weeks ago, and now he stands up before all Jerusalem and charges these very Jews with the murder of Jesus."

The moment he got his eye off the Master he failed; and every man, I don't care who he is—even the strongest—every man that hasn't Christ in him, is a failure. John, the beloved disciple, was noted for his meekness; and yet we hear of him wanting to call fire down from heaven on a little town because it had refused the common hospitalities.

> But he that lacketh these things is
> blind, and cannot see afar off.
> (II Peter 1:9)

I heard a man, some time ago, speaking about Abraham. He said "Abraham was not tempted by the well-watered plains of Sodom, for Abraham was what you might call a long-sighted man; he had his eyes set on the city which had foundation—'whose Builder and Maker is God.'" But Lot was a short-sighted man; and there are many people in the Church who are very short-sighted; they only see things right around them they think good. Abraham was long-sighted; he had glimpses of the celestial city. Moses was long-sighted, and he left the palaces of Egypt and identified himself with God's people—poor people, who were slaves; but he had something in view yonder; he could see something God had in store. Again there are some people who are sort of long-sighted and short-sighted, too. I have a friend who has one eye that is long-sighted and the other is short-sighted; and I think the Church is full of this kind of people. They want one eye for the world and the other for the Kingdom of God. Therefore, everything is blurred, one eye is long and the other is short, all is confusion, and they "see men as trees walking." The Church is filled with that sort of people. But Stephen was long-sighted; he looked clear into heaven; they couldn't convince him even when he was dying, that Christ had not ascended to heaven. "Look yonder," he says, "I see Him over there; He is on the throne, standing at the right hand of God"; and he looked clear into heaven; the world had no temptation for him; he had put the world under his feet. Paul was another of those long-sighted men; he had been caught up and seen things unlawful for him to utter; things grand and glorious. I tell you when the Spirit of God is on us the world looks very empty; the world has a very small hold upon us, and we begin to let go our hold of it. When the Spirit of God is on us we will just let go the things of time and lay hold of things eternal. This is the Church's need today; we want the Spirit to come in mighty power, and consume all the vile dross there is in us. Oh! that the Spirit of fire may come down and burn everything in us that is contrary to God's blessed Word and Will.

> He must increase, but I must
> decrease. (John 3:30)

Sometimes it looks as if God's servants fail. When Herod beheaded John the Baptist, it looked as if John's mission was a failure. But was it? The voice that rang through the valley of the Jordan rings through the whole world to-day. You can hear its echo upon the mountains and the valleys yet, "I must decrease, but He must increase." He held up Jesus Christ and introduced Him to the world, and Herod had not power to behead him until his life work had been accomplished. Stephen never preached but one sermon that we know of, and that was before the Sanhedrim; but how that sermon has been preached again and again all over the world! Out of his death probably came Paul, the greatest preacher the world has seen since Christ left this earth. If a man is sent by Jehovah, there is no such thing as failure. Was Christ's life a failure? See how His parables are going through the earth to-day. It looked as if the apostles had made a failure, but see how much has been accomplished. If you read the book of Acts, you will see that every seeming failure in Acts was turned into a great victory. Moses wasn't going to fail, although Pharaoh said with contempt, "Who is God that I should obey Him?" He found out who God was. He found out that there was a God.

> I will be with him in trouble; I will
> deliver him and honour him.
> (Ps. 91:15)

First, "I will deliver." When God called Moses to go down into Egypt to deliver the children of Israel from the hand of the Egyptians, in all the world there wasn't a man who, humanly speaking, was less qualified than Moses. He had made the attempt once before to deliver the children of Israel, and he began by delivering one man. He failed in that, and killed an Egyptian, and had to run off into the desert, and stay there forty years. He had tried to deliver the Hebrews in his own way, he was working in his own strength and doing it in the energy of the flesh. He had all the wisdom of the Egyptians, but that didn't help him. He had to be taken back into Horeb, and kept there forty years in the school of God, before God could trust him to deliver the children of Israel in God's way. Then God came to him and said, "I have come down to deliver," and when God worked through Moses three million were delivered as easy as I can turn my hand over. God could do it. It was no trouble when God came on the scene.

Learn the lesson. If we want to be delivered, from every inward and outward foe, we must look to a higher source than ourselves. We cannot do it in our own strength.

> And the LORD said, I have surely
> seen the affliction of my people . . .
> and I am come down to deliver
> them. . . . (Exod. 3:7–8)

We all have some weak point in our character. When we would go forward, it drags us back, and when we would rise up into higher spheres of usefulness and the atmosphere of heaven, something drags us down. Now I have no sympathy with the idea that God puts us behind the blood and saves us, and then leaves us in Egypt to be under the old taskmaster. I believe God brings us out of Egypt into the promised land, and that it is the privilege of every child of God to be delivered from every foe, from every besetting sin.

If there is some sin that is getting the mastery over you, you certainly cannot be useful. You certainly cannot bring forth fruit to the honor and glory of God until you get self-control. "He that ruleth his spirit is better than he that taketh a city." If we haven't got victory over jealousy and worldly amusements and worldly pleasure, if we are not delivered from all these things, we are not going to have power with God or with men, and we are not going to be as useful as we might be if we got deliverance from every evil. There isn't an evil within or without but what He will deliver us from if we will let Him. That is what He wants to do. As God said to Moses, "I have come down to deliver." If He could deliver three million slaves from the hands of the mightiest monarch on earth, don't you think He can deliver us from every besetting sin, and give us complete victory over ourselves, over our temper, over our dispositions, over our irritableness and peevishness and snappishness? If we want it and desire it above everything else, we can get victory.

> Casting all your care upon him; for
> he careth for you. (I Peter 5:7)

A great many people seem to embalm their troubles. I always feel like running away when I see them coming. They bring out their old mummy, and tell you in a sad voice:

"You don't know the troubles I have!"

My friends, if you go to the Lord with your troubles, He will take them away. Would you not rather be with the Lord and get rid of your troubles, than be with your troubles and without God? Let trouble come if it will drive us nearer to God.

It is a great thing to have a place of resort in the time of trouble. How people get on without the God of the Bible is a mystery to me. If I didn't have such a refuge, a place to go and pour out my heart to God in such times, I don't know what I would do. It seems as if I would go out of my mind. But to think, when the heart is burdened, we can go and pour it into

His ear, and then have the answer come back, "I will be with him," there is comfort in that!

I thank God for the old Book. I thank God for this old promise. It is as sweet and fresh today as it has ever been. Thank God, none of those promises are out of date, or grown stale. They are as fresh and vigorous and young and sweet as ever.

> With long life will I satisfy him, and
> shew him my salvation. (Ps. 91:16)

J esus Christ came into the world to destroy death, and we can say with Paul, if we will, "Oh, death, where is thy sting?" And we can hear a voice rolling down from heaven saying, "Buried in the bosom of the Son of God." He took death unto His own bosom. He went into the grave to conquer and overthrow it, and when He arose from the dead said, "Because I live, ye shall live also." Thank God, we have a long life with Christ in glory.

My dear friends, if we are in Christ we are never going to die. Do you believe that? If sometime you should read that D. L. Moody, of East Northfield, is dead, don't believe a word of it. He has gone up higher, that is all; gone out of this old clay tenement into a house that is immortal, a body that death cannot touch, that sin cannot taint, a body fashioned like unto His own glorious body. Moses wouldn't have changed the body he had at the transfiguration for the body he had at Pisgah. Elijah wouldn't have changed the body he had at the transfiguration for the body he had under the juniper tree. They got better bodies; and I too am going to make something out of death.

# George Matheson

## (1842–1906)

We remember George Matheson for two great hymns: "O Love That Wilt Not Let Me Go" and "Make Me A Captive, Lord." But he was a great scholar and a beloved pastor and preacher. Even though he was blind, he carried on his duties with distinction and discipline, and he was a blessing to many. Matheson also wrote many devotional books, as well as studies of Bible personalities.

Early in his ministry, Matheson experienced "an eclipse of faith," and he candidly shared the problem with his church leaders. Wise and understanding men, they told him that many young pastors had such experiences, but that he should hold on and give God time. Their counsel proved true, and Matheson came through the valley with a deeper understanding of the grace of God.

Matheson served the church at Innellan, one of Glasgow's resort areas, and when he resigned to become pastor of St. Bernard's Church, Edinburgh, his leaving threatened the economy of the resort! Summer visitors used to come just to hear the blind preacher.

A new heart also will I give you.
Then shall ye remember your own
evil ways. (Ezek. 36:26, 31)

The prophet says that the memory of our badness only comes after we have become good. "A new heart will I give you; *then* shall ye remember your own evil ways." One would have expected the opposite statement. We should have looked for such words as these: "You must expect for a little to be troubled with old memories. You must not be surprised, when you are in the first stage of reformation, to experience the remorse of conscience for bad deeds in the past. When your new nature is complete, when the weaning process is over, when you become accustomed to the corn of the land, you will forget all about your struggles and failures; you will remember your shortcomings no more." The prophet says it is only then you *will* remember them. He says the valleys of your life will not become visible until you have scaled the height and stood upon the mountain's brow. And truly he is right; experience cries "Amen!" The memory of sin is the latest gift of my Father. His earliest gifts are incentives to move forward; they rather discourage a retrospective view. God says to the beginner, "Forget the things which are behind; press toward the mark of the prize!" But when the mark of the prize is won, when the top of the hill is gained, then for the first time He says, "Look back!" Then, for the first time, memory wakes, and our yesterday appears; and the valley of the past looks lowly and the shadows of the past seem deep. We beat upon our breast and say, "O wretched man that I am!"

> When they saw the boldness of
> Peter and John . . . they took knowl-
> edge of them, that they had been
> with Jesus. (Acts 4:13)

These two men drew one quality from the same source; they had both become bold from living with Jesus. Yet it was not the same kind of boldness. Peter and John were both courageous; yet the courage of Peter was as unlike the courage of John as the sun is unlike the moon. When Christ gives the same quality to two men He does not thereby make them the same man. The light which shines on the wall comes from the same source as the light which shines on the river; but no one would mistake the light on the river for the light on the wall. Even so, no one would mistake the courage of Peter for the courage of John. They are not only different; they are in some sense opposite. Peter has the courage that strikes; John has the courage that waits. Peter is a force of action; John is a force of bearing. Peter draws the sword; John lies on the bosom. Peter crosses the sea to meet Jesus; John tarries till the Lord comes. Peter goes into the sepulchre where the body of Jesus has lain; John merely *looks* in—keeps the image of sorrow in his heart.

Christ needs each of these types. There are times when His kingdom requires the courage of the hand—the power of actual contact with danger. There are times when it needs the courage of the heart—the power to wait when nothing can be done, and to keep the spirit up when the hand must be let down. Life has both its Galilee and its Patmos—its place for work and its place for waiting; and for both it requires courage.

> Against thy holy child Jesus . . . both Herod and Pontius Pilate, . . . were gathered together, For to do what-soever thy hand and thy counsel determined before to be done.
> (Acts 4:27–28)

The sentence ends just in the opposite way to what we are prepared for. We expect it to read thus: "Against Thy holy child Jesus both Herod and Pilate were gathered together to *circumvent* the course of Thy Divine will." Instead of that, we read, "Against Thy holy child Jesus both Herod and Pilate were gathered together to do whatever Thy counsel had *determined* to be done." The idea is that their effort of opposition to the Divine will proved to be a stroke of alliance with it. The measures they took to wreck the ship became the very means of keeping the ship afloat. They met together in a council of war against Christ; unconsciously to themselves

217

they signed a treaty for the promotion of Christ's glory. They thought they were making a will in favour of His enemies; they were really bequeathing all their wealth to the Man of Nazareth. They decreed that He should die; that decree was their contribution of palm-leaves.

My brother, God never thwarts adverse circumstances; that is not His method. I have often been struck with these words—"He rideth upon the wings of the wind." They are most suggestive. Our God does not *beat down* the storms that rise against Him; He rides upon them; He works through them. You are often surprised that so many thorny paths are allowed to be open for the good—how that aspiring boy Joseph is put in a dungeon—how that beautiful child Moses is cast into the Nile. You would have expected Providence to have interrupted the opening of these pits destined for destruction. Well, He might have done so; He might have said to the storm, "Peace, be still!" But there was a more excellent way—to ride upon it.

> It is good that a man should both
> hope and quietly wait for the salva-
> tion of the Lord. (Lam. 3:26)

What a singular combination—hope and quiet waiting! It is like a union of poetry and prose. Does it not seem an incongruous mixture of sentiments! We associate hope with impulse; quiet waiting is surely the want of impulse! Hope is a state of flight; waiting implies repose. Hope is the soul on the wing; waiting is the soul in the nest. Hope is the eagerness of expectancy; waiting is a condition of placid calm. Is not that a strange union of feelings to put into one breast! No; it is a sublimely happy marriage—the happiest conceivable. There is no test of hope like quiet waiting.

If you want to measure the strength of a man's hope, you must measure the quietness of his waiting. Our hope is never so weak as when we are excited. I have seen two men who were engaged in the same cause, and who were equally bent on the cause, affected quite differently in an argument. The one was fiery, impetuous, vehement, tempted to lose temper and prompted to be abusive; the other was calm, cool, quiet, disposed to be deferential and inclined to be conciliatory. Yet the second was the man of sure hope. He was calm because he was fearless, he was silent because he was sanguine. He had seen the star in the east and he knew it was travelling westward. He did not care to argue about it, to protest about it, to lose his temper about it. He was so sure of its coming that he was willing to make concessions. He could afford to be gentle, he could afford to be generous, in the light of the morning star.

> Thou shalt not number the tribe of Levi. . . . The Levites shall keep the charge of the tabernacle of testimony. . . . (Num. 1:49, 53)

Here was apparently a neglected set of men—a class overlooked in the enrolment of the people. They were to be uncounted, discounted. A spectator would have said they were a specimen of those unfit for survival. In all the work of the nation they had neither part nor lot. We read, in the parable, of the Levite passing by on the other side; but here the Levite seems to be *passed* by. He is left behind by the stream of the world's activities; and, with the prophet, the beholder is disposed to say that his way is hid from the Lord and his judgment overlooked by his God.

And yet the beholder would be wrong. These men have not been overlooked, have not been shunted from the race of life. If they are left behind by the stream it is because there is a special duty to do which can only be done by those who are left behind. That special duty is to wait and watch. The Levites are to "keep charge of the tabernacle"—to see that no harm comes to the ark and what it contains. It seems a poor service when contrasted with the work of the numbered. In reality it was the greatest service of all. If anything had befallen the tabernacle, Israel would have collapsed immediately. The loss of ten thousand of her soldiers would have been nothing to the putting-out of her altar fire; the one might have weakened her strength, but the other would have killed her hope.

Thou who art unnumbered among the people, thou to whom there has been assigned no active work, there is a message here for thee. There is a service for the unnumbered—for those who only stand and wait. There are Levites as well as priests in the temple of thy Father. There are those who have been laid aside from active duty—who have no district to visit in, no church to preach in, no mission to serve in. Through sickness, through poverty, through the requirement to attend on others, they have been retained indoors—their names are not enrolled. Weep not that thou art among these! Lament not that thy life has been lived behind the scenes! It is behind the scenes that all great things are born.

> The Lord brought an east
> wind . . . and when it was morning,
> the east wind brought the locusts.
> (Exod. 10:13)

One is inclined to ask, Why bring the east wind at all? God was about to send a special providence for the deliverance of His people from Egypt. He was about to inflict the Egyptians with a plague of locusts. The locusts were to be His special providence, the evidence of His supreme power. Why, then, does He not bring the locusts at once! Why evoke the intervention of an east wind! Would it not sound more majestic if it had simply been written, "God sent out a swarm of locusts created for the purpose of setting His people free"! Instead of that, the action of God takes the form of natural law, "The Lord brought an east wind; and, when it was morning, the east wind brought the locusts." Why send His message in a common chariot when it might fly on heavenly wings!

Is there not even something disappointing in the words "when it was morning"! Why should God's act have been so long in working the cure! Is not the whole passage an encouragement of men to say, "Oh, it was all done by natural causes"! Yes—and to add, "All natural causes are Divine causes." For, why is this passage written? It is just to tell us that when we see a Divine benefit coming through an east wind, or any other wind, we are not to say that on this account it comes less direct from God. It is just to tell us that when we ask God's help we ought to expect that the answer will be sent through natural channels, through human channels. It is just to tell us that when the actual heavens are silent we are not to say that there is no voice from our Father. We are to seek the answer to our prayers, not in an opening of the sky, not in an angel's wing, not in a mystic trance, but in the seeming accidents of every day—in the meeting with a friend, in the crossing of a street, in the hearing of a sermon, in the reading of a book, in the listening to a song, in the vision of a scene of beauty. We are to live in the solemn expectation that, any day of our lives, the things which environ us may become God's messengers.

. . . the law of liberty. (James 2:12)

There are two theories in the world about the human will. One says, "Man is a slave; he is bound hand and foot; he is for ever under law." The other says, "Man is free; he is master of his own actions; law has no dominion over him." St. James suggests terms of peace between the opposing views. He says that each of them assumes something which is wrong—that "to be free" is the opposite of "to be bound." He declares that on the contrary there is such a thing as a "law of liberty"—a compulsion whose very essence consists in the strength of human will.

What is this mysterious union of contraries—this law of liberty? It can be expressed in one word—love. Love is at once the most free and the most bound of all things. We say habitually that one in love is "captivated"—made prisoner. And yet the prison is his own choice. He would not lose his chain for all the world. It is to him a golden chain—the badge not of his servitude but of his empire. It represents the freest thing in his nature—the desire of his heart. My love is my heart's desire, my heart's hunger, my heart's prayer. It is the strongest exercise of will conceivable. Nothing shows the power of my will like my love. It is the power of my personality to pass out of itself and to claim a share in yours—to say, "You are mine." James is right when he says that love is the marriage of opposites—liberty and law.

# Frederick Brotherton Meyer

## (1847–1929)

F. B. Meyer was one of the most popular conference speakers of his day. He ministered around the world, was pastor of several churches in England, and wrote dozens of books that still minister to believers today.

Meyer probably would have remained an ordinary minister had not D. L. Moody come to Britain and held meetings in his church. The Spirit of God used Moody to transform Meyer's ministry from mediocre to miraculous. The churches he served prospered under his personal, penetrating ministry of the Word. When one church put obstacles in the way of his ministry, Meyer resigned and started a new church. Melbourne Hall in Leicester still stands as a center of evangelical outreach.

When I was a new believer in my teens, somebody gave me a copy of Meyer's *The Christ-Life for the Self-Life*. The book influenced me for life. The following selections are from three of Meyer's other books.

> . . . that ye may prove what is that
> good, and acceptable, and perfect,
> will of God. (Rom. 12:2)

But how may we know God's will? That is not always easy. Yet the difficulty is not in Him. He does not wish us to grope painfully in the dark. Nay, He is ever giving us many signs and hints as to the way we should take, too delicate to be perceived by the coarse eye of sense, but clear enough to those

223

who are divested of self-will and pride, and only anxious to know and do the holy and acceptable and perfect will of God.

It is a mistake to seek a sign from heaven; to run from counsellor to counsellor; to cast a lot; or to trust to some chance coincidence. Not that God may not reveal His will thus; but because it is hardly the behaviour of a child with its Father. There is a more excellent way. Let the heart be quieted and stilled in the presence of God; weaned from all earthly distractions and worldly ambitions. Let the voice of the Son of God hush into perfect rest the storms that sweep the lake of the inner life, and ruffle its calm surface. Let the whole being be centered on God Himself. And then, remembering that all who lack wisdom are to ask it of God, and that Jesus Christ is already made unto us wisdom, let us quietly appropriate Him, in that capacity, by faith; and then go forward, perhaps not conscious of any increase of wisdom, or able to see far in front; but sure that we shall be guided, as each new step must be taken, or word spoken, or decision made. It is an immense help in any difficulty to say, "I take thee, Lord Jesus, as my wisdom," and to do the next thing, nothing doubting; assured that He will not permit those who trust in Him to be ashamed.

Thou shalt call his name JESUS: for he shall save his people from their sins. (Matt. 1:21)

Your foes may be numerous as the devils in hell, strong and wily; but *He will save*. Your temperament may be as susceptible to temptation as an aspen-leaf is to the wind; but *He will save*. Your past years, by repeated acts of indulgence, may have formed habits strong as iron bands; but *He will save*. Your circumstances and companions may be most unfavorable to a life of victory; but *He will save*. Difficulties are nought to Him; the darkness shineth as the day. It were rank blasphemy to suppose that our Creator could have given us a body which He could not keep; or have placed us in circumstance in which He could not restrain. Is it not written, without a single hint at limitation or reserve?—"He shall save His people from their sins." And shall He not do so?

If there be, therefore, perpetual failure in your life, it cannot arise from any weakness or impotence in the Mighty God; but from some failure on your part. That failure may probably be discovered in one of three hiding places—imperfect surrender; deficient faith; or neglected communion. But when the intention of the soul is right with God, without doubt HE WILL SAVE.

> I the LORD do keep it; I will water it
> every moment: lest any hurt it, I will
> keep it night and day. (Isa. 27:3)

In the scorching Oriental heat the vineyard needs incessant watering, else the vines fail. And our spirits are equally dependent on the refreshment which only God's tender love can afford. The heat of temptation and of sore discipline is so oppressive, that we must faint beneath either one or the other, except for the alleviating succor which our faithful God is constantly administering.

Every moment—literally, every time the eye twinkles—God is watering us. We have become so accustomed to it, that we hardly realize how much we owe to it. Sometimes by the gentle distillation of dew, that gathers almost imperceptibly on our spirits, and we hardly know whence or how it has come. Sometimes by the touch of a moistening sponge, applied by the very hand of God. Sometimes by a shower of grace. By a text suggested to our memory; a holy thought; the look, or act, or word of some companion; a paragraph in a paper; a sentence in a book—God waters us, and we become fresh and green, where the leaf showed signs of becoming shriveled and sere.

How blessed is life like this! In such hands—watched and

guarded by such care—nurtured with such tenderness! May the result in each of us be—not the disappointment of wild grapes, but—the abundant clusters that will make glad the great Husbandman of our souls.

>   Therefore will the LORD
>   wait . . . wait for him. (Isa. 30:18)

*He does not delay because of any caprice.* We must not think that heaven has favorites, who are always served first. There is no partiality or favoritism with our Father. He chastens those whom He loves. The first come last. Each is dealt with according to his own merits, and on the ground of the peculiar necessities of his case.

*He does not delay because of any neglect.* A woman may forget her sucking child, but our Saviour cannot forget us. We are graven as with a point of the rugged nail on the palms of his hand. We are his babes, needing hourly attention; the members of His body, fed by His constant life; the constituent parts of His Bride, whom He nourishes and cherishes as Himself. Sooner might His right hand forget its cunning than he not count us above His chief joy.

*He does not delay because He denies.* Our heart sometimes so interprets His dealings; but they do not really mean what our timorous faith reads into them. The remittance is not sent as asked; yet that does not prove that it is not there in our name, but only that it is being kept at interest, accumulating till it reach a higher figure and be more of service, because coming at a time of greater need. No! His delays are the children of his love. He waits that He may be gracious, He dams up the current, that by holding it back it may become a swifter, fuller stream.

> Blessed be God, even the Father of
> our Lord Jesus Christ, the Father of
> mercies, and the God of all comfort.
> (II Cor. 1:3)

In God there is the mother-nature as well as the Fatherhood. All love was first in Him, ere it was lit up in human hearts. The fires that burn so brightly on the altars of motherhood the world over, were lit in the first instance from the Heart of God; and He keeps them alight. And therefore the love that is so quick to detect and so swift to hush the wail of the babe; which is so sensitive to discover that something ails the troubled heart; which is so inventive of little methods of solace, now by tender touch, and again by delicate suggestion—this love is in the great heart of God, and awaits our need to enwrap us in the embrace of an infinite sympathy and comfort.

The apostle had known this many a time; and when he tells out his experiences on this matter, we feel we are listening to one who knew whereof he spake. Few have suffered more than he did, from the moment that he gave up all for Christ, to the hour in which he died a martyr for the faith—the break with old friends; the physical sufferings of his lot; the homelessness, and privations, and continual journeyings; the care of all the churches, the opposition of false brethren. Every epistle bears some evidence of the anguish constantly being inflicted on his noble and tender heart. And yet he said, *God comforteth us.* "Who comforteth in all our tribulations, that we may be able to comfort them which are in any trouble, by the comfort wherewith we ourselves are comforted of God." (2 Cor. 1:4)

> And when he putteth forth his own
> sheep, he goeth before them, and
> the sheep follow him: for they know
> his voice. (John 10:4)

**W**hatever awaits us is encountered first by Him—each difficulty and complication; each wild beast or wilder robber; each yawning chasm or precipitous path. Faith's eye can always discern His majestic presence in front; and when that cannot be seen, it is dangerous to move forward. Bind this comfort to your heart: that the Saviour has tried for Himself all the experiences through which He asks you to pass; and He would not ask you to pass through them unless He was sure that they were not too difficult for your feet, or too trying for your strength. The Breaker always goes up before us. The Woodsman hews a path for us through the trackless forest. The broad-shouldered Brother pushes a way for us through the crowd. And we have only to follow.

This is the Blessed Life—not anxious to see far in front; not careful about the next step; not eager to choose the path; not weighted with the heavy responsibilities of the future: but quietly following behind the Shepherd, *one step at a time.*

> But when he was yet a great way
> off, his father saw him, and had
> compassion, and ran, and fell on his
> neck, and kissed him. (Luke 15:20)

**W**hat a blessing it was for the prodigal that he did not meet his elder brother before his father! Had the two, by any sad mischance, met face to face in the field, it is certain that the ragged wanderer would never have gone another step. His brother would have upbraided him with leaving home, and wasting his patrimony, and coming back in so disgraceful a state. Assuredly he would not have killed the fatted calf; but he would have killed all hope in that sad and sinstained soul.

With one farewell glance at the dear old home, the penitent would have turned back to the far-country and the swine. Those upbraidings would have broken the bruised reed, and quenched the smoking flax in densest midnight.

But mercifully the prodigal first met his father, whose heart had never ceased to yearn for him, and whose eye strove against the blinding touch of grief and years, that it might still scan the road along which that prodigal child had gone. Was there upbraiding in his look or tone? Never! Was there upbraiding mingled with the first glad notes of welcome? Not a trace! Not a word about the long absence, the wild and evil life! If the son had had his way, he would have carried his confession to the end, and chosen for himself the servant's lot; but even in that he was stopped, and silenced with the warm rush of his father's love. "He gave liberally, and upbraided not."

This is a true picture of God. He gives, and gives again. He gives tears and blood. He gives His darling and His All.

# Peter Taylor Forsyth
## (1848–1921)

I bless the day that I met P. T. Forsyth! I think the first of his books that came to my hands was *Positive Preaching and the Modern Mind,* his Yale lectures given in 1907. I had to get accustomed to his paradoxical way of expressing truth, but once I did a whole new world opened up to me. This is not to say that I always understood him, or agreed with what I did understand. But he has always made me think and has challenged me to see the other side of the question.

Forsyth was born in Scotland, educated there as well as in Germany, and ordained to the Congregational ministry. At first he was very liberal, but he soon discovered that his liberal theology had nothing to offer the needy and the dying. He discovered the grace of God as seen in the cross of Christ, and from that time on was a champion of the doctrine of the cross. The last twenty years of his life he served as principal of Hackney College, London, and exercised a wide influence as a speaker and writer.

There is none that calleth upon thy
name, that stirreth up himself to
take hold of thee. . . . (Isa. 64:7)

The worst sin is prayerlessness. Overt sin, or crime, or the glaring inconsistencies which often surprise us in Christian people are the effect of this, or its punishment. We are left by God for lack of seeking Him. The history of the saints shows often that their lapses were the fruit and nemesis of slackness or neglect in prayer. Their life, at seasons, also tended to become inhuman by their spiritual solitude. They left men, and were left by men, because they did not in their contemplation find God; they found but the thought or the atmosphere of God. Only living prayer keeps loneliness humane. It is the great producer of sympathy. Trusting the God of Christ, and transacting with Him, we come into tune with men. Our egoism retires before the coming of God, and into the clearance there comes with our Father our brother. We realize man as he is in God and for God, his Lover. When God fills our heart He makes more room for man than the humanist heart can find. Prayer is an act, indeed *the* act, of fellowship. We cannot truly pray even for ourselves without passing beyond ourselves and our individual experience. If we should begin with these the nature of prayer carries us beyond them, both to God and to man. Even private prayer is common prayer—the more so, possibly, as it retires from being public prayer.

Not to want to pray, then, is the sin behind sin. And it ends in not being able to pray. That is its punishment—spiritual dumbness, or at least aphasia, and starvation. We do not take our spiritual food, and so we falter, dwindle, and die. 'In the sweat of your brow ye shall eat your bread.' That has been said to be true both of physical and spiritual labor. It is true both of the life of bread and of the bread of life.

> . . . the Spirit himself maketh inter-
> cession for us with groanings which
> cannot be uttered. (Rom. 8:26)

If our prayer reach or move Him it is because He first reached and moved us to pray. The prayer that reached heaven began there, when Christ went forth. It began when God turned to beseech us in Christ—in the appealing Lamb slain before the foundation of the world. The Spirit went out with the power and function in it to return with our soul. Our prayer is the answer to God's. Herein is prayer, not that we prayed Him, but that He first prayed us, in giving His Son to be a propitiation for us. The heart of the Atonement is prayer—Christ's great self-offering to God in the Eternal Spirit. The whole rhythm of Christ's soul, so to say, was Godhead going out and returning on itself. And so God stirs and inspires all prayer which finds and moves Him. His love provokes our sacred forwardness. He does not compel us, but we cannot help it after that look, that tone, that turn of His. All say, 'I am yours if you will'; and when we will it is prayer. Any final glory of human success or destiny rises from man being God's continual creation, and destined by Him for Him. So we pray because we were made for prayer, and God draws us out by breathing Himself in.

The secret of the LORD is with them
that fear him; and he will shew them
his covenant. (Ps. 25:14)

Not to pray is not to discern—not to discern the things that really matter, and the powers that really rule. The mind may see acutely and clearly, but the personality perceives nothing subtle and mighty; and then it comforts and deludes itself by saying it is simple and not sophisticated; and it falls a victim to the Pharisaism of the plain man. The finer (and final) forces, being unfelt, are denied or decried. The eternal motives are misread, the spell of the Eternal disowned. The simplicity in due course becomes merely bald. And all because the natural powers are unschooled, unchastened, and unempowered by the energy of prayer; and yet they are turned, either, in one direction, to do Christian work, active but loveless, or, on the other, to discuss and renounce Christian truth. It is not always hard to tell among Christian men those whose thought is matured in prayer, whose theology there becomes a hymn, whose energy is disciplined there, whose work there becomes love poured out, as by many a Salvationist lass, and whose temper is there subdued to that illuminated humility in which a man truly finds his soul. 'The secret of the Lord is with them that fear Him, and He will show them His covenant.' The deeper we go into things the more do we enter a world where the master and the career is not to talent but to prayer.

> For this thing I besought the Lord
> thrice, that it might depart from me.
> (II Cor. 12:8)

We pray for the removal of pain, pray passionately, and then with exhaustion, sick from hope deferred and prayer's failure. But there is a higher prayer than that. It is a greater thing to pray for pain's conversion than for its removal. It is more of grace to pray that God would make a sacrament of it. The sacrament of pain! That we partake not simply, nor perhaps chiefly, when we say, or try to say, with resignation, 'Thy will be done.' It is not always easy for the sufferer, if he remain clear-eyed, to see that it is God's will. It may have been caused by an evil mind, or a light fool, or some stupid greed. But, now it is there, a certain treatment of it is God's will; and that is to capture and exploit it for Him. It is to make it serve the soul and glorify God. It is to consecrate its elements and make it sacramental. It is to convert it into prayer.

God has blessed pain even in causing us to pray for relief from it, or profit. Whatever drives us to Him, and even nearer Him, has a blessing in it. And, if we are to go higher still, it is to turn pain to praise, to thank Him in the fires, to review life and use some of the energy we spend in worrying upon recalling and tracing His goodness, patience, and mercy. If much open up to us in such a review we may be sure there is much more we do not know, and perhaps never may. God is the greatest of all who do good by stealth and do not crave for every benefit to be acknowledged. Or we may see how our pain becomes a blessing to others. And we turn the spirit of heaviness to the garment of praise. We may stop grousing and get our soul into its Sunday clothes. The sacrament of pain becomes then a true Eucharist and giving of thanks.

> Delight thyself also in the LORD; and
> he shall give thee the desires of thine
> heart. (Ps. 37:4)

So far is this 'pray without ceasing' from being absurd because extravagant that every man's life is in some sense a continual state of prayer. For what is his life's prayer but its ruling passion? All energies, ambitions, and passions are but expressions of standing *nisus* in life, of a hunger, a draft, a practical demand upon the future, upon the unattained and the unseen. Every life is a draft upon the unseen. If you are not praying toward God you are towards something else. You pray as your face is set—towards Jerusalem or Babylon. The very egotism of craving life is prayer. The great difference is the object of it. To whom, for what, do we pray? The man whose passion is habitually set upon pleasure, knowledge, wealth, honor, or power is in a state of prayer to these things or for them. He prays without ceasing. These are his real gods, on whom he waits day and night. He may from time to time go on his knees in church, and use words of Christian address and petition. He may even feel a momentary unction in so doing. But it is a flicker; the other devotion is his steady flame. His real God is the ruling passion and steady pursuit of his life taken as a whole. He certainly does not pray in the name of Christ. And what he worships in spirit and in truth is another God than he addresses at religious times. He prays to an unknown God for a selfish boon. Still, in a sense, he prays. The set and drift of his nature prays. It is the prayer of instinct, not of faith. It is prayer that needs total conversion. But he cannot stop praying either to God or to God's rival—to self, society, world, flesh, or even devil. Every life that is not totally inert is praying either to God or God's adversary.

And all things, whatsoever ye shall
ask in prayer, believing, ye shall
receive. (Matt. 21:22)

Do not allow your practice in prayer to be arrested by scientific or philosophic considerations as to how answer is possible. That is a valuable subject for discussion, but it is not entitled to control our practice. Faith is at least as essential to the soul as science, and it has a foundation more independent. And prayer is not only a necessity of faith, it is faith itself in action.

Criticism of prayer dissolves in the experience of it. When the soul is at close quarters with God it becomes enlarged enough to hold together in harmony things that oppose, and to have room for harmonious contraries. For instance: God, of course, is always working for His Will and Kingdom. But man is bound to pray for its coming, while it is coming all the time. Christ laid stress on prayer as a necessary means of bringing the Kingdom to pass. And it cannot come without our praying. Why? Because its coming is the prayerful frame of soul. So again with God's freedom. It is absolute. But it reckons on ours. Our prayer does not force His hand; it answers His freedom in kind. We are never so active and free as in prayer to an absolutely free God. We share His freedom when we are 'in Christ.'

Call unto me, and I will answer thee,
and show thee great and mighty
things, which thou knowest not.
(Jer. 33:3)

Prayer is for the religious life what original research is for science—by it we get direct contact with reality. The soul is brought into union with its own vaster nature—God. Therefore, also, we must use the Bible as an original; for, indeed, the Bible is the most copious spring of prayer, and of power, and of range. If we learn to pray from the Bible, and avoid a mere *cento* of its phrases, we shall cultivate in our prayer the large humane note of a universal gospel. Let us nurse our prayer on our *study* of our Bible; and let us, therefore, not be too afraid of *theological* prayer. True Christian prayer must have theology in it; no less than true theology must have prayer in it and must be capable of being prayed. 'Your theology is too difficult,' said Charles V to the Reformers; 'it cannot be understood without much prayer.' Yes, that is our arduous puritan way. Prayer and theology must interpenetrate to keep each other great, and wide, and mighty. The failure of the habit of prayer is at the root of much of our light distaste for theology.

# *James Stalker*
## (1848–1927)

After he was pastor of churches in Kirkcaldy and Glasgow, James Stalker became professor of church history in Aberdeen at the United Free Church College. He was another Scotsman who was greatly affected by the ministry of D. L. Moody.

We remember Stalker for his books, especially *The Life of Jesus Christ* and *The Life of Paul*. But in his time, he was known primarily for his preaching. His emphasis on the social applications of the gospel troubled some people.

Stalker also delivered the Lyman Beecher lectures on preaching at Yale in 1891 (*The Preacher and His Models*). Stalker preached the sermon "The Four Men" in the Yale chapel. Moody heard it and insisted that it be printed for wider distribution. It was just like Moody to promote another man's ministry!

A man can receive nothing, except it
be given him from heaven.
(John 3:27)

There is, indeed, no greater mystery in providence than the unequal proportion in which temptation is distributed among different individuals. Some are comparatively little tempted; others are thrown into a fiery furnace of it, seven times heated. There are in the world sheltered situations, in which a man may be compared to a ship in the harbor, where the waves may sometimes heave a little, but a real storm never comes; there are others, where a man may be compared to the vessel which has to sail the high seas and face the full force of the tempest. Many of you must know well what this means. Perhaps you know it so well that you feel inclined to say to me, Preacher, you know little about it: if you had to live where we live—if you had to associate with the companions with whom we have to work and hear the kind of language to which we have to listen—you would know better the truth of what you are saying. Do not be too sure of that. Perhaps my library is as dangerous a place for me as the market-place or the workshop is for you. Solitude has its temptations as well as society.

Ye shall not surely die. (Gen. 3:4)

The great tempter of men has two devices with which he plies us at two different stages. Before we have fallen, he tells us that one fall does not matter: it is a trifle; why should we not know the taste of the forbidden fruit? We can easily recover ourselves again. After we have fallen, on the contrary, he tells us that it is hopeless: we are given over to sin, and need not attempt to rise.

Both are false.

It is a terrible falsehood to say that to fall does not matter. Even by one fall there is something lost that can never be recovered. It is like the breaking of an infinitely precious vessel, which may be mended, but will never be again as if it had not been broken. And, besides, one fall leads to others; it is like going upon very slippery ice—even in the attempt to rise you are carried away again. Moreover, we give others a hold over us. If we have not sinned alone, to have sinned once involves a tacit pledge that we will sin again; and it is often almost impossible to get out of such a false position. God keep us from believing that to fall once does not matter!

My sin is ever before me. (Ps. 51:3)

But then, if we have fallen, our enemy plies us with the other argument: It is of no use to attempt to rise; you cannot overcome your besetting sin. But this is falser still. To those who feel themselves fallen I come, in Christ's name, to say, Yes, you may rise. If we could ascend to heaven today and scan the ranks of the blessed, should we not find multitudes among them who were once sunk low as man can fall? But they are washed, they are justified, they are sanctified, in the name of the Lord Jesus and by the Spirit of our God. And so may you be.

It is, I know, a doctrine which may be abused; but I will not scruple to preach it to those who are fallen and sighing for deliverance. St. Augustine says that we may, out of our dead sins, make stepping stones to rise to the heights of perfection. What did he mean by that? He meant that the memory of our falls may breed in us such a humility, such a distrust of self, such a constant clinging to Christ as we could never have had without the experience of our own weakness.

Does not the Scripture itself go even further? David fell deep as man can fall; but what does he say in that great fifty-first Psalm, in which he confesses his sin? Anticipating forgiveness, he sings,

> Then will I teach Thy ways unto
> Those that transgressors be,
> And those that sinners are shall then
> Be turned unto Thee.

But the thing that David had done
displeased the LORD. (II Sam. 11:27)

This is a strange and solemn power which conscience wields. In your secret soul you commit a sin: it is a mere passing thought perhaps; no human eye has seen it, no tongue will ever speak of it; yet even in the dark it makes you blush; you are degraded in your own eyes; you feel guilty and wretched. And this guilty wretchedness does not pass away; it may at any time revive. Conscience comes to us in lonely hours; it wakens us in the night; it stands at the side of the bed and says, Come, wake up and listen to me! And there it holds us with its remorseless eye; and our buried sins rise out of the grave of the past; they march by in melancholy procession; and we lie in terror looking at them. Nobody knows but ourselves. Next morning we go forth to business with a smiling face; but conscience has had its revenge.

Speaking lies in hypocrisy; having their conscience seared with a hot iron. (I Tim. 4:2)

The Scripture speaks of some whose consciences are seared as with a hot iron. As a hot iron, touching the fingertips, would harden the skin, so that the fine sense of touch located there could not act, so may the conscience be seared in such a way that it does not prompt to do the right or inflict pain when the wrong is done. It is appalling to what lengths this moral insensibility may go. You will see a young man, after a few years of the sins of the city, breaking his mother's heart and bringing his father's grey hairs down with sorrow to the grave, apparently without a qualm. The hardened debauchee will ruin a fair life and introduce shame and desolation into a honored home, and then go among his companions and boast of it. But we may all see now and then the beginnings of this hardening process in ourselves. Acts which at first we touch with shame and fear we do at last without any inward pain. The conscience is ceasing to perform its functions, and atrophy is setting in.

What produces such a state? It is disobedience. If the conscience is constantly called upon to condemn the same sin, which is constantly repeated, it gradually ceases to perform the useless function. If its warnings are neglected, they become less and less distinct, and at last cease altogether. On the contrary, obedience to conscience sharpens it, and makes it a more and more perfect instrument. There are virgin souls which blush in secret at the most transient thought of sins in which others wallow without remorse. There are men who wince, as high-blooded horses do at the touch of the whip, at the first sound in their hearing of words which in other companies form the staple of conversation. The conscience may be trained to tremble at the least approach of dishonor, as the needle of a perfect compass indicates the least turn of the ship. This is the path to all fineness of character. It gradually elevates the whole man, stamping the aspect of dignity and purity even on the external appearance. A hardened conscience coarsens and brutalises soul and body, but a tender conscience refines both.

> Blessed is he whose transgression is
> forgiven, whose sin is covered.
> (Ps. 32:1)

Can this defilement be removed? This surely is the question for every child of Adam; for what conscience is there which has not been stained with sin? It is a question which the conscience itself cannot answer. Conscience prescribes our duty and rewards us if we perform it. If we fail, it fills us with alarms and forebodings, but it cannot tell how these may be removed. This honor belongs to the Gospel of Christ. Like the law, conscience is a schoolmaster to bring us to Christ. Conscience may be compared to a stern guide, who gives a lantern to a cripple and orders him to go the way which the light reveals on pain of death; but it has no concern for his pitiful inability to surmount the difficult path. It is Christ who heals the cripple, putting strength into his feet and ankle-bones, so that he walks and leaps and praises God. Yet it is questionable if anyone can appreciate the blood which cleanseth us from all sin who has not felt the shame and pain of a conscience defiled, or if anyone can understand the easiness of the yoke of Christ who has not felt his bones broken by the yoke of the law. Though conscience does not of itself know the way to reconciliation, yet it wanders restless and excited till it catches sight of Calvary, when its eye kindles like that of the exile who sees on the horizon the cliffs of his native land; and, when it reaches the cross, it pitches its tent there forever.

> . . . and who knoweth whether thou
> art come to the kingdom for such a
> time as this? (Esther 4:14)

We all, I suppose, begin like Esther. We are the center of all things to ourselves; our happiness is the supreme end for which all other persons and things ought to be conspiring. We are proud of our abilities, and eager to shine and command admiration. Perhaps, like Esther, we are brought by circumstances into competition with others, and the verdict of our superiors and our equals confirms the estimate of our powers which we have secretly formed ourselves. The prizes of life glitter ahead of us; we feel confident that we can win them; and we are hungry to taste as many pleasures as we can.

But it is a transfiguring moment when the thought first penetrates a man that perhaps this is not the purpose for which he has received his gifts at all—when the image of humanity rises up before him, in its helplessness and misery, appealing to him, as the weak appeal to the strong; when his country rises before him, as an august and lovable mother, and demands the services of her child; when the image of Christ rises before him and, pointing to His cause struggling with the forces of evil yet heading towards a glorious and not uncertain goal, asks him to lend it his strength—when a man ceases to be the most important object in the world to himself, and sees, outside, an object which makes him forget himself and irresistibly draws him on.

# Henry Drummond
## (1851–1897)

Henry Drummond was D. L. Moody's dear friend and helped to edit Moody's sermons for publication. He influenced hundreds of students to decide for Christ. By profession he was a scientist and a college professor, but his spiritual ministry was remarkable. His devotional booklet, *The Greatest Thing in the World,* has been distributed far and wide.

And yet Drummond was an evolutionist and a defender of higher criticism. Moody was repeatedly criticized by his conservative brethren for asking Drummond to speak at his conferences and meetings, but Moody defended his friend. However, Drummond saw what this association was doing to Moody's ministry, so he graciously stopped participating, and it broke Moody's heart.

Drummond sought to make the gospel meaningful to people who were being strongly influenced by the scientific theories of that day. Some of his writings are museum pieces today, but others still pulsate with power.

For the wrath of man worketh not
the righteousness of God.
(James 1:20)

O nly temper," they call it: a little hot-headedness, a momentary ruffling of the surface, a mere passing cloud. But here the passing cloud is composed of drops, and the drops betoken an ocean, foul and rancorous, seething somewhere within the life—an ocean made up of jealousy, anger, pride, uncharity, cruelty, self-righteousness, sulkiness, touchiness, doggedness, lashed into a raging storm.

This is why temper is significant. It is not in what it is that its significance lies, but in what it reveals. But for this it were not worth notice. It is the intermittent fever which tells of unintermittent disease; the occasional bubble escaping to the surface, betraying the rottenness underneath; a hastily prepared specimen of the hidden products of the soul, dropped involuntarily when you are off your guard. In one word, it is the lightning-form of a dozen hideous and unchristian sins.

> For it is God which worketh in you
> both to will and to do of his good
> pleasure. (Phil. 2:13)

One of the futile methods of sanctifying ourselves is trying; effort—struggle—agonizing. I suppose you have all tried that, and I appeal to your own life when I ask if it has not failed. Crossing the Atlantic, the *Etruria*, in which I was sailing, suddenly stopped in mid-ocean—something had broken down. There were a thousand people on board that ship. Do you think we could have made it go if we had all gathered together and pushed against the sides or against the masts? When a man hopes to sanctify himself by trying, he is like a man trying to make the boat go that carries him by pushing it—he is like a man drowning in the water and trying to save himself by pulling the hair of his own head. It is impossible. Christ held up the mode of sanctification almost to ridicule when He said: "Which of you by taking thought can add a cubit to his stature?" Put down that method forever as futile.

Another man says: "That is not my way. I have given up that. Trying has its place, but that is not where it comes in. My method is to concentrate on some single sin, and to work away upon that until I have got rid of it." Now, in the first place, life is too short for that process to succeed. Their name is legion. In the second place, that leaves the rest of the nature for a long time untouched. In the third place, it does not touch the seed or root of the disease. If you dam up a stream at one place, it will simply overflow higher up. And for a fourth reason: Religion does not consist in negatives—in stopping this sin and stopping that sin.

> We all, with unveiled face, reflecting
> in a mirror the glory of the Lord, are
> changed into the same image from
> glory to glory even as by the Lord,
> the Spirit. (II Cor. 3:18, ERV)

Observe: "We are *changed*." The mistake we have been making is that we have been trying to change ourselves. That is not possible. We are changed into the same image. Now, if we are to get the benefit of the relief that these words ought to give to the man who has been spending half his nights and half his life in a frenzied struggle for holiness without having fulfilled the necessary conditions, let us carefully mark the condition demanded. For that condition being fulfilled, we are infallibly changed into the same image. The condition is that we reflect in a mirror the glory of Christ. That condition I shall refer to in a moment; but one word requires an explanation in passing. "Reflecting in a mirror the glory of the Lord." What is the glory of the Lord? The word "glory" suggests effulgence—radiance. It recalls the halo that the old masters delighted to paint around the heads of their saints and *Ecce Homos*. But this is all material. What does that halo, that radiance, symbolize? It symbolizes the most radiant and beautiful thing in man, as in the man Christ Jesus, and that is, character. *Character.* The glory of Christ is in character.

> Abide in me, and I in you. . . . I am
> the vine, ye are the branches.
> (John 15:4–5)

How disturbed and distressed and anxious Christian people are about their growth in grace! Now, the moment you give that over into Christ's care—the moment you see that you are *being* changed—that anxiety passes away. You see that it must follow by an inevitable process and by a natural law if you fulfill the simple condition; so that peace is the reward of that life and fellowship with Christ. Peace is not a thing that comes down solid, as it were, and is fitted somehow into a man's nature.

We have very gross conceptions of peace, joy, and other Christian experiences; but they are all simply effects and causes. We fulfill the condition; we cannot help the experiences following. I have spoken about peace, but how about joy? In the 15th of John you will see when Christ gave His disciples the Parable of the Vine, He said: "I will tell you why I have told you that parable. It is that your joy might be full." Did you ever notice that? He did not merely throw it into space as a fine illustration. It was not merely a statement of the doctrine of the indwelling Christ. It was that, but it was more. "These words have I spoken unto you," He said, "That My joy might remain in you, and that your joy might be full." That is the way to get joy. It is to abide in Christ. Out of this simple relationship we have faith, we have peace, we have joy. Many other things follow. A man's usefulness depends to a large extent upon his fellowship with Christ. That is obvious. Only Christ can influence the world; but all that the world sees of Christ is what it sees of you and me. Christ said: "The world seeth Me no more, but ye see Me." You see Him, and standing in front of Him, reflect Him, and the world sees the reflection. It cannot see Him. So that a Christian's usefulness depends solely upon that relationship.

> Take my yoke upon you, and learn
> of me . . . and ye shall find rest unto
> your souls. (Matt. 11:29)

It is only when we see what it was in Him that we can know what the word Rest means. It lies not in emotions, nor in the absence of emotions. It is not a hallowed feeling that comes over us in church. It is not something that the preacher has in his voice. It is not in nature, or in poetry, or in music—though in all these there is soothing. It is the mind at leisure from itself. It is the perfect poise of the soul; the absolute adjustment of the inward man to the stress of all outward things; the preparedness against every emergency; the stability of assured convictions; the eternal calm of an invulnerable faith; the repose of a heart set deep in God. It is the mood of the man who says, with Browning, "God's in His Heaven, all's well with the world."

Two painters each painted a picture to illustrate his conception of rest. The first chose for his scene a still, lone lake among the far-off mountains. The second threw on his canvas a thundering waterfall, with a fragile birch-tree bending over the foam; at the fork of a branch, almost wet with the cataract's spray, a robin sat on its nest. The first was only *Stagnation;* the last was Rest. For in Rest there are always two elements—tranquillity and energy; silence and turbulence; creation and destruction; fearlessness and fearfulness. This it was in Christ.

> It is good for a man that he bear the
> yoke in his youth. (Lam. 3:27)

After the statement, "Learn of Me," Christ throws in the disconcerting qualification, *"Take My yoke upon you and learn of Me."* Why, if all this be true, does He call it a *yoke?* Why, while professing to give Rest, does He with the next breath whisper *"burden"?* Is the Christian life, after all, what its enemies take it for—an additional weight to the already great woe of life, some extra punctiliousness about duty, some painful devotion to observances, some heavy restriction and trammeling of all that is joyous and free in the world? Is life not hard and sorrowful enough without being fettered with yet another yoke?

It is astounding how so glaring a misunderstanding of this plain sentence should ever have passed into currency. Did you ever stop to ask what a yoke is really for? Is it to be a burden to the animal which wears it? It is just the opposite. It is to make its burden light. Attached to the oxen in any other way than by a yoke, the plough would be intolerable. Worked by means of a yoke, it is light. A yoke is not an instrument of torture; it is an instrument of mercy. It is not a malicious contrivance for making work hard; it is a gentle device to make hard labor light. It is not meant to give pain, but to save pain. And yet men speak of the yoke of Christ as if it were a slavery, and look upon those who wear it as objects of compassion.

And the Word was made flesh, and
dwelt among us. . . . (John 1:14)

The purpose of revelation is to exhibit the mind of God . . . The vehicle is words . . . What words? Words which are windows and not prisons. Words of the intellect cannot hold God—the finite cannot hold the infinite. But an image can. So God has made it possible for us by giving us an external world to make *image-words*. The external world is not a place to work in, or to feed in, but to see in. It is a world of images, the external everywhere revealing the eternal. The key to the external world is to look not at the things which are seen, but in looking at the things which are seen to see through them to the things that are unseen. Look at the ocean. It is mere water—a thing which is seen; but look again, look through that which is seen, and you see the limitlessness of Eternity.

Look at a river, another of God's images of the unseen. It is also water, but God has given it another form to image a different truth. There is Time, swift and silent. There is Life, irrevocable, passing.

But the most singular truth of this is the Incarnation. There was no word in the world's vocabulary for Himself. In nature we had images of Time and Eternity. The seasons spoke of change, the mountains of stability. The home-life imaged Love. Law and Justice were in the Civil system. The snow was Purity, the rain, Fertility. By using these metaphors we could realize feebly Time and Eternity, Stability and Change. But there was no image of Himself. So God made one. He gave a word in Flesh—a word in Image-form. He gave the man Christ Jesus the express image of His person. This was the one image that was wanting in the image-vocabulary of truth, and the Incarnation supplied it.

# William M. Clow

## (1853–1930)

William M. Clow was born in Glasgow, educated in Glasgow and New Zealand, and was pastor of several churches. He taught theology at the United Free Church College in Glasgow, and became principal of the school.

As both a preacher and writer, Clow's emphasis was on the sacrifice and victory of Jesus Christ. *The Cross in Christian Experience* is a classic.

The secret of the LORD is with them
that fear him, and he will shew them
his covenant. (Ps. 25:14)

There is a threefold distinction in religion which is as simple as it is profound. Religion, in its simplest aspect, is a life. It is to live soberly, righteously, and godly in this present world. It is to do the will of God from the heart. It is to visit the widows and the fatherless in their affliction, and to keep oneself unspotted from the world. But religion is more than a life. It is also a faith. It is to see the invisible. It is a trust in the being, and wisdom, and power, and love of God. It is a conviction and assurance of spiritual truth which every man fashions into his creed, whether he sets it down in statement and article, or leaves it unexpressed.

But religion is more than a faith. It is an experience, not to be shared with the world, and never to be uttered to alien ears. It is an experience which a man dare not tell, cannot tell, to the outsider. It is solemn, mystic, incommunicable. It is a knowledge of God and of His ways, and purposes, and desire, which issues into the peace which passeth all understanding, the hope which maketh not ashamed, the joy unspeakable and full of glory. It is this experience which the Psalmist named the secret of the Lord. Here he sets down its law. It is "with them that fear Him." He adds the seal of the law when he writes, "and He will show them His covenant."

> For whosoever will save his life shall
> lose it: and whosoever will lose his
> life for my sake shall find it.
> (Matt. 16:25)

On the face of it nothing can be more contradictory than to say that to save one's life is to lose it, and to lose one's life is to find it. Sometimes this paradox is explained by declaring that Jesus had two different kinds of life in view. We are told that Jesus meant us to sacrifice a lower life for a higher, an earthly and a temporal life for a spiritual and an eternal, the life of the body for the life of the soul. We are taken, for the noblest instance and proof of this interpretation, to the Roman amphitheatre. We are shown the martyrs awaiting the onrush of the lions. As they are set upon by the hungry and merciless beasts, and as the mangled remains of their bodies are carried away, we are told to see in their tragic loss their splendid gain. They have lost their lives for Christ's sake, but they have found the life eternal. But the martyrs' loss and gain touches the fringe, but only the fringe, of Christ's truth.

Jesus has enshrined a deeper meaning in His paradox. He is stating a law of universal life. He does not mean two different kinds of life, a lower and a higher, set in contrast. He is thinking of the same life in each case. He is stating the still unaccepted and, for many men, incredible truth, that to be eager to save life is the way to lose it, and that the way to find it

251

is to be willing to lose it, and, if need be, to pour it out in a splendid waste.

> And he was transfigured before
> them: and his face did shine as the
> sun. . . . (Matt. 17:2)

He was transfigured while He prayed. This element of the experience we can understand. No one of us ever prayed as Jesus prayed. We are all poor, fearful, darkened, sinful beings in the presence of God. We never have had Christ's perfect trust, His unclouded assurance, His undimmed vision of God. Yet we understand how a man may be transfigured as he prays. His whole inner being will become illuminated, and the sheen of it will be seen in his face. "They looked unto Him and were lightened; and their faces were not ashamed." As Jesus prayed, and as He yielded Himself up, in this hour of communion with God, to an entire consecration to God's will, the inner ecstasy of His spirit shone out, not only in the radiance of His face, but also in the lustre of the tabernacle of His flesh. The face of Moses shone with so heavenly a light that he was compelled to veil it when he came down from his mount. The face of Stephen was like the face of an angel as he stood in his holy place. All faces shine when they lose themselves in the rapture of prayer. It is no marvel that Christ's face was transfigured and His raiment shone on this night of high communion with God.

> . . . Moses knew not that the skin of
> his face shone while he talked with
> him. (Exod. 34:29)

But there is a height in prayer above communion. What shall I call it? It may be named the prayer of surrender. Very few ever utter that prayer to its utmost syllable. Few ever really lay themselves, spirit and soul and body, on God's altar. We are always withholding something, keeping back from God some dear and cherished possession, some gift or talent or power, some love or pleasure or passion. We will not yield up some one dear and tightly held joy. Yet when we do pray this prayer we pass on to an experience, which seals us with a seal that cannot be broken, to the service of God for ever. Then on the transparent mirror of the face the light leaps and flashes, and some of it abides. That is the secret of that heavenly and almost intolerable radiance on the face of Moses which men feared to look upon. He had come out of that most holy place and offered up his prayer of surrender in those solemn words, "But if not . . . blot out my name from Thy book." That is why Stephen's face shone in the council. His clear and discerning mind saw his martyr death before him, and he yielded himself up to God's will. Could we have seen Paul's face when he heard God's words, "My grace is sufficient for thee," and meekly accepted God's will, we would have seen the sheen of the transfiguring light also upon it. He did not know whether he was "in the body" or "out of it." That is why Christ's face shone as He prayed. And that is how our faces also shall be transfigured.

> O death, where is thy sting? O grave,
> where is thy victory? (I Cor. 15:55)

He has three names for death. He calls it a *falling asleep.* He is using one of the phrases which daring and trustful men had coined, and He is giving it proof and reality. When He stands beside the bed of Jairus' little daughter He softly says, "Talitha cumi," "My little lambie, arise."

He calls it a *going to the Father.* This is the word which remained unspoken until the end, but it was His most cherished thought. When He gathers His disciples together in the upper room, and He is upon the eve of His dying, then the word is like a refrain in a song, a recurring note of music in His addresses. Again and again He repeats, "I go to My Father." He is like an emigrant who has been for years in another hemisphere and in the land of strangers. He has been busy with its life and its industries. He has endured its hardships and isolation. Now the time of His sojourn is over and the hour of His return is come. He is going to the Father. He is going home.

He calls it, in the conversation, by a singular word. "They spake of His decease." In the literal and significant meaning of the word it was His *"exodus."* We cannot doubt why the word was chosen. It is the thought of death from the point of view of one who is about to go out by it as by a door. How full of light is this word. Death is an exodus, a going out from the land of the stranger, from the house of bondage, from affliction and thankless toil, from the state of the slave. Death is a deliverance and a boon. It is a going through a wilderness, with its loneliness and its pain and privation, but it is a going through a wilderness upon a journey which is to end in the land which is the promise of God.

> This is my beloved Son, in whom I
> am well pleased; hear ye him.
> (Matt. 17:5)

**H**ear Him." This is the message which in some form is given to men who fear as they enter the cloud. Out of every cloud which shall fall over men, on their knowledge, or faith, or understanding of God's will, or interpretation of His ways, there comes this one word, "Hear Him." When God's being has become dim and uncertain, and the cloud of doubt so overshadows your heart that you cannot pray, hear Him who calls, "He that hath seen Me hath seen the Father." When God's character seems dark and unlovely, and your heart rebels against some grim word which has been taught you by men who have not considered God's great mind, and the cloud overshadows you, hear Him who saith, "He is kind unto the unthankful and to the evil." When God's providence seems estranged, and the cloud has fallen upon your daily life, and all that makes it gracious has been taken away, hear Him who saith, "If God so clothe the grass of the field, which today is, and tomorrow is cast into the oven, shall He not much more clothe you, O ye of little faith?" If the will of God seems hard and stern and bids you pass through a baptism, until you find the cloud upon your spirit and you lie under its fear, hear Him who saith, "I have given you an example that ye should do as I have done to you." Whatever cloud you enter, the cloud of guilty conscience, of a chilled faith, of a searching loneliness, as you fear, hear Him who has a word for every hour. In time to come, if not while trembling under the shadow, you will learn the significance of the cloud, the fear, and the voice.

> This is the victory that overcometh
> the world, even our faith. (I John 5:4)

There lies the noblest victory of the men who believe. To John and to his generation, and to all men who have had the vision of God, the world is the blinding, seducing, terrifying reality. By the world, John does not mean the realm of earth and sea and sky, or the things which God hath made beautiful in their season. He does not mean the world of men and women, with their joys and sorrows, their hopes and fears. That is the world God loves. By the world John meant that merely earthly order and fashion and mode of life, with its hates, greeds, foul habits, and dark mutinies against goodness and truth. It was that pagan world in which he lived, sometimes lovely in its forms of passion, often alluring in its fascination, but always deadly to the purities and simplicities of the soul. It was that world which Demas loved, and for whose indulgences he became a deserter. That world we face when we go down to our businesses, enter into our pleasures,

255

suffer our trials and losses, meet our scornings and our disappointments.

The man who has had his moment of vision, who receives in every hour the energy of God's Holy Spirit, will face its temptations, endure its trials, and he will overcome. We may feel ourselves far from the attainment of this victory. We conquer it in proportion as we believe. We might say, as the great believers have said, to the mountain which seems to hinder the coming of the kingdom of God and to blot out the very light of heaven, "Be thou removed," and it would be removed. All the splendid achievements and all the victory over the wrong, and the tyranny, and the cruelty of the past, however strongly these have been entrenched, have been gained by men of faith. Nothing has been impossible to them. But only One has gotten Him the faultless victory. That One is Jesus, the beginner and the consummator of faith, who endured the Cross, and despised its shame, and is now set down, in the victor's place, at the right hand of God.

# William Henry Griffith Thomas
## (1861–1924)

I once walked around Portman Square in London, looking for St. Paul's Church but unable to find it. Finally I asked a gentleman where it was, and he informed me that the original church had been demolished and a new building constructed adjacent to the square. "But why are you interested in St. Paul's?" he asked me. "Because Griffith Thomas pastored there," I replied, and I walked away, leaving him wondering who Griffith Thomas was!

Pastor, teacher, theologian, writer—all of these only begin to describe the varied ministries of this man. W. H. Griffith Thomas was pastor not only at St. Paul's, Portman Square, but also at St. Aldate's Church, Oxford. He served as principal of Wycliffe Hall, Oxford, a center for the training of evangelical Anglican ministers. (Lawrence of Arabia used to attend his Sunday afternoon Bible studies.) He was one of the founding fathers of Dallas Theological Seminary but did not live long enough to participate in the actual ministry of the school. The library at Dallas Seminary is named in his honor.

Thomas wrote many books, all of them helpful to Christians. His "outline studies" are a treasury of truth.

Since we heard of your faith in
Christ Jesus, and of the love which
ye have to all the saints, For the
hope which is laid up for you in
heaven. . . . (Col. 1:4–5)

This hope is said by St. Paul to be "laid up" for believers "in the heavens," and the verb is particularly worthy of notice

257

because of its use elsewhere. Thus, a crown of righteousness is said to be "laid up" for those who love Christ's appearing (II Tim. 4:8, *A.S.V.*), while it is also recorded that it was "laid up" for men once to die (Heb. 9:27). Another solemn contrast is drawn in our Lord's parable of the pounds, where the unfaithful servant "laid up" his master's gift instead of using it (Luke 19:20). In two Old Testament passages, moreover, it is declared that the Lord has "laid up" His goodness for those who fear Him (Ps. 31:19) and "sound wisdom for the righteous" (Prov. 2:7). No Christian life, then, is complete which does not include in it this forward look of joyous certitude toward a bright future, for hope as a grace is not a mere spirit of what we call hopefulness, or a natural buoyancy of temperament. It is a distinctly Christian virtue, the result of union with God in Christ; and it has for its immediate object the Lord Jesus at His glorious appearing, and for its ultimate, eternal and exhaustless substance the glories of heaven and God as our all in all.

> Since we heard of your faith in
> Christ Jesus, and of the love which
> ye have to all the saints, For the
> hope which is laid up for you in
> heaven. . . . (Col. 1:4–5)

Faith rests on the past, love works in the present, and hope presses toward the future; or, faith looks backward and upward, love looks outward, and hope looks forward. These three constitute the true, complete Christian life and not one of them should be omitted or slighted. We are only too apt to emphasize faith and love and forget hope but, inasmuch as hope is invariably connected with the coming of the Lord, "that blessed hope" (Titus 2:13), it is a vital part of our Christian life. Faith accepts, hope expects; faith appropriates, hope anticipates; faith receives, hope realizes; faith is always and only concerned with the past and present, hope is always and only concerned with the future. We know that faith comes by hearing; we shall find that hope comes by experience. Faith is concerned with a person who promises, hope with the thing promised; and faith is the root of which hope is a fruit.

> For this cause we also . . . do not
> cease to pray for you, and to desire
> that ye might be filled with the
> knowledge of his will in all wisdom
> and spiritual understanding.
> (Col. 1:9)

The difficulty with so many people today is that they are superficial in their knowledge and shallow in their experience, and so are a prey to various errors, "carried about with every wind of doctrine" (Eph. 4:14). We may safely aver, then, that to be "filled with the knowledge of his will in all wisdom and spiritual understanding" means for its complete realization a constant touch with those writings which present the clearly expressed plan of God. The divine will is in that Book, and when it, the Word of God, is illuminated by the Spirit of God we, His children, come to know His will concerning us. Indeed, no one will ever have the full knowledge of that will, no one can possibly be mature in Christian experience, if the Word of God is not his daily, definite, direct study and meditation. It purifies the perceptive faculties by its cleansing power; it illuminates the moral faculties with its enlightening power; it controls the emotional faculties with its protective power; and it energizes the volitional faculties with its stimulating power. Thus, in the constant, continuous use of the Word of God in personal practice, with reverent meditation and earnest prayer, we shall indeed, to paraphrase the apostle's words, "become filled with the full knowledge of His will in every avenue of perception and in their spiritual applications."

> That their hearts might be com-
> forted, being knit together in love,
> and unto all riches of the full assur-
> ance of understanding. . . . (Col. 2:2)

He prayed that these Christians might be joined together, knit together, and kept together. Solitary Christians are apt to be weak Christians, for in this sphere as in all others "union is strength." If Christian people are not truly knit together, the cause of Christ may suffer, for through the severances caused by division the enemy can keep thrusting his darts which must be parried alone. That is why the apostle elsewhere urges believers earnestly to strive "to keep the unity of the Spirit in the bond of peace" (Eph. 4:3). One of the greatest powers that Satan wields today is due to disunion among the genuine people of God. It is true alike of the Christian home, congregation, and denomination that this wedge of discord can become one of the enemy's most powerful weapons. On the other hand, where the brethren are able to "dwell together in unity," there the Lord commands His blessing (Ps. 133:3).

This unity, however, is only possible "in love." It is the love of God to us that unites us to Him and it will be the love of God in us that unites us to our brethren. Indeed, there is no power like love to bind Christians together. We may not see eye to eye on all aspects of the truth we hold; we may not all use the same methods of worship and service; but if we love one another God dwells in us and among us, and He can add His own seal of blessing to the work done for Him. Let every evangelical Christian be fully assured that, in so far as he is striving, praying, and laboring for the union of God's people in love, he will be doing one of the most influential and blessed pieces of work for his Master and, at the same time, one of the greatest possible pieces of disservice to the kingdom of Satan. Contrariwise, the Christian man or Christian church practicing separateness and exclusiveness because of non-essential differences of opinion or policy is one of the best allies of Satan and one of his most effective workers.

And ye are complete in Him. . . .
(Col. 2:10)

The emphasis on the words "in Him" (vv. 9–11) very plainly shows that the source of all spiritual power lies in the union of the soul with Christ. But not only so—we are circumcised, and buried, and raised, and made alive *"with* Him" (vv. 11, 12, 13), suggesting a spiritual fellowship. All this is associated with a definite confidence in God as the object of our trust and as the source of all spiritual blessing. Scripture is very emphatic in regard to the way in which faith links us to God as the means of obtaining grace and power.

Thus at every point Christ and the believer are identified. When our Lord was circumcised, we were circumcised with Him; when our Lord died, we died in Him; when He was buried, we were buried; when He rose, we were raised; and when He was quickened, we were quickened. To these great truths we may add that when He ascended, we ascended; and, as in one of the parallel passages, Ephesians 2:4–6, now that He is at God's right hand we are seated with Him in heavenly places. In this spiritual unity will be found the only guarantee of faithful adherence to what is true and of fearless abhorrence of what is false. This emphasis on the spiritual life as distinct from mere knowledge and even philosophy (v. 8) will be found as potent today as ever. When faced with ideas which under specious guises of one sort or another tend to lead us astray, it is not too much to urge that a careful attention to a passage like this one will do more than anything else to protect against them. Thus, old errors, which continue to appear in new forms, may be met and vanquished just as in St. Paul's day. Yes, union with Christ affects both thought, the full exercise of mental powers, and action, the translation of thought into redeemed, victorious living.

> If ye then be risen with Christ, seek
> those things which are above, where
> Christ sitteth on the right hand of
> God. (Col. 3:1)

The apostle first calls attention to his readers having been "raised together with Christ" (*A.S.V.*). The English word "if" is employed here in its sense of "since"—"in view of," and the verb is in the indicative mood, so that Paul is clearly assuming this resurrection as a fact, admissive of no doubt. That is to say, these Christians were raised spiritually when Christ was raised physically; and this identification was the foundation of their spiritual position. The resurrection is variously presented in the New Testament as at once a proof, a pattern, a power, a promise, and a pledge. It is the proof of our acceptance of Christ's death and of our acceptance with Him (Rom. 4:24, 25): it is to be the pattern of our holy life (Rom. 6:4); it is also the power for Christian character and service (Eph. 1:18–20); it contains the promise of our own physical resurrection (I Thess. 4:14); and it is the pledge of our life hereafter (John 14:19). In the present passage our resurrection is associated with Christ's because we are united with Him in such a way that, whatever He did, we are regarded by God the Father as having done also (2:12; Rom. 6:8).

> And let the peace of God rule in
> your hearts. . . . (Col. 3:15)

What does the peace of Christ do? Primarily it gives assurance of acceptance with God (cf. Rom. 5:1), and the protection of God (cf. Phil. 4:7, Gr., "shall garrison," a paradoxical use of a warlike term). But here Christ's peace is to be received into the heart as the arbiter deciding the course and ruling the life (Gr., "umpire"). A similar idea and practically the same Greek word is found in 2:18, as we have seen, where the apostle is warning his readers not to let anyone judicially deprive them of their reward as though they were unworthy. This word, translated here "rule," suggests that which settles differences, especially where there is any conflict of thoughts and feelings. Under such circumstances "the peace of Christ" is to decide; and if it be asked how peace is able to do this perhaps the explanation is that just as peace with God is the result of our acceptance of Christ as Savior (Rom. 5:1), so the experience of peace in the soul, in union with Christ and through the presence of the Holy Spirit, will at once settle every difficulty, resolve every conflict, and show us what is the will of God. In this case there is a special reason for such divine peace—the essential unity of the body of Christ, the Church, and to this peace, we are told, every believer has been called. When we are one with Christ, in whom God "called us with an holy calling" (II Tim. 1:9), and also one with Christians, "called in one body," as Paul says here, there is no question as to the great power of divine peace in our lives. We read of "government and peace" (Isa. 9:7), of "righteousness and peace" (Ps. 85:10; cf. Isa. 32:17), and of "grace . . . and peace" (Titus 1:4). Until these prevail universally, however, "the God of peace himself" (I Thess. 5:23, *A.S.V.*) will be with us, keeping us meanwhile "in perfect peace" (Isa. 26:3).

# George Campbell Morgan
## (1863–1945)

G. Campbell Morgan was known as "The Prince of Exposi-tors" both in America and Great Britain, and he lived up to that title. A self-taught teacher, Morgan never attended a Bible school or seminary, yet he was on several faculties, lectured widely, and even served as a college president for a time.

Like F. B. Meyer, Morgan was "discovered" by D. L. Moody. In fact, Morgan had a wide ministry in the United States before he was called to Westminster Chapel in London, where he was pastor from 1904 to 1917. The church was ready to die when Morgan arrived, but his ministry of the Word transformed it into a vibrant center of evangelical activity. Morgan returned to Westminster in 1938 for five more years of ministry, resigning in 1943. His associate D. Martyn Lloyd-Jones succeeded him.

Morgan was a tireless traveler, a speaker much in demand, and a prolific author. When asked the secret of his success, he would say, "Work—hard work—and again, work!" He was at his desk at 6 A.M. each day and permitted no interruptions.

. . . the church of the living God, the
pillar and ground of the truth.
(I Tim. 3:15)

The Church of God apart from the Person of Christ is a useless structure. However ornate it may be in its organiza-tion, however perfect in all its arrangements, however rich and increased with goods, if the Church is not revealing the Person, lifting Him to the height where all men can see Him, then the Church becomes an impertinence and a sham, a blasphemy and a fraud, and the sooner the world is rid of it, the better. The Church, apart from the shining of a light, is a lampstand, dark, valueless, effete. The Church that fails to proclaim the Word is a sound, a voice without articulation, sounding brass and a clanging cymbal; of no value.

With all reverence, let me state the other side, which is to my own heart full of grave solemnity. That supernal Person, apart from the Church, is hidden. Jesus Christ has no means of showing Himself save through His Church. The light that flashes from His eyes cannot be seen save as it beams and shines and burns and flashes and flames from the eyes of His people. The tenderness and strength of His teaching can be felt only as the Church becomes the instrument through which He speaks to humanity to direct, instruct, and bless it. The great central Person is hidden unless the Church reveals Him. The Light that lighteth every man, and which came into the world, and was focused, centralized for a brief period in a Person, has passed out of human sight, and is no longer shining save through the Church. The Word of God today has no voice apart from the Christian Church.

> And he gave some, apostles; and some, prophets; and some, evangelists; and some, pastors and teachers. (Eph. 4:11)

The business of those within the Church is to teach the word of truth in such form and fashion that the Church will be able to incarnate the Word, and flash the light on the world's darkness. The apostolic function, which, technically is expressing truth in its balanced form and proportion, is always to that end. The pastoral function is breaking the Bread of Life, feeding the flock of God, leading individual souls to new appreciation, in order that by obedience thereto they may proclaim the truth. These gifts within the Church are bestowed in order that the Church may fulfill her function of being the pillar and the ground of the truth.

The Church must not only fulfill its function by incarnation, she must do it also by proclamation. In order to do this, she has her prophets and evangelists. The function of the prophet is to proclaim the evangel, call men to repentance and faith. The prophet and the evangelist must speak on behalf of the Church, explaining the secrets of the Church's experience. If there be no experience to explain, the declaration of a theory is of no avail. For one brief moment let us go back to the Day of Pentecost. Think of the significant and important fact, that Peter's preaching was made possible by the Church's enthusiasm. What attracted the crowd? A Church with its eyes aflame with light and its lips filled with song! All Jerusalem gathered together, and they were amazed, and they were perplexed, and they said, What meaneth this? The Church attracted the crowd by its enthusiasm, and so the opportunity of the preacher was created. This is the supreme work of the Christian Church, and it is only as she does her work that men and nations and the world will live by the Bible.

> And Nadab and Abihu, the sons of
> Aaron, took either of them his
> censer, and put fire therein, and laid
> incense thereon, and offered strange
> fire before the LORD. . . . (Lev. 10:1)

This is without question a story full of solemnity. It gives pause to all who are called to service, as it reminds us of the necessity for a constant and sustained loyalty to God in our methods of service. It calls the Christian Church ever and anon to halt in her progress in order that she may readjust her relationships with her Lord. It calls us to examine every organization that is springing up, lest haply we find that they are not in accordance with the Divine method, even though they desire the realization of the Divine purpose. I am not at all sure that if the Church would give herself to such solemn consideration and readjustment, she would not find many organizations which are merely fungus growths, sapping her life, and contributing nothing to the work of God.

When we turn from the larger outlook to the more particular, with what awful solemnity does this word speak to us of our work for God. The dark appalling hint of the story needs emphasizing in all its applications; the worker for God must never touch God's work in the strength of any false stimulant. To attempt God's work under the stimulus of passion for fame, or desire for notoriety, is to burn false fire on the altar. To us, I repeat, prescribed forms are no more; but the living and ever-present Spirit of God is with us, and the greatest matter in all our Christian service is that we seek to know His will and submit ourselves to His direction.

> For we know that the whole creation
> groaneth and travaileth in pain
> together until now. (Rom. 8:22)

It may be well that we remind ourselves that pain presents no *problem* to any man except to the man who believes in God. Pain becomes a problem only in the presence of faith. When, ever and anon, some believer, it may be one whose faith at the moment is trembling, challenges the world's agony, the challenge is always uttered in the presence of the consciousness of God. When the soul cries out in revolt in the presence of the abounding suffering of men, the cry is always born of the wonder how God can permit this. There is no other problem. Blot God out of His universe and you will still have pain, but no problem to assault the soul. It is only faith that has to face this perplexity. It is Habakkuk who suffers most in the day of the declension of the people of God. It is Habakkuk who says, "Oh, Lord, how long?" I cry murder and

Thou dost not hear. I cry violence and there is no answer. What is God doing?

It was Carlyle, rough, rugged, peculiar in many ways, and yet a man of the greatest faith, who, when Froude attempted to comfort him by telling him that God is in His heaven, said, "Yes, but He is doing nothing." I never repeat that without being inclined to say to believing souls, Do not be angry with Carlyle. It was not true, God *was* doing something, but there is neither man nor woman in this house who has ever come very near, and remained near to the world's agony, who has not had that thought at some time or another. The whole creation groaneth and travaileth together in pain, and the proportion of our nearness to God is the proportion of our sense of this problem of pain, for it is the love of God shed abroad in the heart that renders the heart keen and sensitive to the world's agony. The heart of man, taught by the Divine love, questions the Divine love, until, presently, the heart of the man discovers that the very agony he feels which makes him question is the result of the presence in his soul of the God of love, and, indeed, it is an expression of God's own agony. It is when we become sensible of that prevalent pain that we need hope; and unless hope shall save us, then we shall indeed be lost.

> That I may know him . . . and the
> fellowship of his sufferings. . . .
> (Phil. 3:10)

Do not miss the blessedness of the fact that the fellowship of His sufferings means that He has fellowship with us. When I enter into the fellowship of His sufferings I am not alone, for He is forever with me. I can endure no pain for Him that He does not share with me. When I stand in the presence of sin and suffer—if I have climbed high enough, in that moment He is with me, He is feeling the same pain, He is suffering with me. When my heart is moved with hot anger because God is misunderstood, He is suffering with me. My fellowship with Him means His fellowship with me. When through pity born of His love my heart breaks over the awful punishment that is falling on the head of the sinner, never let Satan suggest I have reached a higher level than the Lord, for He is having fellowship with me, my pity is born of His pity, and His love is suffering with my love.

Paradox of Christianity which no man can explain—there is no joy like the fellowship of His suffering! What is the sense of sin that causes you pain, dear child of God? It is the outcome of purity. The measure of purity is the measure of suffering in the presence of sin. In the infinite mystery of pain there is the deeper heart and core of holy joy. What is that suffering of your heart in the presence of misunderstanding of God? It is born of your perfect satisfaction in God. Why are you angry when that man libels God? Because you know Him. Your hot pain and great sorrow come out of the quiet rest of intimate knowledge. What is that pity for the sinner that throbs through your soul, fills your eyes, breaks your heart? It is the outcome of the love of God shed abroad in your heart.

> . . . he brake in pieces the brasen
> serpent that Moses had made: . . .
> and he called it Nehushtan [a piece
> of brass]. (II Kings 18:4)

I see a people hungering after what they have lost. An idol always means this. An idol created by the fingers of men, or chosen by men and appointed to the place of a god, is forevermore a revelation of the sense of need, the sense of lack. It is an evidence that the deepest thing in the human heart is its cry after God. This is not to defend idolatry, not to defend the action of these people in the deification of the brazen serpent, but to say that when people lose their consciousness of God they do not lose their sense of need for God. Whereas I look back on these people in this hour and say they have lost their vision of God, have lost the sense of His nearness, have wandered far away from that spiritual communion with Him which is in itself a fire and a force, I say also that having lost the vision and having lost the sense, they are restless. When the one true and living God, having been revealed and known, is lost to consciousness the heart will clamantly cry for that which is lost. This worship of the serpent was certainly a revelation of the hunger of the people after God.

There is one other matter which I think this event reveals. Having lost their vision of God, and still being conscious of the necessity for some object of worship around which their spiritual life could gather, their deification of the serpent was a revelation of the utmost confusion. It was history misinterpreted. A blessing of the olden days was made a curse in the present moment by that misinterpretation of their own history. Setting up the brazen serpent as an object of worship suggested that the serpent itself had been the means of their healing on the past occasion. Their vision of God lost, and the cry of their souls after such a God, and the blundering confusion of a people who, looking back at their own history, emphasized it wrong, interpreted it falsely, and treated the serpent as though it had been the means of their healing in the past—such was the abuse of the brazen serpent.

> For I am not ashamed of the gospel
> of Christ. . . . For therein is the right-
> eousness of God revealed. . . .
> (Rom. 1:16–17)

Salvation is righteousness made possible. If you can tell me that salvation is deliverance from hell, I tell you that you have an utterly inadequate understanding of what salvation is. If you tell me that salvation is forgiveness of sins, I shall affirm that you have a very partial understanding of what salvation is. Unless there be more in salvation than deliverance from penalty and forgiveness of transgressions, then I solemnly say that salvation cannot satisfy my own heart and conscience.

. . . mere forgiveness of sins and deliverance from some penalty cannot satisfy the profoundest in human consciousness. Deep down in the common human consciousness there is a response to righteousness, an admission of its call, its beauty, its necessity.

Salvation, then, is making possible that righteousness. Salvation is the power to do right. However enfeebled the will may be, however polluted the nature, the gospel comes bringing to men the message of power enabling them to do right. In the gospel is revealed a righteousness of God, which, as the Apostle argues and makes quite plain as he goes on with his great letter, is a righteousness which is placed at the disposal of the unrighteous man so that the unrighteous man may become righteous in heart and thought and will and deed.

# John Henry Jowett
## (1864–1923)

The newspapers hailed him as "the greatest preacher in the English-speaking world." Yet when he arrived in New York harbor, about to become pastor of Fifth Avenue Church, and one of the city's greatest chefs waited to prepare the meal of his choice, John Henry Jowett asked for—bread and milk!

Jowett was a great preacher, a master with words. Above all else, he magnified the grace of God. God's grace was the theme of his ministry, both to lost sinners and self-satisfied saints. He was not an expositor in the traditional sense. He was a textual preacher who held every text up to the bright light of God's grace the way a jeweler holds a diamond in the sunlight. Jowett shows us the many beautiful facets of God's truth, and he explains how we can experience truth in our lives.

Jowett followed R. W. Dale at Carr's Lane, Birmingham, and enjoyed a rich ministry. He left New York in 1918 to succeed G. Campbell Morgan at Westminster. He devoted his closing years to a futile crusade for world peace.

Peace I leave with you, my peace I give unto you. (John 14:27)

There are two ways in which this gift of peace differs from the gifts of the world. In the first place, it differs in the matter of the gift. When the world seeks to give peace it addresses itself to conditions; the Lord addresses Himself to character. The world deals with things; the Lord deals with kinships. The world keeps in the material realm; Jesus Christ moves in the spiritual realm. The world offers to put us into a fine house; the Lord offers to make a fine tenant. The world will introduce us into "fine society"; Jesus will make us at home with God.

In the second place, our Lord differs from the world in the manner of His giving. The world always gives its best at the beginning. It offers gaudy garlands, brimming cups, and glittering crowns. "But knowest thou not it shall be bitterness in the latter end?" It makes an imposing fire, but we are speedily left with the ashes. It leads us to a showy feast, but we soon encounter aches and pains. It blinds us with the "garish day"; then come chill twilight and uncompanionable night. "Not as the world giveth give I." He keeps His good wine until last. He leads us from grace to grace, from faith to faith, from glory to glory. "Greater things than these shall we see." His gifts grow deeper, richer, fuller, right through the eternal years.

> They have gone from mountain to
> hill, and have forgotten their
> restingplace. (Jer. 50:6)

I think this word is very descriptive of much of our modern life. It is a vagrancy rather than a crusade. We go from "mountain to hill," and from hill to mountain. We are always on the move. We are ever seeking something else and never finding satisfaction. We get weary and tired with one thing and we trudge to another! We are here, there, and yonder, and our lives become jaded and stale. But the extraordinary thing is that in all our goings we forget our resting-place. "Return unto thy rest, O my soul." Yes, but we turn anywhere and everywhere rather than to this. Our lives can become so vagrant that God is exiled from our minds. It seems as though there is something in vagrancy that stupefies the soul, and renders us insensitive to our true home and rest in God.

When I first came to New York, during the first few months

of my ministry, I was continually asked by people, "Have you got into the whirl?" The very phrase seems so far removed from the words of the psalmist, "He maketh me to lie down in green pastures. He leadeth me beside the still waters." Not that the psalmist luxuriated in indolence, or spent his days in the fatness of ease; the rest was only preparative to a march. "He leadeth me in the paths of righteousness." But from the march he returned to his resting-place. But we can be caught in such a whirl in our modern life that we just rush from one thing to another, and we forget the glorious rest that is ours in God. I think the enemy of our souls must love to get us into a whirl! If once we are dizzied with sensations we are likely to lose the thought of God.

> And He healed many that were sick
> of divers diseases, and cast out
> many devils . . . and He departed
> into a solitary place and there
> prayed. (Mark 1:34–35)

But what need was there to pray just then? He was most evidently engaged in doing good. The newly-opened eyes of the blind were radiant with thanksgiving. The once lame man leaped as a hart. The Master abounded in good works, and some measure of popular favour rested upon Him. Then why go apart to pray?

First of all, He retired to pray in order to provide against nervous exhaustion. All this healing, all this giving, all this sympathy meant large expenditure of vital power. "Virtue is gone out of Me." And, therefore, He prayed in order that His vital resources might be restored. There is some work that cannot be done without resort to Divine communion. When the soul is drained in the ministry of sympathy, there is nothing for it but resort to the springs, and there is nothing which so readily and powerfully restores a man like drinking the water of life. "They that wait upon the Lord shall renew their strength."

But there is a second reason why our Saviour prayed when He was in the midst of successful public work. He prayed in order to make His soul secure against the perils of success, against "the destruction that wasteth at noonday." Success may bruise the spirit more than failure. Heat can ruin a violin quite as effectually as the chilly damp. Prosperity slays many a man whose health was preserved in adversity. And so I think our Lord prayed in the hour of popular favour lest His very success should maim His life of service. And there is significant counsel in His practice for all the children of men. When we are busily successful, let us pray, and we need not "be afraid for the arrow that flieth by day."

> Great and marvellous are Thy
> works! (Rev. 15:3)

These works are not primarily the works of nature, but the works of grace. The singers are contemplating the truth in its conflict with falsehood. They are watching the wonders of holiness in its hallowing ministries among the children of men. They are recalling the romance of God's providence as they see it unrolled through the generations of their own troubled national history. And their doxology of providence and grace gathers about two names, the names of Moses and the Lamb. In their songful recital of providential deliverances these two names seem to crystallize and tell the story. And what is the significance of the names? Surely it is this: Moses signifies emancipation from social bondage; the Lamb signifies emancipation from spiritual bondage. Moses stands for deliverance from wrong. The Lamb stands for deliverance from sin. Moses delivers from the wrong which man may suffer from himself. Moses delivers from the Pharaoh outside man. The Lamb delivers from the devil within man. Moses delivers from the gall of oppression and pain. The Lamb delivers from the gall of guilt and sin. This is the song the singers sing, the "Song of Moses and the Lamb"—Thy marvellous works in Moses against all wrong; Thy marvellous works in the Lamb against all sin!

> . . . for he oft refreshed me, and was
> not ashamed of my chain.
> (II Tim. 1:16)

This kind of service is the one that is most needed in the Church of Christ. We want people who carry atmosphere and are ministers of refreshment. And such people will instinctively go where the ministry is most required. It is a beautiful lineament in the character of Onesiphorus which is given in the Apostle's phrase, "He was not ashamed of my chain." The great scholar, and convert, and saint, and apostle was held in servitude, but we know what a name he gave to his chain. He called it "my bonds in Christ." He linked his very servitude to the Lord. He took his restrictions, his limitations, his impediments, and surveyed them in their association with the Christ. But a man's chain often lessens the circle of his friends. The chain of poverty keeps many people away, and so does the chain of unpopularity. When a man is in high repute he has many friends. When he begins to wear a chain the friends are apt to fall away. But the ministers of the morning breeze love to come to the shades of night. They delight to minister in the region of despondency, and where the bonds lie heaviest upon the soul. "He was not ashamed of my chain." The chain was really an allurement. It gave speed to his feet and urgency to his ministry.

And is not this the very friendship of the Lord Jesus? He is not ashamed of our chains. When He was with us in the flesh He amazed people by His familiarity with the victims who were held in bonds. "He is gone to be guest with a man that is a sinner." He was not ashamed of his chain. "He eateth and drinketh with publicans and sinners." Their chains did not

repel Him. "He remembereth us in our low estate." He brings
the ministry of refreshment to those who languish in prison.
"He is the Lord of the morning to the children of the night."

For as the rain cometh down, and
the snow from heaven, and
returneth not thither, but watereth
the earth. . . . (Isa. 55:10)

Winter possesses a life. The grey days come and the cold,
dark nights. And then some grace appears, some fine reverence, some chaste reserve, some beautiful modesty, some
violet of the spirit, like crocus or gentian revealing itself under
the melting coverlet of Alpine snows. It was not there before
the snow had fallen, but now it lifts its lowly head before the
face of an approving heaven.

Let me quote one or two examples of spiritual graces and
purposes which have been gendered and nourished beneath
the snow robe. Here is one: "Before I was afflicted I went
astray, but now I have kept Thy word." Something was born in
the severities of affliction; the virtue of fidelity was nourished
in the wintry day. And here is another: "It is good for me that I
have been afflicted, that I might learn Thy statutes." Here is a
faculty that is strengthened by the frost. Affliction adds to the
man's worth. The grace of refined perception was found in
the day of the falling snow. There is a third suggestive
example in the life of Hezekiah: "In those days was Hezekiah
sick unto death." The gloom of affliction settled upon his soul;
the snow was falling! Now, if we turn to the day when the
winter is over, we shall find "flowers appear on the earth."
Listen to this word when Hezekiah was recovered of his
sickness: "I shall go softly all my years." The snow brought the
flowers of delicacy and gentleness and considerateness, and
never again would he break the bruised reed.

If Thou hadst been here, my brother
had not died. (John 11:21, 32)

That is a Scriptural example of a very familiar experience. It illustrates a most commonplace form of grief. It is an example of needless regrets. If we had arranged things a little differently, how different might have been the issues! If we had taken another turning, what a contrast in our destiny! If only we had done so-and-so, Lazarus might have been with us still! My readers will recognize the familiarity of the utterance. It is the expression of a common human infirmity. Its sound travels through the years like the haunting sigh of a low moan. "If only . . . !" "If only . . . !" And the pathetic cry is with us today. It is usually born on the morning after a crisis, and it sometimes continues until the plaintive soul itself goes home to rest. It is a sorrow that consumes like a gangrene. It drains away the vital strength. If by some gracious ministry it could be ended, and the moan changed into trustful quietude, an enormous load would be lifted from the heart of the race. Men and women are being crushed under needless regrets. And here is one of them: "Lord, if Thou hadst been here my brother had not died!" It was a regret that shut out the kindly light of the stars which God has ordained should shine and cheer us in our nights.

# John Daniel Jones
## (1865–1942)

My wife and I were driving through Bournemouth, England, and we remembered that J. D. Jones was a pastor there for thirty-eight years. We found Richmond Hill Congregational Church and paid our respects to the memory of a fine man and a faithful preacher.

Jones was not a spellbinder. He did not traffic in the sensational. His sermons were consistently good—biblical, practical, pastoral. No high flights of sacred oratory carried him along from week to week. But he loved his people and sought to encourage them along the way. That is the word that best describes the preaching of J. D. Jones—encouragement.

We visited his grave in the Bournemouth cemetery. On the gravestone it says: "John Daniel Jones, Preacher of the Gospel. 'Simply to Thy cross I cling.'"

And he ordained twelve, that they
should be with him. . . . (Mark 3:14)

No one would have imagined Jesus would have chosen the disciples He did. When men are starting a new enterprise, they try to get distinguished and influential men to give it their backing. When a new company is being launched they try to get the names of widely-known and honored men upon the directorate. Even in our local affairs—the running of a concert or exhibition—we like to get a number of local celebrities to act as patrons. Jesus was starting a society whose

279

object it was to win the wide world to faith and obedience. In that case, you would have expected Him to have chosen as His helpers men who were influential in the religious circles of His day. But He didn't do what men expected of Him. He did the most quixotic and paradoxical thing. "He called twelve, that they might be with Him." And of those twelve the majority were fishermen from the Galilean lake, one was an ex-tax-gatherer, and one a Sinn Feiner. There was only one—Judas, the man of Kerioth—who may have been of some better social standing; and he turned traitor. The rest were the humblest of the humble—unlettered, uninfluential, unknown. Not many wise, not many mighty, were called by Jesus. But He called the foolish things of the world, and the weak things of the world, and the base things of the world, and the things that are not. It was an almost unbelievable choice. They cast His disciples up against Him. "Hath any of the rulers believed on Him, or of the Pharisees?" they asked in scornful contempt. If Jesus had done what most people would have called the wise and prudent thing, He would have secured the support of some influential Rabbis or well-known Pharisees, and He would have put their names in the forefront of His prospectus. Instead of that, He entrusted His cause to eleven poor and unlettered men. It was a fantastic choice! And yet, after all, absurd though it seemed, Jesus knew what He was about. The success of Christianity could not be put down to the genius of its advocates! The treasure was in earthen vessels; that made it all the more evident that the excellency of the power was of God.

> For the preaching of the cross is to them that perish foolishness; but unto us which are saved it is the power of God. (I Cor. 1:18)

He chose to redeem the world by dying for it. This was not the method the Jews had anticipated. This was not the method even His own disciples anticipated. They expected Christ to take possession of the world by right of conquest. They were always dreaming about thrones, quarrelling as to which of them should occupy the throne nearest Christ's when His Kingdom was actually established. The temptation to take possession of the world in that way presented itself to Jesus. It constituted part of the Temptation in the wilderness. The Devil promised Him all the kingdoms of the world and the glory of them if He would stoop to the use of worldly weapons. But Jesus thrust the temptation away and deliberately set His face toward the Cross. He set His faith, not on force, but on sacrificial love. He chose to win the world by dying for it. But that was so unexpected a method, that for the moment it shattered the faith of the disciples. The unbelieving Jews thought that by the Cross they had brought an impostor's career to an end; the disciples thought the Cross meant final defeat and failure. Their hopes of the Kingdom died with the death of Jesus. Even though Jesus Himself had spoken of it to them again and again, they had refused to believe it, and when it really took place all their dreams collapsed. Well, it did seem a strange way of winning the world—to accept defeat at its hands, to go down to death and shame, to suffer on a Cross! When the Apostles went about preaching Christ crucified, people laughed at their message. Paul talks about the "offence of the Cross." It seemed absurd to suggest that a person who died on the gibbet was the world's Saviour. The Cross was a stumbling-block to the Jews and foolishness to the Greeks. But this foolish, paradoxical method of saving and redeeming the world proved itself, in experience, to be the very power and wisdom of God.

> Every one that falleth on that stone
> shall be broken to pieces; but on
> whomsoever it shall fall, it will
> scatter him as dust. (Luke 20:18)

We think of Him as the "gentle Jesus"—"Gentle Jesus, meek and mild," as our child's hymn puts it. He spoke of Himself as being "meek and lowly in heart." He dealt tenderly with the sinful and the erring. He never broke a bruised reed or quenched a flickering wick. As we picture to ourselves this gracious, loving Person who went about doing good, "formidable" is about the last word in the world we should think of applying to Him. But is there any essential and irreconcilable antagonism between *gentleness* and *formidableness*? Is it quite impossible for these two qualities to exist in one and the same Person? If a person's gentleness never became formidableness, would that person be anything like a complete person? Would not gentleness that never became formidable in face of evil and wrong—would it not cease to be a virtue and become a rather contemptible vice? A man who does not become formidable, terrible even, to the wrong-doer can lay no claim to being a perfect man. Now our Lord was meek; but His meekness was not softness. And He was gentle; but His gentleness was not a foolish and easy good-nature. Jesus was formidable as well as gentle, terrible as well as meek. The Bible is never afraid of combining seeming opposites in its descriptions of Jesus. For example, it speaks of "the wrath of the Lamb." "Wrath" and "Lamb" don't somehow seem to fit each other. The Lamb is the symbol of patience, meekness, gentleness, and so has come to stand for Him who went as a Lamb to the slaughter, and, "as a sheep before its shearers is dumb, so He opened not His mouth." Wrath would seem to fit lion rather than Lamb. But the Bible talks of the "wrath of the Lamb"—the wrath of Him who bore with unmurmuring patience the rude insults and murderous cruelty of evil men. It declares that that gentle and infinitely patient Jesus can blaze out into holy anger, and the wrath is the more terrible just because it is the wrath of the *Lamb*.

Good Master, what good thing shall I
do, that I may have eternal life?
(Matt. 19:16)

Jesus confronted this young ruler with his own words. "Good Master," He said. "Why callest thou Me good?" replied Jesus, as if to ask, "Do you mean what you say?"—What is this—a true word or just a compliment? It was more than a protest against the loose use of words; it was a demand for *reality*. The merely conventional and formal was hateful to Jesus. He demanded truth in the inward parts. He didn't want this young ruler to use towards Him the language that should be the expression of his real soul. Reality, sincerity, was what our Lord demanded. If there was one thing He loathed more than another it was pretence, formalism; what He called hypocrisy. And nowhere is pretence and unreality more utterly hateful than in religion. Perhaps I am not forcing my text unduly if I see in it a warning against *religious cant*. What exactly do we mean by *cant?* My dictionary defines it as "speaking with affectation about religion." It means using religious terms which we do not sincerely mean. And there is a sore temptation to do that, partly because people expect to hear certain terms and partly because men wish to gain a certain reputation for orthodoxy. But it is a fatal thing to do. It is an insult to Him who is the Truth to speak to Him, or about Him, in words which are insincere.

If I then, your Lord and Master,
have washed your feet; ye also
ought to wash one another's feet.
(John 13:14)

The pitchers and the basin and the towel were all there, ready for use, but no one pretended to see them. They took their place at the table, but no one gave any sign of intending to play the part of servant that night. And why was that?

283

Because on the way to the Upper Room they had been contending which of them was greatest. It was not the first time they had quarrelled about their places in Christ's Kingdom. James and John, you remember, had tried to steal a march upon the rest of the disciples by getting their mother Salome to ask Jesus to promise beforehand that the two highest thrones should be given to them. On this particular evening, I should judge, the contention had been particularly keen and bitter, and so they came into the room, as Dr. Dods says, hot and angry and full of resentment, like so many sulky schoolboys. And no one would condescend to discharge this humble but grateful duty of feet-washing. John would not wash the feet of Peter; Peter would not wash the feet of Simon the Canaanite; Simon would not wash the feet of Thomas. For to wash the feet of the rest was to declare oneself the servant of all, and that was precisely what each was resolved he would not do. They stood on their dignity—a poor sort of thing to stand upon. There they sat, looking at the table, looking at the ceiling, arranging their dress, each resolved he would not confess himself a whit inferior to the others by performing the slave's office of washing their feet.

> Be sober, be vigilant; because your
> adversary the devil, as a roaring lion,
> walketh about, seeking whom he
> may devour. (I Peter 5:8)

Peter did not fall for lack of warning. He fell because he paid no heed to the warnings given. More than once our Lord told him in set terms what would happen. But, so far as Peter was concerned, the warnings fell on absolutely deaf ears. He could not claim that the rock on which his barque struck and well-nigh foundered was a sunken and uncharted rock; he sailed straight on to it, though its bells were clashing out their warnings and telling him of danger. The reason for Peter's neglect of these repeated warnings was, I believe, twofold.

First of all, he had complete confidence in his own courage. He was by nature a strong and forceful personality, and he honestly believed he could stand up to any menacing peril without flinching. And, secondly, he was so entirely and completely devoted to Jesus that the very idea of defection and cowardice seemed wildly and absurdly impossible. Peter really meant what he said when he declared that with Jesus he was ready to go both to prison and to death. For his love for Jesus was, in very truth, the master-passion of Peter's life. That a man thus strong in will and so entirely devoted to Jesus as Peter was should fall so shamefully and disastrously as he did lends peculiar point and emphasis to the apostolic exhortation, "Let him that thinketh he standeth take heed lest he fall."

> By what authority doest thou these
> things? and who gave thee this
> authority to do these things?
> (Mark 11:28)

There is no moral authority without character. "As the man is, so is his strength." Office in itself will never confer moral authority. The sons of Eli had office. But they had not character. What was their influence? Nothing; worse than nothing. Because of them men abhorred the offering of the Lord. If we want to wield power for God, we must first of all be ourselves men of God. To do good we must be good. Without character, though we have all official guarantees, we are no better than sounding-brass or a tinkling cymbal.

The ultimate source of authority to teach and preach is God. No man is ordained unless he is ordained of God. Nobody is really "in orders" unless he is placed in them by God. All that men can do is to ratify God's ordaining. No man, called of God, needs human authority to speak for Him. I have no word to say by way of disparagement of human ordination; I have been ordained myself. I have myself been set aside by the laying on of the hands of the presbytery. I believe that ordination tends to orderliness in the Church. And yet I would never forget that the real authority to preach comes from a higher source—it comes from God. And He can and does give it to men on whom no human hands have ever been laid. The Spirit bloweth still where He listeth, and the man dowered with the Spirit is the man ordained of God.

# George H. Morrison
## (1866–1928)

One typically wet Scottish day, I found Wellington Church, Glasgow, telephoned the office, and got permission to go in. It was a high and holy hour when I stood in George Morrison's pulpit, for he has been my "pastor" for many years. His many books of sermons hold a special place in my library, and I read them often.

Morrison worked on the *New English Dictionary* with Sir James Murray before he started his ministerial studies. In his sermons you can detect his love for words and his ability to choose just the right one. He assisted Alexander Whyte for a time and then was pastor of two other churches before going to Wellington Church, where he ministered for twenty-six years.

Now I know in part. . . . (I Cor. 13:12)

You and I know God through the Lord Jesus Christ. All that we know of God from outward nature, and all that we gather from the world's long history, is but the outwork and flanking of that revelation which is ours through the life and death of Jesus. Now tell me, is God less mysterious to us in the light of that revelation of Christ Jesus? 'God without mystery were not good news.' God was a Sovereign once, now He is Father, and there are more mysteries in Fatherhood than in Kingship. God was a God of power once; He is a God of love now; and all the power of all the thunderbolts of Jove are not so mysterious as the slightest spark of love. And God was alone once,

287

or there were many Gods. Now, baffling comprehension, yet most real, we have a vision of Three in One and One in Three. Christ has intensified the mystery of God.

I trust that you see, then, how true it is, that Jesus deepened the mystery of things. And I trust that you begin to understand what the spirit of Christ longs to achieve in you. The Christian view is always the deepest view. The Lord who inspired it saw kingdoms in mustard-seeds. There is more in the world, and in man, and in the Bible, than the nicest calculation can discover, but we only see it through the eyes of Christ.

> Ye blind guides, which strain at a
> gnat, and swallow a camel.
> (Matt. 23:24)

This failure to see things in their true proportions is often seen in relation to our grievances. When a man has a grievance—and many men have them—he is almost certain to have distorted vision. You can block out the sun by the smallest coin if you hold the coin near enough to the eye. And we have a way of dwelling on our grievances, till we lose sight of the blue heaven above us. How ready we are to brood on petty insults! How we take them home with us and nurse and fondle them! How we are stung by trifling neglects! A little discourtesy, and our soul begins to fester! And though hearts are just as warm to us today as they were yesterday, when we responded to them; and though the great tides of the deep love of God rise to their flood, still, on every shore, it is strange how a man will be blind to all the glory, when a little bitterness is rankling within. We are all adepts at counting up our grievances. Open a new column and count your mercies now. It is supremely important to see things in their magnitudes, and perhaps you have never learned that lesson yet. The man who suspects is always judging wrongly. A jealous woman sees everything out of focus. If there be any virtue, if there be any praise, think on these things, says the apostle.

> And they [Peter and the angel] went
> out, and passed on through one
> street; and forthwith the angel
> departed from him. (Acts 12:10)

I wonder if you grasp, then, what I should venture to call the helpful doctrine of the departing angel? I think it is a feature of God's dealing that has been somewhat neglected in our thought. It means that in extraordinary difficulties we may reasonably look for extraordinary help. It means that when we are shut in prison walls, and utterly helpless to extricate ourselves, God has unusual powers in reserve, that He is willing to dispatch to aid His own. But when the clamant need goes, so does the angel. In the open street, under the common sky, do not expect miraculous intervention. It was better for Peter's manhood, and it is better for yours, that only the hour of the dungeon should bring that. The angel departs, but the law of God abides. The angel departs, but the love of Christ remains. And I think that all God's leading of His people, and all the experience of the Christian heart, might be summed up, with not a little gain, in the departing angel and the remaining Lord.

> The slothful man roasteth not that
> which he took in hunting.
> (Prov. 12:27)

It is the picture of a hunter—he is a sportsman, but a lazy fellow. But some fine autumn morning this hunter wakens early. The air is keen; the dogs are baying; the old enthusiasm

289

of the chase stirs in his heart. He will go forth and hunt today,
and his right hand has not lost its cunning. So far all is well.
Laden with bird and beast he gets back to his tent. Then comes
the waste, the sin. The impulse is gone; the morning's glow is
dead—he cannot be troubled cooking what he caught. So
bird and beast lie there, day after day; until for very shame
the hunter casts them out. Unused, they become useless. It is
a case of wasted gains. For all the good he gets from them, he
might as well have stayed at home, and left his bow hanging
upon the wall.

Such is the picture. Now do you see the meaning of it? It
may be, that huntsman is not far away. By toil, by tears, by
sharing in the toil and tears of others, our life is rich in gains.
Trophies have fallen to our bow, and to the bow of the nation
with which we are one, and to the bow of the gospel we
believe; and we have never roasted what we took in hunting.
The gains are wasted; the trophies are unused.

> Grey hairs are here and there upon
> him, yet he knoweth not. (Hosea 7:9)

Some losses reveal themselves at once. There are things
which, lost, leave the heart blank and desolate. We see at a
glance, by the naked gap among the grass, that some tree has
been uprooted there; but many of life's worst losses are not so.
There is loss, but there is no sense of loss. Virtues, ideals,
things bright and strong and beautiful, steal away silently
from us in the dark. . . .

But the great cause of our neglected losses lies in the
gradual and slow method of the loss. There are men whose
hair has whitened in a night. I warrant you they saw that in
the morning. But it is not of that Hosea speaks, when he uses
the happy figure of our text. All that was best had perished
out of Israel. Why was Israel ignorant of that? The loss had
come so slowly, surely, silently, Israel had failed to detect it
when it came. If all the birds ceased singing in the summer,

the dullest city ear would note the silence. If the forest were swept bare by one swift gale, the blindest of us would find cause for wonder. But the music of the woods ceases so gradually, and the trees are stripped so silently and slowly, that winter is with us, songless and desolate, before we have eyes for what is being lost. Some sins carry immediate penalties; their consequences leap into light at once. The moment a man commits them he is ruined. And we know that: perhaps therefore we avoid them. But there is another ruin quite as sure as that, wrought silently through deterioration of the years, and it steals on the spirit of a man so gradually that grey hairs are on him and he knows it not.

My Father worketh hitherto, and I work. (John 5:17)

Christ was supremely certain that His Father was present and working in the world. Above all sorrow and sin, and struggle and failure, Christ felt the pressure of a sovereign power, and the movement of the infinite love of heaven. In the Old Testament men had described God's sovereignty, but it was an awful and tremendous sovereignty. With Jesus it has become a much more gentle attribute; it clothes the grass and sees the sparrow fall. You remember the famous line of Robert Browning, 'God's in His heaven, all's right with the world'? That was one source of the optimism of Browning; but the optimism of Jesus went a great deal deeper. It was the fact that God was in His *earth*, so that the ravens were fed and the lilies were adorned, and so that the very hairs of a man's head are numbered—it was that which gave a radiant quietude to Christ.

Then Jesus believed, with a faith that was magnificent, in the freedom and the worth of personality, and whenever a man comes to believe in that, it is impossible to hold that life is a tragedy.

> For who hath known the mind of
> the Lord? or who hath been his
> counsellor? (Rom. 11:34)

If the gospel of Christ appeals to men and women, and if its appeal has been powerful through the chance and change of time, one secret of its power has been this, that it has dared to give great answers to the great questions of the human heart. It is well to distrust solutions that solve everything. I had a professor in my university who made things so plain that we were all perplexed. There is something lacking in every creed and system that is too ready with universal answers. But the gospel has no easy explanations. It is *good* news, because it is *great* news. It says: 'The questions of the soul are mighty, and I shall furnish them with mighty answers.' You say to it, 'What must I do to be saved?' And does it bid you go and show some little kindnesses? It says, 'Believe on the Lord Jesus Christ, and thou shalt be saved,' and belief is the whole manhood roused to heroism. You say to it, 'What about my sin?' And does it bid you be happy, and do the best you can? It talks of Blood, and shows you a Saviour crucified, and says, 'Though your sin be as scarlet, it shall be white as snow'—and that appeals to the very depths of me. Beware of cheap and easy substitutes for Christ. They will not last, they do not satisfy. Ask those who have gone by the way whether they do. I have a gospel I shall never be ashamed of, for it scorns to give little answers to great questions.

# Hugh Black
## (1868–1953)

Hugh Black was ordained in 1891 and served Sherwood Free Church, Paisley, Scotland, until 1896, when he became associate to Alexander Whyte in Edinburgh. More liberal in theology than Whyte, Hugh Black drew large crowds of eager listeners. It was jokingly said that Whyte blackened the people at one service while Black whitewashed them at the other!

But Black was not to stay in Scotland very long. He accepted a call to teach at Union Seminary, New York, and there he served for nearly fifty years. He felt that his calling was to interpret the gospel in terms that modern man could understand and accept. Black also published many books, including collections of sermons.

Then Lot chose him all the plain of
Jordan . . . and they separated
themselves the one from the other.
(Gen. 13:11)

Lot lost his chance of meeting Abram's generosity with equal generosity. All that Lot possessed had come to him through Abram. He might have said, 'Nay, it is not for me to choose. All I have is thine. Take thy choice and give me what is right.' He would have kept his life from being compassed about with many sorrows, and have saved his old age from shame. But the world had taken possession of his heart. Egypt, which had been to Abram a discipline, had been to Lot a temptation. His imagination there was inflamed by the sight of wealth beyond dream. His soul was taken captive by the desire to be rich; and Lot lifted up his eyes and beheld all the plain of Jordan, that it was well watered everywhere, even as the garden of the Lord, like the land of Egypt.

Worldly advantage was the first element in his choice. He judged according to the world's judgment; he judged by the eye. His heart was allured by the beauty and fertility of the plain, and it seemed only prudence and common sense to prefer that to a barren and scanty living among the hills. From the worldly standpoint he was right. There could be no hesitation to a worldly mind between the two alternatives. On the one side was the promise of wealth, its easy acquisition, and its seeming security of tenure—a well-watered land, rich and fertile. On the other side the gain was limited and hardly-won, and any day another drought could occur and sweep away everything, as before when hunger drove them to Egypt.

> By faith Moses . . . refused. . . .
> (Heb. 11:24)

Faith is the refusal of the small, for the sake of the large. Faith will make no decision, take no step, merely from worldly motives; for it sees past the immediate good to a richer, grander good. Worldly-wisdom is not wisdom; it is folly, the blind grasping at what is within reach. It is folly, for any present good, to cut yourself off from your true life. A good conscience, peace of heart, faith, the vision of God, the hope of glory—it is a fool's bargain (let pot-house moralists prate as they may) to barter these for any mess of pottage. To rake in the dust-heap for scraps of treasure heedless of the golden crown to be had for the looking and the taking—that was Lot's choice, and that is the choice of every soul who seeks *first* the world. Demas thought he was doing a wise thing in leaving Paul when earthly success seemed lost, but this present world, seductive though it was to him, however much it brought him, was a poor, a contemptible exchange for the days and nights with Paul, and the life lived by the Son of God. And his name is an infamy. Lot thought he was doing a wise thing in making the choice he did, but a share in the wealth of Sodom was a pitiful substitute for a place in Abram's company, and a share in Abram's thoughts and faith. And the end was a ruined home, a desolate life, and a broken heart.

Which is the wiser choice? Paul and a Roman prison and Jesus Christ—or Demas and the present world and an apostate's mind? Abram and the barren hillside and God—or Lot and the cities of the plain and Sodom's shame?

> Thy statutes have been my songs in
> the house of my pilgrimage.
> (Ps. 119:54)

Statutes need to be turned into songs before their work can be completed. The note is struck in the very first Psalm, which speaks of the blessedness of loving the Law and the curse of hating it. The Psalter is the blossom of the Law, preparing for its perfect fruit in obedient and joyful hearts. When the law of God is turned into songs in this the house of our pilgrimage, it has reached its destined end. Thus this verse is really typical of the whole Psalter. Our text, then, is spiritually set in the very center of the Psalter, and in the very center of the Old Testament. The law is really obeyed, when it is no longer mere rule and precept, and no longer something to be feared as when it flashed out its solemn warnings from Sinai, but when it becomes a delight, as music to the soul, changed into inner harmony, when it is a flooding passion of love for the Law of God, when the statutes are turned into songs in the house of man's pilgrimage. It ceases to be law in the rigid legal sense, and becomes perfect freedom.

And at midnight Paul and Silas
prayed, and sang praises unto God.
(Acts 16:25)

What can turn the statutes into songs, take the sting out of
the commandments, make the will of God a delight? When it
is all transfigured by the glory of love. Love inspires obedience to law, and makes it easy. If we see law not as something
external, an obligation imposed on us from without, a despot-
ism against which we cannot rebel, and to which we can only
sullenly submit; if we see law as the law of our own life, the
fruit of the tenderest and highest love, the commandments
are seen not to be grievous, and obedience becomes sweet
and natural. We know the difference between obedience
dictated by fear and obedience dictated by love. When we are
brought into a personal relation to God and enter into fellowship with Him, we realise that even in the making of our own
moral life, in the creating of our own character, we are fellow-
workers with God. We desire the same end as He does, and it
is the best end.

The love of Christ is the great instrument of sanctification;
for it breeds in us a passion to do God's will and keep His
commandments. 'Ye are complete in Him,' says St. Paul. He
fills out our incompleteness, and for the first time we feel that
we are truly ourselves, and for the first time really possess our
souls, and are in harmony with the great end of our existence.
When our heart is enlarged we can run in the way of God's
commandments. Life breaks out into music and light.

Wisdom is before him that hath
understanding; but the eyes of a fool
are in the ends of the earth.
(Prov. 17:24)

We all know something of the attraction of distance, the
romance of the unknown; and we are inclined to minimise

296

present opportunities by dreaming about some larger sphere where we would do great things. Not here, but somewhere in the ends of the earth, is the occasion we need to draw out our unsuspected powers. The first duty is the duty near at hand; but that is too small for the fool whose eyes are in the ends of the earth. The distant, the far-away affects imagination easily; it can soar and fly without breaking wings against hard facts. Some think that it is because they are of superior nature, of a finer texture of imagination, that they take no interest in the life around them, but divert themselves with vain dreams, building castles in the air, turning ever towards the ends of the earth for their high thoughts and noble aspirations. But really, such an imagination is of the commonest and lowest type. It is lack of imagination to be unable to enter with insight and sympathy into the common life around, to see only the commonplace in what is common, to see none of the romance and pathos and heroism of lowly life. Even from the point of view of art that is the triumph of imagination, to throw a glory round the usual and interpret the common in loving sympathy. Any one can imagine thrilling adventures in China or Peru or in the islands of the sea, but few can show us the treasures of heart and soul in the common life ungilded by the halo of romance. Truly wisdom is before the face of him that hath understanding, but the eyes of a fool are in the ends of the earth.

He that is not against us is for us.
(Mark 9:40)

When we think of the *tolerance of God* with all of us, His patience, His longsuffering with our slowness of heart, His wide, rich mercy, His free gospel of grace, how miserable are the petty barriers and limits which we set up, how sinful is our arrogance with which we unchurch and excommunicate all who do not see eye to eye with us, and follow not *us!*

It is the mark of spiritual insight to be able to recognise

goodness everywhere, and assert kinship with it, to feel in sympathy with it, to accept it, and thank God for it, to claim fellowship with every good man, to share in every good work, however unauthorised by man, if only it have the stamp of God's approval. Also, it is the highest triumph of grace in us to be willing even to be set aside, to see others do the work our own hands long to do, to be willing to be superseded, to rejoice in every victory of the Cross through others, to stand aside and praise God for every evidence of His power and mercy to the world through other channels than our own, to tear away all pride and prejudice and receive as brethren all who love the Lord Jesus in sincerity, to comfort ourselves with the inspiring thought that He has so many instruments beyond our narrow circle, to find peace and joy in believing that he who is not against us is for us.

> If thou hast run with the footmen,
> and they have wearied thee, then
> how canst thou contend with
> horses? and if in the land of peace,
> wherein thou trustedst, they
> wearied thee, then how wilt thou do
> in the swelling of Jordan? (Jer. 12:5)

Does it seem an unfeeling answer? It was the answer Jeremiah needed. He needed to be braced, not pampered. He is taught the need of endurance. It is a strange cure for cowardice, a strange remedy for weakness; yet it is effective. It gives stiffening to the soul. The tear-stained face is lifted up calm once more. A new resolution creeps into the eye to prove worthy of the new responsibility. God appeals to the strength in Jeremiah, not to the weakness. By God's grace I will fight, and fighting fall if need be. By God's grace I will contend even with horses; and I will go to the pride of Jordan though the jungle growl and snarl. This was the result on Jeremiah, and it was the result required. Only a heroic soul could do the heroic work needed by Israel and by God, and it was the greatest heroism of all which was needed, the *heroism of endurance.*

Nothing worth doing can be done in this world without something of that iron resolution. It is the spirit which never knows defeat, which cannot be worn out, which has taken its stand and refuses to move. This is the 'patience' about which the Bible is full, not the sickly counterfeit which so often passes for patience, but the power to bear, to suffer, to sacrifice, to endure all things, to die, harder still sometimes to continue to live. The whole world teaches that patience. Life in her struggle with nature is lavish of our resources. She is willing to sacrifice anything for the bare maintenance of existence meanwhile. Inch by inch each advance has to be gained, fought for, paid for, kept. It is the lesson of all history also, both for the individual and for a body of men who have espoused any cause.

# Frank W. Boreham

## (1871?–1959)

"Tell his mother to put a pen in his hand and he'll never want for a living." Those words from a gypsy woman to Frank Boreham's nurse proved prophetic. Not only did he become a prolific writer with more than fifty books to his credit, but he also became a successful pastor and lecturer whose world-wide ministry encouraged many.

Boreham fans (and there are many of them) like to debate the merits of his various books of essays. I prefer the essays about his pastoral experiences in New Zealand, Tasmania, and Australia. But I also enjoy his sermons, especially the series about "Texts That Made History." His autobiography, *My Pilgrimage,* is delightful.

Blessed are they that mourn: for
they shall be comforted. (Matt. 5:4)

*Blessed are they that mourn!* the Saviour says; and I think that I begin to understand him. "Blessed are those who *feel!*" he seems to say. The tendency is to become insensitive. We get used to things. Our susceptibilities become seared. The doctor, who nearly fainted at his first operation, learns in time to look upon pain without emotion. The minister is so much among the sorrowing and the bereaved that he is in peril of regarding the tears of the mourner with professional non-chalance. He takes them for granted. It is not easy under such conditions to keep the spirit fresh and the heart tender. *Blessed are they that mourn!* Mourning implies a soft, copious, heartfelt grief—a grief that has broken all restraint and finds relief in welcome floods of tears. There is all the difference in the world between a keen, cutting wind with just a dash of rain in it, and a warm tropical shower. There is just the same difference between the stiff and formal expression of our sympathy and the deep and heartfelt sorrow that is the earnest and surety of real blessedness.

Unless we are constantly on our guard against it, we are all in danger of being drawn into the horrible vortex of insensibility.

> Blessed are the meek: for they shall
> inherit the earth. (Matt. 5:5)

It is absurd to deplore the possession of a fiery temper. The temper of Moses was, to the end of his days, one of the secrets of his strength. Aaron and the idolaters trembled when, in a fit of holy wrath, Moses broke the two tables in pieces at the foot of the mount. And, turning from the Old Testament model to the New, we have a vision of Jesus, the meekest of all, who, in his righteous indignation, overthrew the tables of the money changers and the seats of them that sold doves, and, with a scourge of small cords, drove the cattle from the temple precincts. It is a fine thing to own a dog, provided he does not seize your brother's throat and lick the burglar's hand; it is a good thing to possess a spirited horse, so long as it remains your own prerogative to determine the place and the pace of each journey; it is a good thing to own a gun, so long as it is entirely subject to the cunning of your hand; and, similarly, it is a good thing to possess a temper that feels deeply and acutely and keenly, provided that you have it in complete subjection. The very word "meekness," one authority assures me, is the word used by the Greeks to describe a colt which had been broken in and harnessed. It was once careering wildly over the waste: but now it is disciplined for service. Its strength is not reduced; but its real value has been developed.

301

The souls that, through the ages, have been the deliverers of Israel, have been the meekest of men—calm men, sensitive men, strong men—not doves, but eagles; not timid hares, but lions with eyes of fire and all their mighty forces under magnificent control.

Blessed are the pure in heart: for they shall see God. (Matt. 5:8)

Two stupendous principles underlie this searching utterance. The *first* is that heart-purity is the essential condition to the reception of a divine revelation. God can reveal himself more readily to the pure in heart than to the mighty in intellect. The testimony of a little child who has learned to love God is, in spiritual matters, more to be trusted than the witness of gray-haired sages whose hearts are alienated from him. It is the pure-hearted Samuel who, while Eli slumbers, hears the voice divine. *"With the pure thou wilt show thyself pure." "The pure in heart shall see God."*

The *second* is that, in the spiritual life, there is a law of action and reaction constantly at work. Those who are pure in heart see God; the vision of the Eternal intensifies the purity of their hearts; and this again increases their desire and their capacity for fresh revelations. When a leak occurs in the famous dykes of Holland, the water rushes through the cavity with such tremendous force that it tears the opening larger and larger. The enlarging vacuum makes room for a greater rush of water, while the growing volume of water constantly expands the vacuum. The two processes act and react one upon the other. The leaves of the tree inhale vitality from the atmosphere, and thus minister to the life of the remotest roots. Simultaneously, the invigorated roots suck up the nutriment from the earth and communicate strength to the loftiest boughs. There is constant action and reaction. Every vision of God increases a Christian's hatred of sin and intensifies his struggle after holiness; while at every inch of progress in that divine path he gets a more radiant vision of the face of God.

This law of reaction proceeds unbroken until time melts into eternity. The pure in heart become purer and yet purer as the revelations of the divine become clearer and yet clearer, till at last, pure as God is pure, they stand in his insufferable presence and behold with seraphic rapture the beauty of his face. The blurred gaze of the impure, on the contrary, deepens into total blindness until, destitute of all moral perception and spiritual vision, they stagger tragically out into the everlasting dark.

Behold, thou desirest truth in the
inward parts. . . . (Ps. 51:6)

The heart is the throne; and on the throne Purity must reign supreme. The will—so difficult to control—must yield unreserved allegiance to Purity's beneficent rule. The imagination—so hard to confine—must no longer deck the mind with its seductive pictures; it must bow to the lofty beauty of unsullied purity. The thoughts must be brought into absolute dominion; every purpose and intent must recognize the regal sway. Purity must reign in unquestioned authority.

All this may take time. The revolutionary and reactionary elements among my members cannot be subdued and subjugated in a single day. The flesh is mighty and does not readily capitulate; the fancy, accustomed to unfettered freedom, does not easily abandon its hectic flights. But there is all the difference in the world between that state of things in which the heart condones and secretly enjoys this waywardness and that state of things in which the heart forbids and deplores it.

> Blessed are the peacemakers: for
> they shall be called the children of
> God. (Matt. 5:9)

The world will see in the peacemaker a softened, hallowed mirroring of the divine glory. "He gives offense to none, even when fiercely provoked," men will say; "he takes offense from none, even when directly insulted; he seeks to heal all wounded hearts about him. This is godlike; it is divine! He must be none other than a son of God!" The world will see the august descent of the peacemaker in the beautiful and tranquil sublimity of his spirit.

In such an one the world recognizes a striking likeness to *the* Son of God. "We saw a Peacemaker once before," the world will say. "We remember him as One who went about, not merely saying, 'Peace be to this house!' but actually conferring peace on every home he entered; we remember him as One who, living, said: *'My peace I give unto you!'* and, dying, bequeathed that peace to his disciples as a priceless legacy; we remember him as One whose advent into the world was heralded with angel songs of peace on earth and of good will toward men, and whose death was undertaken that he might make peace by the blood of his cross. Remembering *him*, we feel that this new peacemaker of our acquaintance must be related to him; he has the same nature, the same griefs, the same delights, the same characteristics; he must be, like him, a son of God." This is the blessedness of the peacemaker. He has no need to tell men that he is a Christian. They tell him, what he himself sometimes doubts, that he is directly related to the Prince of Peace. They take knowledge of him that he has been with Jesus. *"Blessed are the peacemakers: for they shall be called the sons of God."*

Blessed are they which are persecuted for righteousness' sake: for
theirs is the kingdom of heaven.
(Matt. 5:10)

Indeed, he had his whole Church in mind—the Church of all times and of all climes. For the eighth beatitude includes us all. It would be a thousand pities to confine its scope to those heroes of the faith whose names are writ large in Master Foxe's famous volume.

Every Christian worth his salt has suffered persecution. I like to think that, fearful lest some of us should feel ourselves excluded from this final blessing, the Master went out of his way to amplify its scope and define its terms. "Blessed are *ye*," he added, dividing persecution into *three* distinct classifications, "blessed are ye when men shall revile you, persecute you, and say all manner of evil against you falsely for my sake." Paul adheres to the same threefold division in writing to the Corinthians: "Being *reviled*, we bless; being *persecuted*, we suffer it; being *defamed* we entreat." One or other of these words leads every true Christian who ever lived into the felicity of the last beatitude. At some time or other he has probably been actually *persecuted*. He has been harassed, annoyed, tormented, involved in some severe penalty or subjected to some disability for his Saviour's sake. Or he has been *reviled*—affronted to his face; openly snubbed, insulted, or jeered at. Or at least he has been *defamed*. Behind his back men have said all manner of evil against him, falsely.

Blessed are ye, when men shall
revile you, and persecute you, and
shall say all manner of evil against
you falsely, for my sake. (Matt. 5:11)

The persecuted are blessed by reason of the factors that led to their persecution. They have been permitted to see truth to which other eyes were blind. They have been like those snow-capped summits that, because of their altitude and purity, are first to catch the crimson flush of dawn. It is one of the striking facts of history that, wherever men have sought sincerely after truth, the truth has been revealed to them. And, having found the pearl for which they sought, they have paid the price with a smile. In the secrecy of their souls they have heard voices which seemed to convey to them the congratulations of highest heaven. *"Blessed,"* exclaimed those voices, *"blessed are the eyes which see the things that ye see; for I tell you that many prophets and kings have desired to see those things which ye see, and have not seen them; and to hear those things which ye hear, and have not heard them."* Every martyr, ancient and modern, has rejoiced in the truth that led him to suffer, and would ten thousand times rather possess that truth and die in torture, than live, either never having seen it, or having seen and betrayed it. In view of the wealth of the spiritual treasury which has been entrusted to him, he smiles at the stake, hurls defiance at death, and greets the unseen with a cheer.

He feels too a thrill of exultation at the thought of the company he keeps. His sufferings identify him with an exalted and triumphant brotherhood. *"If,"* said the Master, under the shadow of the cross, *"if ye were of the world, the world would love its own, but because ye are not of the world, therefore the world hateth you. If they have persecuted me, they will also persecute you."* The man who goes without the camp bearing the reproach of the cross, shares the fellowship of his Saviour's sufferings and experiences the joy of identification with him. Persecution is the world's testimony to the Church's purity. A wolf will not worry a painted sheep; a cat will not seize a toy mouse. The world may despise, but it will not persecute, a counterfeit Christian; it may scorn, but it will not burn, a hypocrite. Crucifixion is the evidence of Christliness.

# Arthur John Gossip
## (1873–1954)

What a full and varied ministry A. J. Gossip had! During his long life he was pastor of four churches, ministered as an army chaplain, and taught practical theology at Trinity College, Glasgow. He wrote several books of sermons and gave the Warrack lectures on preaching which were published in 1925 as *In Christ's Stead.*

Gossip's best-known sermon was titled "But When Life Tumbles In, What Then?" He preached it shortly after the sudden death of his beloved wife. It throbs with the assurances of a man who has been through the deep waters and has felt the solid rock beneath.

> But many of the priests and Levites
> and chief of the fathers, who were
> ancient men, . . . wept with a loud
> voice; and many shouted aloud for
> joy. (Ezra 3:12)

I don't think these weeping folk helped very much. The mood was natural enough, perhaps, but certainly not overmanly and little likely to do anything except dishearten those around them. And a mind that is perpetually looking back, and talking scornfully of all things present as a sad decadence, that is gloomy and pessimistic, that knows the reins have broken in God's hands, and that all things are hurtling hideously down to ruin, that keeps clutching the seat nervously, ready to jump when the disaster it is always forseeing

307

comes—well, it's a rather miserable role to fill, and surely not a little blasphemous.

But what about you who are young? Ah, well, you can be trying and exasperating too. That airy assumption of yours that all who went before you were incompetent bunglers, that you are the people and wisdom will die with you, or at least that suddenly the slow, dour thing has blossomed into full flower in your day, is less than just by far to that innumerable company of valiant souls who, with hard breathing, toil and pain and sheer dare-devil heroism, won for you with their bare hands nearly all you have inherited. Look again at your possessions, at the simplest of them; and, like David, with that water from the well at Bethlehem which valiant men had risked their lives to bring, you too will feel, in an awed and even ashamed way, that these are vastly too valuable, have cost far too much, to make it seemly you should use them as if they were common nothings; will make you want rather to pour them out before God, who alone is worthy to receive them—these things how wonderful when you look at them closer, for has it not taken human blood and brains and lives to win each one of them? Don't forget that.

> Any one who does not take up his
> cross and follow where I lead is not
> worthy of Me.
> (Matt. 10:38, *Weymouth*)

Look at the Cross, if you would measure sin aright, your little daily trespasses and falls; look at its cost to God; look at the man Christ Jesus on the tree, and take it in. That is the perfect picture of how God always is affected by it, every time so hurt, so wounded, so heartbroken! So will you grasp its hideousness and horror, and be filled with loathing for this awful thing. Our one chance, Newman thought, is that we be shocked by sin. Look upon Him whom we have pierced, and surely that must shock us, till we hate what caused Him that, fly from it, find a new power surging up within us that gives the strength to cast it forth, and make an end of it.

Or take the biggest thing in the whole universe, the deepest, the most inexhaustible, God's love. How busy we have been all down the ages with our wretched little foot-rules upon that, complacently meauring the immeasurable, marking it off— this is its length, and this its breadth—fixing the bounds and limits of this illimitable thing, setting up barriers which we declare it never passes, and marks which we say with assurance it can never overflow, declaring confidently this and that it cannot overlook, and that and this it never does, judging of God, in short, by our own petulant, foolish, sullen, earthly human hearts!

> If thou hast run with the footmen,
> and they have wearied thee, then
> how canst thou contend with
> horses? and if in the land of peace,
> wherein thou trustedst, they
> wearied thee, then how wilt thou do
> in the swelling of Jordan? (Jer. 12:5)

But then so many people's religion is a fair-weather affair. A little rain, and it runs and crumbles; a touch of strain, and it snaps. How often out at the front one lay and watched an airplane high up in the blue and sunlight, a shimmering, glistening, beautiful thing: and then there came one shot out of a cloud, and it crashed down to earth, a broken mass of twisted metal. And many a one's religion is like that. So long as God's will runs parallel to ours, we follow blithely. But the moment that they cross, or clash, that life grows difficult, that we don't understand, how apt faith is to fail us just when we have most need of it!

You remember our Lord's story of the two men who lived in the same village, and went to the same synagogue, and sat in the same pew, listening to the same services: and how one day some kind of gale blew into their lives, a fearsome storm. And in the one case, everything collapsed, and for a moment there were some poor spars tossing upon wild waters, and then, nothing at all. For that unhappy soul had built on sand, and in his day of need, everything was undermined, and vanished. But the other, though he too had to face the emptiness, the loneliness, the pain, came through it all braver and stronger and mellower and nearer God. For he had built upon the rock. Well, what of you and me? We have found it a business to march with the infantry, how will we keep up with the horsemen: if the small ills of life have frayed our faith and temper, what will we do in the roar and the black swirl of Jordan?

> For I say unto you, That except your righteousness shall exceed the righteousness of the scribes and Pharisees, ye shall in no case enter into the kingdom of heaven.
> (Matt. 5:20)

The truth is, says Christ, that what is wrong is that you are all using far too low a standard, with the result that you are much too quickly satisfied. It is not nearly enough to be just; though even that, God knows, is hard to practice; or to claim no more than your bare dues; or to pay your fellows their full rights; or to deal with men as they deserve. All that is far less than your bounden duty. When you use such things as your scale of measurement you are taking custom, or the conventions, or other people round about, or at the best the worthiest of them, as your index of how you ought to live and what you ought to be. And none of these will do. For your standard is God. For you to live deliberately on a lower moral plane than God is failure. And look yonder! There is an open sinner; yet you see the sunshine does not skip his fields! And there a scandalously immoral man; yet on his croft the rains fall just

310

as healingly as upon any other. And you too in God's generous way must blot out enmity however well deserved as men judge things, and must forget ingratitude, and must meet rank unworthiness and worse with a queer stubborn love that keeps on obstinately loving in despite of everything. So only shall you prove yourselves the children of that Father who, whatever you have done, still unaccountably persists in loving you.


Come unto me, all ye that labour
and are heavy laden, and I will give
you rest. (Matt. 11:28)

**W**ho are the happiest people that you meet? The man who thinks of no one but himself, and whose narrow horizons are bounded by his own selfish interests? Certainly not. But mothers living for their children—listen how they sing about the house. And men spending themselves for some great cause; and youths and maidens so full of the other that they have never a thought to spare for self. And, above all, those to whom to live is Christ.

The Lord God fashioned us for mighty ends, and nothing less than following that for which He made us can heal our restlessness of heart. He called us, says Paul, He called you and me "to be partners with His Son Jesus Christ" in His amazing enterprise. And, made for that, do you imagine we can be content with pottering at these shabby little nothings with which people seek to fill their days? For a time it may seem to satisfy, but not for long. No, not the cleanest and most beautiful that this life has to offer. Did not even Ruskin cry out in a sobbing anguish, "Oh, why did no one tell me that the colors would fade, and that the glory of the earth would vanish; and that the soul asks and must have something bigger and better and more splendid than this earth can give it?" You may be long in realizing that. But if so, one day you must stand with life all spent, and all for which you paid it faded and gone out, and you, poor dupe, left empty-handed, hungry-hearted, fooled! Why should we hesitate to close with Christ? It is so glorious a chance He offers us.

> And this word, Yet once more, signi-
> fieth the removing of those things
> that are shaken, as of things that are
> made, that those things which
> cannot be shaken may remain.
> (Heb. 12:27)

God will not allow us to settle down with any second best, however splendid; He keeps breaking in on us, disturbing and upsetting us, much to our own chagrin. Each time that we drop anchor in some snug haven out of the wind, and straighten our stiff backs, and stretch ourselves luxuriously, meaning henceforth to take our ease, He calls to us imperatively, bidding us hoist sails at once and make for the wild tossing of the open seas again. And it is slowly and grudgingly we lift our anchors and very wistfully that we stare at the fading shores, yet we must go. We knock together a scheme of things we think will do, and propose to rest satisfied with that, and not bother ourselves about such matters any further; and He thrusts upon us some new fact that makes the whole thing, even to our prejudiced eyes, quite out of date and hopelessly inadequate, and we perforce must start anew. We run up a mode of life that is well enough, we say, and He flashes before us a vision of what it might be that makes us flush and hurriedly bury out of sight that poor thing grown impossible now, and build again more boldly and on a far ampler plan. We know Christ as well as we want to do, have taken from Him as much as we wish, and God so orders things that one day we come on Him face to face; and with that we must rise and follow Him into far lands we never thought to travel. Our ambition is to live a dull, tame, uneventful life, pottering to and fro at little nothings,

"In a sleepy land where under the same wheel
The same old rut is deepened year by year."

But He won't let us be, keeps crying to us, "Up! Up! Rise, ye, and depart, for this is not your rest"; is urgent and insistent with us; brutally rough, we sometimes whimper, rubbing ruefully at the shoulder He has shaken till we opened drowsy eyes, and grumbled slowly to our heavy feet. At all events He won't take a refusal, but forces us to go; and, if we try to tarry, there and then shakes down about our ears the comfortable resting-places where we meant to loll and take our ease.

# Oswald Chambers
## (1874–1917)

When I first began to use *My Utmost for His Highest,* I could get nothing out of it. I confessed this to a friend, and she advised, "Lay it aside and give yourself time to grow." I did—and the book began to speak to me. It still does.

Chambers was a Scot; his father was converted under Spurgeon and became a Baptist minister. Chambers began his career studying art in London and Edinburgh, and his aesthetic sensitivity shows in his books. He felt a call to ministry and attended Dunoon College. During his formative years, he learned to walk by faith and to depend on the inner power of the Spirit.

Chambers was principal of the Bible Training College in London (1911–1915). He traveled widely, sharing his message of surrender and power. His last ministry was as director of a YMCA in Egypt, where he ministered effectively to the troops stationed there.

Come up hither, and I will shew thee
things. . . . (Rev. 4:1)

**A**n elevated mood can only come out of an elevated habit of personal character. If in the externals of your life you live up to the highest you know, God will continually say—"Friend, go up higher." The golden rule in temptation is—Go higher. When you get higher up, you face other temptations and characteristics. Satan uses the strategy of elevation in temptation, and God does the same, but the effect is different.

When the devil puts you into an elevated place, he makes you screw your idea of holiness beyond what flesh and blood could ever bear, it is a spiritual acrobatic performance, you are just poised and dare not move; but when God elevates you by His grace into the heavenly places, instead of finding a pinnacle to cling to, you find a great table-land where it is easy to move.

> I have to lead my life in faith,
> without seeing Him. . . .
> (II Cor. 5:7, *Moffatt*)

A gilt-edged saint is no good, he is abnormal, unfit for daily life, and altogether unlike God. We are here as men and women, not as half-fledged angels, to do the work of the world, and to do it with an infinitely greater power to stand the turmoil because we have been born from above.

If we try to re-introduce the rare moments of inspiration, it is a sign that it is not God we want. We are making a fetish of the moments when God did come and speak, and insisting that He must do it again; whereas what God wants us to do is to "walk by faith." How many of us have laid ourselves by, as it were, and said—"I cannot do any more until God appears to me." He never will, and without any inspiration, without any sudden touch of God, we will have to get up. Then comes the surprise—"Why, He was there all the time, and I never knew it!" Never live for the rare moments, they are surprises. God will give us touches of inspiration when He sees we are not in danger of being led away by them. We must never make our moments of inspiration our standard; our standard is our duty.

Where there is no vision, the people
cast off restraint. (Prov. 29:18)

There is a difference between an ideal and a vision. An ideal has no moral inspiration; a vision has. The people who give themselves over to ideals rarely *do* anything. A man's conception of Deity may be used to justify his deliberate neglect of his duty. Jonah argued that because God was a God of justice and of mercy, therefore everything would be all right. I may have a right conception of God, and that may be the very reason why I do not do my duty. But wherever there is vision, there is also a life of rectitude because the vision imparts moral incentive.

Ideals may lull to ruin. Take stock of yourself spiritually and see whether you have ideals only or if you have vision.

That the life also of Jesus might be
made manifest in our mortal flesh.
(II Cor. 4:10)

We have to form habits to express what God's grace has done in us. It is not a question of being saved from hell, but of being saved in order to manifest the life of the Son of God in our mortal flesh, and it is the disagreeable things which make us exhibit whether or not we are manifesting His life. Do I manifest the essential sweetness of the Son of God, or the essential irritation of "myself" apart from Him? The only thing that will enable me to enjoy the disagreeable is the keen enthusiasm of letting the life of the Son of God manifest itself in me. No matter how disagreeable a thing may be, say— "Lord, I am delighted to obey Thee in this matter," and instantly the Son of God will press to the front, and there will be manifested in my human life that which glorifies Jesus.

Behold the fowls of the air. . . .
Consider the lilies of the field.
(Matt. 6:26, 28)

Consider the lilies of the field, how they grow, they simply are! Think of the sea, the air, the sun, the stars and the moon— all these are, and what a ministration they exert. So often we mar God's designed influence through us by our self-conscious effort to be consistent and useful. Jesus says that there is only one way to develop spiritually, and that is by concentration on God. "Do not bother about being of use to others; believe on Me"—pay attention to the Source, and out of you will flow rivers of living water. We cannot get at the springs of our natural life by common sense, and Jesus is teaching that growth in spiritual life does not depend on our watching it, but on concentration on our Father in heaven. Our heavenly Father knows the circumstances we are in, and if we keep concentrated on Him we will grow spiritually as the lilies.

The people who influence us most are not those who buttonhole us and talk to us, but those who live their lives like the stars in heaven and the lilies in the field, perfectly simply and unaffectedly. Those are the lives that mould us.

If you want to be of use to God, get rightly related to Jesus Christ and He will make you of use unconsciously every minute you live.

. . . partakers of the divine
nature. . . . (II Peter 1:4)

What does it matter if external circumstances are hard? Why should they not be! If we give way to self-pity and indulge in the luxury of misery, we banish God's riches from our own lives and hinder others from entering into His provision. No sin is worse than the sin of self-pity, because it obliterates God and puts self-interest upon the throne. It opens our mouths to spit out murmurings and our lives become craving spiritual sponges, there is nothing lovely or generous about them.

When God is beginning to be satisfied with us He will impoverish everything in the nature of fictitious wealth, until we learn that all our fresh springs are in Him. If the majesty and grace and power of God are not being manifested in us (not to our consciousness), God holds us responsible. "God is able to make all grace abound," then learn to lavish the grace of God on others. Be stamped with God's nature, and His blessing will come through you all the time.

Notwithstanding in this rejoice
not, . . . but rather rejoice because
your names are written in heaven.
(Luke 10:20)

Jesus Christ says, in effect, Don't rejoice in successful service but rejoice because you are rightly related to Me. The snare in Christian work is to rejoice in successful service, to rejoice in the fact that God has used you. You never can measure what God will do through you if you are rightly related to Jesus Christ. Keep your relationship right with Him, then whatever circumstances you are in, and whoever you meet day by day, He is pouring rivers of living water through you, and it is of His mercy that He does not let you know it. When once you are rightly related to God by salvation and sanctification, remember that wherever you are, you are put there by God; and by the reaction of your life on the circumstances around you, you will fulfil God's purpose, as long as you keep in the light as God is in the light.

The tendency today is to put the emphasis on service. Beware of the people who make usefulness their ground of appeal. If you make usefulness the test, then Jesus Christ was the greatest failure that ever lived. The lodestar of the saint is God Himself, not estimated usefulness. It is the work that God does through us that counts, not what we do for Him. All that Our Lord heeds in a man's life is the relationship of worth to His Father. Jesus is bringing many *sons* to glory.

Come ye after me. . . . (Mark 1:17)

One of the greatest hindrances in coming to Jesus is the excuse of temperament. We make our temperament and our natural affinities barriers to coming to Jesus. The first thing we realize when we come to Jesus is that He pays no attention whatever to our natural affinities. We have the notion that we can consecrate our gifts to God. You cannot consecrate what is not yours; there is only one thing you can consecrate to God, and that is your right to yourself (Romans 12:1). If you will give God your right to yourself, He will make a holy experiment out of you. God's experiments always succeed. The one mark of a saint is the moral originality which springs from abandonment to Jesus Christ. In the life of a saint there is this amazing wellspring of original life all the time; the Spirit of God is a well of water springing up, perennially fresh. The saint realizes that it is God Who engineers circumstances, consequently there is no whine, but a reckless abandon to Jesus. Never make a principle out of your experience; let God be as original with other people as He is with you.

# J. Stuart Holden

## (1874–1934)

J. Stuart Holden belonged to that exciting fellowship of Anglican divines that experienced and preached the "deeper life" message that centered around the British Keswick convention. He was pastor of St. Paul's, Portman Square, London, a church also associated with his friend and fellow Keswick speaker, W. H. Griffith Thomas.

If Holden had been a member of the Roman Catholic communion, he would have been termed a "spiritual director," because he had a gift for diagnosing spiritual needs and prescribing the right remedies. Holden's preaching was popular, not heavily doctrinal, but always saturated with Christ and the gospel.

He that observeth the wind shall not
sow; and he that regardeth the
clouds shall not reap. (Eccles. 11:4)

There are deterrent influences which ceaselessly play upon Christian life to baffle and thwart its pledged purposes. Unfavourable winds and unseasonable clouds are apt to induce the thought that such unpropitious conditions call for prudence and justify cessation of field-service. How full of rebuke and how searchingly final is the prophet's comment: "He that observeth the wind shall not sow, and he that regardeth the clouds shall not reap." And this trite maxim, a summary of the imperative law of all husbandry, is not just a bit of mere moralizing. It is a positively protective counsel. For a farmer who knows his business does not wait until an ideal day encourages his sowing. Of course he cannot afford to. The proper season is at hand; he sows his seed; and trusts the disintegrating and reintegrating forces of Nature to keep that which he commits to them against the coming autumn. Deterrent prudence would simply be costly faithlessness. Indeed where God and man are in co-operation it always is. The fact is, every farmer is either a man of faith or a dead failure. So, too, our supreme life-duty must be carried on just as whole-heartedly, with just the same faith and courage, when conditions seem unpromising as when prospects flatter. If we wait for ideally favourable weather for the sowing of the good seed, for the investment of our lives in the field of human need and Divine fidelity, we shall die waiting.

My soul is continually in my hand.
(Ps. 119:109)

See how entirely unanswerable is the logic of those demands which the New Testament makes upon us. It lays foundations, and then says "Build!" It declares truth, and then says "Act!" It unveils fountains, and then says "Drink, and be renewed!" It reveals a pathway, and then says "Walk!" It discloses an enemy's dispositions, and then says "Fight!" It says "You have been transplanted; now grow!" In short, it couples the Divine and the human in indispensable association. It proclaims what God has done and is ever doing for His children, and then it lays down what they, in consequence, must also do. It makes known what He is, and then announces what they must become—and why. It unveils the faith of God, and then indicates what must be the responsive and active quality of their faith. It publishes the fact that "it is He that hath made us," and then it goes on to insist that we fashion ourselves. Its unqualified assurances lift us to the very heavens. And then its inescapable imperatives bring us back to earth, to work out here the implicates of our belief and the obligations of our moral and spiritual insights into the concrete realities of Christian character.

> For it is God which worketh in you
> both to will and to do of his good
> pleasure. (Phil. 2:13)

For, in the truest sense of that frequently misused term, every Christian believer is a self-made man. That description is, I know, usually applied to a man who has made a fortune and has in many cases been so busy over the making of it that he has never thought of making himself. He has made money but has all the time been letting his money make him or rather unmake him. Most often when so applied it points to an example which is a terrible warning. But in an entirely different sense from its common misuse in this connection the Christian believer is a self-made man. He chooses his Model because he is aware that his Model has first chosen him. And he humbly, resolutely and prayerfully determines the degree of fidelity with which he pursues its living lineaments. His soul is continually in his hand. Which is not to say that he is always thinking of his soul. That would be quite as injurious, and quite as complete a denial of his Christian faith, as always to be thinking of his body. No! His hand has to work at the tasks it finds to do, tasks that often seem to have no relation whatever to his spiritual aims and hopes, tasks that in themselves may be altogether uncongenial and yield not the slightest satisfaction beyond their economic value—or rather recompense, tasks that promise nothing beyond the inexorable necessity of their own endless repetition. For such are many of the tasks of modern industry. Yet all the time, while engaged upon them, the Christian man is actually fashioning himself. From this supreme task, in which all others are embraced, which is in point of fact carried out through them, he has no discharge.

> For we are his workmanship,
> created in Christ Jesus unto good
> works, which God hath before
> ordained that we should walk in
> them. (Eph. 2:10)

The old Puritan writer who defined Salvation as "the life of God in the soul of man" was entirely right. Only do not fail to bear in mind that the man in whom He dwells is not himself passive. In the nature of the case he cannot be. For indolent inactivity, even in the name of orthodox belief, can never hold fellowship with essential energy—which is what God is.

Yes! There are Hands unseen working with our hands. There is a Will omnipotent energizing our wills. There is a Wisdom ineffable informing our minds. There is a Patience untiring steadying our impulses. There is a Strength untold directing our members. There is a Divine Craftsman repeating Himself in us. And all in such a manner that our individuality is not thereby destroyed but developed. We are ourselves workers together with Him, pledged to do our part, though always aware that without Him we can do nothing, and always sure that "if there be any virtue, and if there be any praise," it belongs to Him alone. For the final explanation of life is that deep and yet how simple statement that "We are His workmanship, created in Christ Jesus unto good works."

> But we have the mind of Christ.
> (I Cor. 2:16)

I do not know that the apostle ever makes a greater claim for himself and his fellow-believers than this. And yet how entirely justified it is. For when a man responds at first to the overtures of our Lord Jesus Christ, unites with Him by faith and appropriates His proffered pardon, cleansing and adjustment with God, when he is thus born again, this is his endowment. For "if any man have not the Spirit of Christ," the

323

expression of Christ Himself dwelling within him, is, in fact, the authentic mark that the great transaction has been effected. A Christian is one who has the mind of Christ in a two fold fashion. He has accepted and enthroned the mind of Christ as the standard of conduct—the mind of Christ declared in His word and in His life as these are recorded in the Gospels. The mind of Christ is the straight-edge by which he tests the horizontal of his life and the plumb-line by which he judges its perpendicular. Then further, he has received the mind, that is, the Spirit of Christ, as an enlightening, restraining, constraining, rebuking, guiding, empowering, creating energy. And the loyal application to life of the standard unfailingly assures the putting forth of the energy in life.

This is not to proclaim any Gospel that leaves men and women mere passive automata. It is of the essence of the truth as it is in Christ that they are made intelligent and active co-workers with Him. Your personality will not be destroyed, nor even impaired, by your yielding to the control of Him Who holds its secret key. It will be developed to its maximum possibility, until your life in its every part makes its full contribution to God's glory in the world.

> Lord, if thou hadst been here, my
> brother had not died. (John 11:21)

Of course she was wrong. The plain truth of the matter is that Lazarus had died just because, in a truer sense than Martha could understand, the Lord was there! She did not know that her brother's sickness was "not unto death," that is, it was not part of Death's campaign and triumph, but was directly ordered "for the glory of God." It was actually planned by the Love that permitted it to take its course, and was meant to set the stage for the mightiest display of Christ's power, the most convincing declaration of His Godhead. But this Martha could not know. She had to learn—and she did learn—that His love outstrips all fleetness of the human mind, that it is always ahead of the conceptions and prayers of His followers, that when the lesser is denied it is as a preparation for the gift of the greater, that the measure of His power is "exceeding abundantly above all that we ask or think"—be our thoughts never so extravagant.

> For a great door and effectual is
> opened unto me, and there are
> many adversaries. (I Cor. 16:9)

Let there be no mistake about this. The place of Christian witness is often a hard and lonely place. But it is under just such conditions, matching the confidence of your faith against the apparent hopelessness of your efforts, that your own personal life will most surely develop. You may not appear to make much of the work entrusted to you. But it will make you! The man you are to be will not emerge from the man you are except by hardness and conflict and by the overcoming of obstacles in the power of Him Who neither dispenses with your personality nor suppresses it as you engage together in the holy warfare.

Look out, then, upon that open door! And get you through it in fellowship with Jesus Christ! Look at the adversaries through the opportunity. Don't make the fatal mistake of looking at the opportunity through the adversaries. And remember, now and always, that Christ our Lord does not ask us to do anything that He does not propose to undertake also with us! "Who shall separate us from the love of Christ?" Many adversaries? "Nay. In all these things we are more than conquerors through Him who loves us!"

# Henry ("Harry") Allan Ironside
## (1876–1951)

When he was twelve years old, Harry Ironside heard D. L. Moody preach. The lad prayed that night, "Lord, help me some day to preach to crowds like these, and to lead souls to Christ." God answered that prayer.

Ironside was a self-taught man, who became blind because he read and studied so much. (At one time, he studied Chinese.) He started in the Salvation Army, but left because he disagreed with their views of sanctification and security. His lifelong ecclesiastical home after that was with the Brethren, and he often ministered in assemblies in the United States and Canada.

Ironside is best remembered for his effective ministry at the Moody Church, Chicago, from 1930 to 1948. An expounder of the Word, he preached through Bible book after book, enriching the people who week by week filled that 4,000-seat auditorium. Many of Ironside's series were stenographically reported and published in book form.

As ye also learned of Epaphras our
dear fellowservant, who is for you a
faithful minister of Christ. (Col. 1:7)

He simply mentions the fact that Epaphras had told them of their love in the Spirit. It was a precious testimony to the happy state of these dear young Christians, so recently brought out of Paganism with all its abominations. Now as a company set apart to the name of the Lord Jesus Christ, they were characterized by the love which the Spirit sheds abroad in the hearts of those who are born of God. This is all-important. To pretend to great zeal for the truth of the one Body, while failing to manifest the love of the Spirit, is to put the emphasis in the wrong place. Doctrinal correctness will never atone for lack of brotherly love. It is far more to God who is Himself love, in His very nature, that His people walk in love one toward another, than that they contend valiantly for set forms of truth, however scriptural. "Truthing in love" (which would correctly convey the thought of Eph. 4:15) is more than contending for formulas. It is the manifestation of the truth in a life of love to God and to those who are His, as well as for poor lost sinners for whom Christ died.

> In whom we have redemption
> through his blood, even the forgive-
> ness of sins. (Col. 1:14)

It is very important to distinguish these things; that is, to have clearly in mind the privileges and blessings which are non-forfeitable, because confirmed to us by God in Christ from the moment we believe on Him who died to make them good to us; and the additional blessings for which we need to pray daily, and concerning which there should be constant soul-exercise lest we fail to enter into and enjoy them. Many believers fail in not distinguishing the two classes of blessings. In certain circles almost every public prayer will be concluded somewhat as follows: "We pray Thee, forgive us our sins, and wash us in the blood of Jesus; receive us into Thy kingdom, give us Thy Holy Spirit, and save us at last for Christ's sake, Amen." Yet every petition in this prayer has already been granted to the believer in Christ! God has forgiven us all trespasses. We are cleansed by the blood of Jesus. He has already translated us out of the kingdom of darkness into that of the Son of His love. He has sealed us with His Holy Spirit, for "if any man have not the Spirit of Christ, he

327

is none of His." And we are saved eternally from the moment we believe the gospel.

Therefore we might far rather cry exultantly in faith: "We thank Thee that Thou hast forgiven all our sins, and washed us from every stain in the blood of the Lamb. Thou hast brought us into Thy kingdom, given us Thy Holy Spirit, and saved us for eternity." Faith says "Amen" to what God has declared in His Word to be true. To go on praying for blessings that He tells us are already ours is the most subtle kind of unbelief, and robs us of the enjoyment that should be our portion if we but had faith to lay hold of the exceeding great and precious promises which are ours in Christ.

> Giving thanks unto the Father, which hath made us meet to be partakers of the inheritance of the saints in light. (Col. 1:12)

This is true of every Christian, and there are no degrees in this divine fitness. We are made meet to be partakers of our glorious inheritance the instant we are cleansed from our sins and receive the new nature, which is imparted by a divine operation when we are born of God. How different are the thoughts of even some of the best of men! How often we hear it said of some devoted and aged believer, "He is fit for heaven at last." But he was just as truly fit for heaven the moment he received Christ as he is at the end of a long life of devoted service. Fitness does not depend upon experience. But in this connection it is well to remember that there is something more than the Father's house, the inheritance of the saints in light, before us. It is important that we should also have in mind the coming glorious kingdom. In 2 Peter 1:10, 11 we are told, "Wherefore the rather, brethren, give diligence to make your calling and election sure: for if ye do these things, ye shall never fall: for so an entrance shall be ministered unto you abundantly into the everlasting kingdom of our Lord and

Saviour Jesus Christ." The expression, "these things," refers to the various Christian virtues enumerated in verses 5–7. It is through these things we are fitted for a place in the coming kingdom, but it is the justifying, regenerating grace of God that alone makes us meet for our heavenly inheritance. In other words, it is important that we distinguish between salvation by grace and reward for service.

> Beware lest any man spoil you
> through philosophy and vain deceit,
> after the tradition of men, after the
> rudiments of the world, and not
> after Christ. (Col. 2:8)

Scripture nowhere condemns the acquisition of knowledge. It is the wisdom of this world, not its knowledge, that is foolishness with God. Philosophy is but worldly wisdom. It is the effort of the human mind to solve the mystery of the universe. It is not an exact science, for the philosophers have never been able to come to any satisfactory conclusion as to either the "why" or the "wherefore" of things. "The Greeks seek after wisdom," we are told; and it was they who led the way for all future generations in philosophical theorizing. Before a divine revelation came it was quite natural and proper that man should seek by wisdom to solve the riddles that nature was constantly propounding, but now that God has spoken this is no longer necessary, and it may become grave infidelity. From Plato to Kant, and from Kant to the last of the moderns, one system has overturned another, so that the history of philosophy is a story of contradictory, discarded hypotheses. This is not to say that the philosophers were or are dishonest men, but it is to say that many of them have failed to avail themselves of that which would unravel every knot and solve every problem, namely, the revelation of God in Christ as given in the Holy Scriptures.

Plato yearned for a divine Word—"logos"—which would

come with authority and make everything plain. That Word is Christ of whom John writes, "In the beginning was the Word, and the Word was with God, and the Word was God." And again, "The Word became flesh, and tabernacled among us, and we beheld His glory, the glory as of the only begotten of the Father, full of grace and truth." The Word is no longer hidden. We do not need to search for it. "The word is nigh thee, even in thy mouth, and in thy heart: that if thou shalt confess with thy mouth the Lord Jesus, and shalt believe in thine heart that God hath raised Him from the dead, thou shalt be saved."

> Blotting out the handwriting of
> ordinances that was against us,
> which was contrary to us, and took
> it out of the way, nailing it to his
> cross. (Col. 2:14)

Pilate wrote out the inscription to be placed over the head of Christ Jesus, and that in three languages, Hebrew, Greek, and Latin, that all might know why the patient Sufferer from Galilee was being publicly executed. "This is Jesus of Nazareth the King of the Jews." As the people read this they understood that he was being crucified because He made Himself a king and was thus disloyal to Caesar.

But as God looked upon that cross His holy eye saw, as it were, another inscription altogether. Nailed upon the rood above the head of His blessed Son was the handwriting of ten ordinances given at Sinai. It was because this law had been broken in every point that Jesus poured out His blood, thus giving His life to redeem us from the curse of the law. And so all of our sins have been settled for. There the law, which we had so dishonored, has been magnified to the full in the satisfaction which He made to the divine justice. Thus Christ has become the end of the law to every one that believeth. It is of course the Jewish believers Paul has in mind when he says

330

"us," for Gentiles were not under the law. But it is true now in principle for us all, to whom the knowledge of the law has come. Christ has, by His death, met every claim against us and cancelled the bond we could not pay.

> Set your affection on things above,
> not on things on the earth. (Col. 3:2)

It is of all importance that we realize that we do not stand before God on the ground of responsibility. The responsible man failed utterly to keep his obligations. There was nothing for him, therefore, but condemnation, but our Lord Jesus Christ has borne that condemnation; He voluntarily, in infinite grace, took the place of the sinner and bore his judgment upon the cross. Now in resurrection, as we have seen, all who believe are not only given a perfect representation by Him before the throne of God, but we are in Him in virtue of being partakers of His life.

It is when the soul enters into this experimentally, realizing that the death of Christ, in which faith has given him part, has severed the link that bound him to the world and all its purposes and has freed him from all necessity to be subject to sin in the flesh, that he will be free to glorify God as he walks in newness of life. Most theological systems fail to apprehend this great truth of the new man in Christ, hence so few believers have settled peace and realize their union with Him who sits at God's right hand, not only as the Head of the Church, but as the Head of every man who has found life through Him.

Occupation, then, with Christ risen in the energy of the Holy Spirit, is the power for holiness. We are called upon to seek those things which are above, where Christ sitteth on the right hand of God. Our real life is there, our truest, best interests are all identified with Him. Heavenly-mindedness is the natural, or I should say, spiritual outcome of this realization.

> . . . always labouring fervently for
> you in prayers, that ye may stand
> perfect and complete in all the will
> of God. (Col. 4:12)

Prayer, is first of all, communion with God. Our blessed Lord Himself, in the days of His flesh, is seen again and again leaving the company of His disciples and going out into some desert place on a mountain side, or into a garden, that His spirit might be refreshed as He bowed in prayer alone with the Father. From such seasons of fellowship He returned to do His mightiest works and to bear witness to the truth. And in this He is our great Exemplar. We need to pray as much as we need to breathe. Our souls will languish without it, and our testimony will be utterly fruitless if we neglect it.

We are told to continue in prayer. This does not mean that we are to be constantly teasing God in order that we may obtain what we might think would add most to our happiness or be best for us, but we are to abide in a sense of His presence and of our dependence upon His bounty. We are to learn to talk to Him and to quietly wait before Him, too, in order that we may hear His voice as He speaks to us. We are bidden to bring everything to Him in prayer, assured that if we ask anything according to His will He heareth us. But because we are so ignorant and so shortsighted we need ever to remember that we are to leave the final disposal of things with Him who makes no mistakes. Without anxiety as to anything, we may bring everything to Him in prayer and supplication with thanksgiving, making known our requests in childlike simplicity; then, leaving all in His hands, we go forth in fullest confidence as our hearts say, "Thy will be done," knowing that He will do for us exceeding abundantly above all that we ask or think.

# William Graham Scroggie
## (1877–1958)

Trained at Spurgeon's College, London, W. Graham Scroggie
climaxed a long and fruitful ministry when he was pastor of
the famous Spurgeon's Tabernacle from 1938–1944. He was
pastor of four other churches, including the historic Charlotte
Chapel in Edinburgh, and traveled widely in a Bible-teaching
ministry. During his seventeen years in Edinburgh, he
became widely known as a Bible teacher and preacher of the
victorious Christian life.

I value the books that Scroggie published. I use them often
and I recommend them. He had a gift for analyzing and
summarizing large portions of Scripture so that you get the
bird's-eye view before you examine the details. But he did
more than analyze Scripture; he was a forceful preacher who
applied the Word to daily life.

The meek will he guide in judgment:
and the meek will he teach his way.
(Ps. 25:9)

We recognize that it is only as God guides us that we can
know what our duty is, which is another way of saying that,
God guides His people by His Word, interpreted and applied
by His Spirit. If therefore, we neglect the Bible, we cannot but
remain in ignorance of the Divine will. The shrewdest calculation and the keenest foresight can never be adequate for our
supreme need, nor be a substitute for the knowledge of the
Divine mind. Just because life is related to truth, and the

highest revelation of truth is preserved in the Scriptures, we must discover from them what is the will of God for us, and having discovered it, we must do it, with a glad and trustful heart.

"The meek will He guide in judgment, and the meek will he teach His way." God will not fail on His part, but we may fail on ours. If we listen at all, "our ears shall hear a word behind us saying, 'This is the way, walk ye in it,' when we turn to the right hand, and when we turn to the left," but if we heed not that voice, we shall continue to wander in perilous by-paths. The mere reading of the Scriptures will not give us guidance for the way; we must obediently seek therein, for our personal need, the will of God and this is done by *prayer.* If we ask, He will answer, but if His guidance of us is to be continuous, our asking must be the reflection of an *attitude* towards Him, on our part, of dependence and trust.

> And he [the elder brother] was
> angry, and would not go in. . . .
> (Luke 15:28)

The greatest hindrance to the progress of Christianity in this world is the elder brother class in the Church; people who make a religion of their morality and who despise others.

His attitude toward himself is ridiculous, his attitude toward his brother is despicable. But that is not all; what is his attitude towards the household, and remember that is the Church? He despised all their expressions of joy. He heard music and dancing, and looked grave, and he sent in for a servant and said, "What is the meaning of all this?" "Oh, everybody in there is glad because your brother is home again." "Oh! Well it should not be, it is not decent, it is a disregard of convention and propriety."

Such people pray for revival in the Church, and immediately revival appears they grow serious and say it is contrary to custom and convention; "We should not do it, we really should not." I do not think the Spirit of God has much use for custom and convention for custom's sake and convention's sake. I am not against custom or against convention; I believe we should do all things decently and in order, but I believe also that if there is ever any excuse for a man or woman dancing, it is when sinners are saved, but that is not when it is done.

These self-righteous people disapprove; they say "it is *unseemly.*"

And this man was incensed at the occasion of their joy; he was angry! A Church member, mind you, *Angry!* What about? About a sinner coming home. Angry!

> And now abideth faith, hope, love,
> these three; but the greatest of these
> is love. (I Cor. 13:13)

The Corinthians had thought that the Gifts were the abiding things, but Paul says these must pass away. "Now," therefore, does not mean *now* in time, for then these three would not differ from the Gifts in any wise. . . . Here we have the anomaly of three nouns governed by a singular verb, "and now abideth Faith, Hope, Love." The great truth preserved in this piece of apparent grammatical irregularity is that Faith, Hope, and Love are one in essence, that they are a trinity in unity and they are therefore coextensive with one another. . . .

We shall never be able to dispense with Faith and Hope, both shall go on for ever. . . . We must all carefully distinguish between Eternal and Final; Eternity does not mean Finality, but to reach finality would be to fall short of Eternity. And we must distinguish also between Perfection and Finality. In Heaven there will be perfection, but there will be differences of attainment even as one star differs from another star in glory. . . . There will be progress from stage to stage. "In My Father's house are many mansions" means "many resting-places," a figure which refers to those stations on the great roads where travellers can get rest and refreshment before proceeding on their journey. The notions both of repose and progress are in the words. . . . Every further acquisition of God will make fuller acquisition possible; every new height of glory scaled will reveal yet more glorious heights beyond: Eternal progress . . .

> For even Christ our passover is sacrificed for us. (I Cor. 5:7)

How then is the Feast to be observed? "Not with old leaven, neither with the leaven of malice and wickedness, but with the unleavened bread of sincerity and truth." That is, by living a holy life, and by separation from all evil. For not keeping the Feast as ordained, we shall be held answerable to God. The observance of the Feast is not in order to obtain our salvation, but because we are saved, and if we do not keep the Feast our security is not affected but our fellowship is. Salvation is by our being under the Blood; communion is by our being unleavened. Here, then, is a message of the most urgent importance to the people of God. On every hand we see laxity, alike of doctrine and of practice, which is most alarming, an indifference to the claims of Christ and a widespread ignorance of the implicates of our Christian profession, and it is this that sufficiently explains our ineffectiveness in the service of Christ. We must be clean, for we are the vessels of the Lord. We must faithfully and fearlessly deal with all known evil, alike in our hearts, and homes, and churches, and businesses, and all our prayer for revival will be worse than useless unless we come to grips with that which hinders God's pouring out His blessing upon us. But this once done, there is no good which He will withhold.

A sea of glass mingled with fire.
(Rev. 15:2)

Peace and energy do not always go together, though they should. Energy need be none the less energetic if it be peaceful, nor peace the less peaceful if it be energetic. Peace without energy may be only stagnation; and energy without peace may be but a form of panic. What we need is that our glassy sea be mingled with fire, and that our fire shall have for its home a glassy sea. Too often the water puts out the fire, or the fire dries up the water; but in every true life these dwell helpfully together. Why should peace exclude passion, and why should passion destroy peace? Why should one moral quality triumph at the expense of another? Yet, too often it is so. Sometimes our sea is not glassy, but tempest tossed; and sometimes our fire burns low. Sometimes it is all calm, and no energy, and sometimes it is all energy and no calm. But what is possible and right is, that the glassy sea be mingled with fire! that our outward energy be regulated by inward peace, and that our inward peace find expression in outward energy. Then shall there be equipoise of power.

. . . what he hath prepared for him
that waiteth for him. (Isa. 64:4)

I suppose most people find it difficult to *wait*. The grace of patience is not common. "In a little room sat two children, each one in his own chair. The name of the eldest was Passion, and the name of the other Patience. Passion seemed to be much discontented, but Patience was very quiet. Then Christian asked, What is the reason of the discontent of Passion? The Interpreter answered, The Governor of them would have him stay for his best things till the beginning of next year, but he will have all now. But *Patience is willing to wait.*"Milton was of the same mind as Bunyan, when of the angels he said,

"They also serve who only stand and wait." Such waiting does not imply indolence or indifference, but is an evidence of spiritual faith and confidence, of true insight, and forsight, and of self-discipline also. While in this worthy way we are passive, our God is active. He works for those who wait for Him. There are some things which He can do for us only as we wait. Blessed passivity, which calls forth such activity! Of course, it is also true that in other things God will wait while we work. He will not do for us what He has bidden us do for ourselves, even as we cannot do for ourselves what He has undertaken to do for us. Thus we become "workers together with God." Are you waiting at His bidding? "Ye shall not need to fight in this battle; set yourselves, stand ye still, and see the salvation of the Lord with you; fear not, nor be dismayed."

> And I sought for a man among
> them. . . . (Ezek. 22:30)

But even God can't work without man. We are called to co-operate. History is the story of the race, of the nation, of the individual; and so, while God has been making His revelation, He has been making it to men and He has been looking for men who will apprehend the revelation and carry forward His purpose here in time. My brethren, I point out to you that God has never wrought anything tremendous by means of masses and crowds in human history. He has wrought His wonders through the ages by individuals—people whom He could trust, people who exercise faith. What is faith? We are told in this first verse of the chapter, "Faith is the substance of things hoped for, the evidence of things not seen." The objects, therefore, of faith, are the future and the unseen; and the office of faith is to give present existence to future things and vital reality to unseen things. And wherever such faith has been exercised, wherever men have laid hold of the divine revelation, God has built a new era in the human story. It is the advent of personality which alters the current of history. The sharp turning points of history are due to the rise of great personalities. It is not so much by ideas as by personalities that God sets the world forward. The mightiest civilizing powers are personalities, and the mightiest civilizing personalities are Christian men.

# Herbert Henry Farmer

## (1892–1981)

A Cambridge graduate, H. H. Farmer was pastor of several Presbyterian churches in England, and then returned to Cambridge to teach theology. He had a gift for making theological concepts meaningful and personal, but he was not a "popularizer." He makes us think.

I first met Farmer's thought in the pages of *The Servant of the Word,* a book every preacher and teacher of the Bible ought to read and ponder. I began to look for other titles, and each new discovery was rewarding. He gave the Yale lectures in 1946; the series is published under the title *God and Men.* It is another good theological work for those who share the Word.

Consider the lilies of the field, how
they grow; they toil not, neither do
they spin: yet I say unto you, That
even Solomon in all his glory was
not arrayed like one of these.
(Matt. 6:28–29)

The beauty of the flowers reveals something about the nature of God.

You remember that Jesus used to set great store by the chance words of men. "Every idle word that men shall speak," he said, "they shall give an account thereof." "Out of the overflow of the heart the mouth speaketh." The unstudied word, the word which we let slip out without thinking and to serve no particular end, the small change of daily intercourse, which we could quite easily dispense with so far as the immediate business of living is concerned,—these, almost more than anything else, reveal the inner man, and are the index of his true quality. So also are the little, superfluous, unnecessary acts of daily life. Most of us manage to do with some grace the necessary things, the things which clamant human need or coercive public opinion demands; but the man who throws little, unnecessary, beautiful acts into his daily conduct, he it is who reveals a truly beautiful soul. The superfluities, the things which flow, not so much out of the pressure of the external situation, as out of the internal pressure of a tender and generous spirit, these declare the man. Now it is the same with beauty as a revelation of God. Beauty in creation is the overflow of God's heart; it is the unstudied Divine word uttered, apparently, for no particular purpose and to serve no particular end; an unnecessary, delightful superfluity; therefore, more eloquent of the Divine mind almost than anything else.

> Woe unto you that are rich! for ye
> have received your consolation.
> (Luke 6:24)

To Jesus the terrible thing about having wrong values in life and pursuing wrong things, is not that you are doomed to bitter disappointment, but that you are *not;* not that you do not achieve what you want, but that you *do.* The way of these people, He says, is to be avoided, not because they are such miserable failures, but because, in their own way, they are such triumphant successes! They get exactly what they are out for. The person who is out to get a reputation for piety can get it, says Jesus. He blows a trumpet when he is about to give an alms, so that he may have glory of men, and he has his reward, and that is exactly why you must not copy him! The man who seeks the power and the comfort of affluence can get the power and comfort of affluence; he receives *his* good things during this present life, and he passes hence with his ambitions perfectly satisfied. But he is not to be envied for that reason—quite the contrary. This is his failure, that by his own standards, he succeeds. For there *are* consolations in riches, for those who have a mind that way. There are few troubles in life wealth cannot lighten and mitigate: and, in any case, if you have come to think, as many wealthy people unconsciously do think, that there is no disaster quite so bad as poverty, there is always some consolation in any trouble in reviewing your possessions. Jesus was too honest to pretend that the consolations of riches cannot be very real and very sweet, just as the pains of poverty can be very real and very bitter. But was the rich man to be congratulated on that account? Not for a moment. What piercing and paradoxical insight is this which says that such a man is really in woe, just at the very point when he is most conscious of being consoled, of being completely justified in his way of life? *Woe* unto you rich, for ye have received your *consolations!* As though one should say, "My friend, your view of life's values is proved wrong by the fact that on experiment it has been proved right; your disaster is that you have had no disaster; your bankruptcy consists in the fact that you are absolutely solvent; your devastating failure is demonstrated by your victorious success. What you asked of life, life has given you. Woe to you!"

They have received their reward.
(Matt. 6:2)

By demanding that worldliness should not be allowed even worldly success, we land ourselves with an insoluble problem[:] directly we discover that life does not work like that at all. The prosperity and success of the wicked have been a source of trouble to pious people in all ages. You find the Psalmist, the author of the book of Job, and again and again the prophets, wrestling with it. And, today, one is continually meeting folk who are puzzled and rebellious, because they feel that somehow it impugns the goodness and providence of God that so many good people are struggling with poverty and so many worldly people have everything the heart could desire. We need to think the whole thing through again.

Is it not clear that to demand that worldliness should be punished by depriving it of worldly success is to set the same value on worldly success as worldliness itself does? Is it not to grant that worldly success *is* worth something after all, that to miss it *is* a real deprivation, a real punishment? If in the end it counts for nothing, why be put out because bad people so often get it? If our desire is to take it away from them and give it to better folk, are we not really in an inverted sort of way congratulating them on having it, agreeing with them, that it is after all a very good thing, worth striving for? This is no quibble. It represents a very serious and solemn fact of our poor, unregenerate, worldly hearts. There is a great deal of denunciation of the rich which is sheer envy, a great deal of puzzlement and rebellion at life which springs from a materialistic outlook only half redeemed. We say, "woe! to the rich," but only because in our hearts we think them happy, happier than they deserve! How different the attitude of Jesus! Here again, His amazing originality and purity appear. He stands quite clear of all these fallacies and self-deceptions. To Him the success of the worldly is not an undeserved reward; on the contrary, it is their most terrible punishment, their entirely appropriate doom. He does not envy them it; He pities them rather. He says "woe to them," because He really thinks it is a most dreadful thing to aim at worldly success and get it. It would have been better for them to have aimed at it and *not* got it. Nowhere, I say, is the purity of His moral perceptions shown more clearly than in this conviction, that the real failure of worldliness lies in its astonishing success, its real woe in its present consolations.

> Son, be of good cheer; thy sins are
> forgiven. (Matt. 9:2)

I do not find for one moment that my sinfulness makes it easier for me to fathom and to sympathize with the moral need of others. Quite the contrary. I find that my own harsh judgments of myself continually make me pass harsh judgments on other people. I find that my own easy judgments on myself continually make me pass easy judgments on other people. Sometimes it works the other way and I cover self-indulgence by being exacting to others. I am, in short, erratic and confused. Always I read into others my moral mood at the moment, and I see them, not as they are, but through the distorting medium of my own profound dissatisfaction and conflict with myself. Furthermore, sin not only fogs the understanding, but it dries up the sympathies and the affections. Moral conflict within dams back and turns inwards the vital energies which are meant to flow outwards in sympathy with, and service to, other lives. Really to love other people, really to enter into their lives and be identified with them and stand beside them, is so difficult and so exacting, that it demands that the soul's energies should be completely released from any exhausting, internal struggle with itself. That sounds like the jargon of modern psychology, but any one can deduce it from a little observation of himself. It is after some renewed experience of forgiveness, when, for a time at any rate, the inner conflict is allayed, that a man's feelings and desires are most responsive to the need of others. When the gospel of God's forgiveness has deeply laid hold of a man he feels for the moment that he could take the whole world to his bosom and that he would do anything to share the benefit with everyone he meets. It is the peaceful heart which is the deeply sympathetic heart. There is no doubt of that. As sin gets hold of us again and the old conflict returns, so we become conscious of a re-hardening of the surfaces of personality, a withdrawal of sympathy with others, an increase of callousness. Sin is like leprosy in the sphere of the spirit. It anesthetizes the skin.

> Are ye able to drink the cup that I
> am about to drink? . . . They say
> unto him, We are able. (Matt. 20:22)

There is always a certain obliquity, a certain element of cross-purpose, a certain displacement of perspective and vision, between a leader and his followers. That is what makes leadership the most difficult and sometimes the most heart-breaking of tasks. To be a leader you must be ahead of others; yet not too far ahead. You must talk two languages at one and the same time, your own and theirs. You must be one of them and yet not one of them, in their world and yet out of it, sometimes entirely out of it. You must see things which they do not see and for the time being perhaps cannot see, things which, none the less, alone determine the path you want them to choose to follow. A leader has to work with his two eyes as it were out of focus, one apprehending the truth, the other the half-truth, or even the untruth, which holds the minds of his disciples in thrall. If he lacks the capacity for this, if he cannot put himself in his disciples' shoes and look out on life in some measure through their eyes, he lacks the first essential of leadership and is doomed to failure. And, of course, the more transcendentally great he is in character and vision and desire, the bigger the distance between him and followers, the more he towers above his contemporaries—then the more urgently necessary, and the more impossibly difficult, will this essential quality of appreciating two worlds at once become.

> And Peter answered him and said,
> Lord, if it be thou, bid me come
> unto thee on the water. (Matt. 14:28)

None of us knows what his weaknesses and his powers are, nor how exactly life will test them; but it is quite certain that we shall never know what they are, nor will life's tests teach us anything, unless we aspire to the highest that we know, and

are continually testing ourselves by the most lofty profes-
sions. To shut out ultimate success through fear of interim
failures, to maintain a worthless consistency by the miserable
expedient of walking always along the mud flats, to fail in
nothing because you had promised nothing, that is a folly
which is only explicable on the ground that it springs from a
narrow and calculating egotism. Far better always is the
generous impulse, which, like Peter, says, "I will, I am able,"
and then goes out to learn through defeat a deeper knowledge of self and a deeper knowledge of Christ. And how can
anyone know with fully proved conviction that Christ is the
Way, the Truth and the Life, before he has gone through the
whole of life in His company and faced all its worst challenges
with Him? Christian discipleship always must begin in ignorance; or to put it in another way, it must always begin in a sort
of plunge, a grand experiment. Something draws us to Him
and we risk our lives upon Him. There is only one way to
prove Him trustworthy and that is to trust Him. We do not ask
of anyone to do more than make honest experiment of Jesus.
Our faith in preaching Him is that, if Jesus is fairly given His
chance, He will be able to make triumphant use of it.

> And he cometh unto the disciples,
> and findeth them sleeping, and saith
> unto Peter, What, could ye not
> watch with me one hour?
> (Matt. 26:40)

There is always that danger in religion,—the danger of
regarding God as a servant, rather than as One utterly to be
served. Of course, we do not put it to ourselves in those terms;
we speak of a God of love and comfort, and we sing praises to
His adequacy to our need, all of which, in its own way, is right.
But we must not stop there. There is a stranger and more
astonishing thought, which sounds blasphemous perhaps to
those who have not been gripped and overwhelmed by it, or

who have not fully apprehended that what we see in Jesus that God is, and that is the thought of God's need of us, of God's infinite desire for our companionship. In this word of Jesus,—spoken from out of the midst of the most solemn experience of His life, when more than at any other time He was close to the heart of His Father and God's suffering became His,—I hear an infinite desire for human companionship. "Could ye not watch *with* me?" We need Jesus, but Jesus quite desperately needs us, and that is what we do not realize when we protest our allegiance to Him.

# Thomas R. Kelly
## (1893–1941)

When I picked up *A Testament of Devotion* in a used-book sale many years ago, I had no idea what a treasure had come into my life. I hastened to order *The Eternal Promise*, and since that time have often reread both books.

Thomas Kelly was a man with a rare blending of scholarship, spiritual intuition, and social concern. His spiritual home was with the Quakers, but his ministry is for all who are weary of the daily "rat race." Kelly was not an impractical mystic, but he was a mystic in the finest sense of that word. He calls us back to the spiritual realities that get our attention off of prices and on to values. Like Thoreau, he pleads for a simplicity of life, a putting off of the excess baggage that wears us out.

Martha, Martha, thou art careful
and troubled about many things:
But one thing is needful. . . .
(Luke 10:41–42)

L et me first suggest that we are giving a false explanation of the complexity of our lives. We blame it upon the complex environment. Our complex living, we say, is due to the complex world we live in, with its radios and autos, which give us more stimulation per square hour than used to be given per square day to our grandmothers. This explanation by the *outward* order leads us to turn wistfully, in some moments, to thoughts of a quiet South Sea Island existence, or to the horse and buggy days of our great grandparents, who went, jingle bells, jingle bells, over the crisp and ringing snow to spend the day with *their* grandparents on the farm. Let me assure you, I have tried the life of the South Seas for a year, the long, lingering leisure of a tropic world. And I found that Americans carry into the tropics their same madcap, feverish life which we know on the mainland. Complexity of our program cannot be blamed upon complexity of our environment, much as we should like to think so. Nor will simplification of life follow simplification of environment. I must confess that I chafed terribly, that year in Hawaii, because in some respects the environment seemed too simple.

> Keep thy heart with all diligence; for
> out of it are the issues of life.
> (Prov. 4:23)

We Western peoples are apt to think our great problems are external, environmental. We are not skilled in the inner life, where the real roots of our problem lie. For I would suggest that the true explanation of the complexity of our program is an inner one, not an outer one. The outer distractions of our interests reflect an inner lack of integration of our own lives. We are trying to be several selves at once, without all our selves being organized by a single, mastering Life within us. Each of us tends to be, not a single self, but a whole committee of selves. There is the civic self, the parental self, the financial self, the religious self, the society self, the professional self, the literary self. And each of our selves is in turn a rank individualist, not co-operative but shouting out his vote loudly for himself when the voting time comes. And all too commonly we follow the common American method of getting a quick decision among conflicting claims within us. It is as if we have a chairman of our committee of the many selves within us, who does not integrate the many into one but who merely counts the votes at each decision, and leaves disgruntled minorities. The claims of each self are still pressed. If we accept service on a committee on Negro education, we still regret we can't help with a Sunday-school class. We are not integrated. We are distraught. We feel honestly the pull of many obligations and try to fulfill them all.

> O send out thy light and thy truth:
> let them lead me. . . . (Ps. 43:3)

Life is meant to be lived from a Center, a divine Center. Each one of us can live such a life of amazing power and peace and serenity, of integration and confidence and simplified multiplicity, on one condition—that is, *if we really want to.* There is a divine Abyss within us all, a holy Infinite Center, A Heart, A Life who speaks in us and through us to the world. We have all heard this holy Whisper at times. At times we have followed the Whisper, and amazing equilibrium of life, amazing effectiveness of living set in. But too many of us have heeded the Voice only at times. Only at times have we submitted to His holy guidance. We have not counted this Holy Thing within us to be the most precious thing in the world. We have not surrendered *all else,* to attend to it alone. Let me repeat. Most of us, I fear, have not surrendered all else, in order to attend to the Holy Within.

John Woolman did. He resolved so to order his outward affairs as to be, *at every moment,* attentive to that voice. He simplified life on the basis of its relation to the divine Center. Nothing else really counted so much as attentiveness to that Root of all living which he found within himself. And the Quaker discovery lies in just that: the welling-up whispers of divine guidance and love and presence, more precious than heaven or earth.

When thou saidst, Seek ye my face;
my heart said unto thee, Thy face,
LORD, will I seek. (Ps. 27:8)

$A$nd under the silent, watchful eye of the Holy One we all are standing, whether we know it or not. And in that Center, in that holy Abyss where the Eternal dwells at the base of our being, our programs, our gifts to Him, our offerings of duties performed are again and again revised in their values. Many of the things we are doing seem so important to us. We haven't been able to say No to them, because they seemed so important. But if we *center down,* as the old phrase goes, and live in that holy Silence which is dearer than life, and take our life program into the silent places of the heart, with complete openness, ready to do, ready to renounce according to His leading, then many of the things we are doing lose their vitality for us. I should like to testify to this, as a personal experience, graciously given. There is a reevaluation of much that we do or try to do, which is *done for us,* and we know what to do and what to let alone.

Be still, and know that I am God.
(Ps. 46:10)

$I$ should like to be mercilessly drastic in uncovering any sham pretense of being wholly devoted to the inner holy Presence, in singleness of love to God. But I must confess that it doesn't take time, or complicate your program. I find that a life of little whispered words of adoration, of praise, of prayer, of worship can be breathed all through the day. One can have a very busy day, outwardly speaking, and yet be steadily in the holy Presence. We do need a half-hour or an hour of quiet reading and relaxation. But I find that one can carry the recreating silences within oneself, *well-nigh all the time.* With delight I read Brother Lawrence, in his *Practice of the Presence of God.* At the close of the Fourth Conversation it is

351

reported of him, "He was never hasty nor loitering, but did each thing in its season, with an even, uninterrupted composure and tranquillity of spirit. 'The time of business,' he said, 'does not with me differ from the time calling for different things, I possess God in as great tranquillity as if I were upon my knees at the blessed sacrament.'" Our real problem, in failing to center down, is not a lack of time; it is, I fear, in too many of us, lack of joyful, enthusiastic delight in Him, lack of deep, deep-drawing love directed toward Him at every hour of the day and night.

> . . . your life is hid with Christ in
> God. (Col. 3:3)

There is a way of life so hid with Christ in God that in the midst of the day's business one is inwardly lifting brief prayers, short ejaculations of praise, subdued whispers of adoration and of tender love to the Beyond that is within. No one need know about it. I only speak to you because it is a sacred trust, not mine but to be given to others. One can live in a well-nigh continuous state of unworded prayer, directed toward God, directed toward people and enterprises we have on our heart. There is no hurry about it all; it is a life unspeakable and full of glory, an inner world of splendor within which we, unworthy, may live. Some of you know it and live in it; others of you may wistfully long for it; it can be yours.

> . . . the love of God is shed abroad in
> our hearts. . . . (Rom. 5:5)

Now out from such a holy Center come the commissions of life. Our fellowship with God issues in world-concern. We cannot keep the love of God to ourselves. It spills over. It quickens us. It makes us see the world's needs anew. We love people and we grieve to see them blind when they might be seeing, asleep with all the world's comforts when they ought to be awake and living sacrificially, accepting the world's goods as their right when they really hold them only in temporary trust. It is because from this holy Center we relove people, relove our neighbors as ourselves, that we are bestirred to be means of their awakening. The deepest need of men is not food and clothing and shelter, important as they are. It is God. We have mistaken the nature of poverty, and thought it was economic poverty. No, it is poverty of soul, deprivation of God's recreating, loving peace. Peer into poverty and see if we are really getting down to the deepest needs, in our economic salvation schemes. These are important. But they lie farther along the road, secondary steps toward world reconstruction. The primary step is a holy life, transformed and radiant in the glory of God.

# Aiden Wilson Tozer

## (1897–1963)

A. W. Tozer was a country boy who, by God's grace, became the conscience of evangelicalism while he was pastor of the Southside Alliance Church in Chicago (1928–1959). An evangelical mystic, Tozer feared nothing but sin, and sought glory for no one save God. He was misunderstood, criticized, attacked, and neglected, but his many books still speak to us and call us back to the essentials.

I heard Tozer speak many times, but I preferred his books to his spoken ministry. In his "spiritual essays" he gave us the *distillation* of his profound thought and lengthy meditation. I have used *The Pursuit of God* as a basic textbook for a seminary class about Christian living, and have had students tell me the book changed their lives. I have read and reread his many volumes, and they always say something new to me.

Tozer was not a run-of-the-mill pastor. He did little pastoral or administrative work. He spent his time reading, praying, thinking, writing, and preaching. He loved the old mystics— Tauler, Suso, Meister Eckhart, St. John of the Cross—but he loved Christ and the Word even more.

Search the scriptures; . . . they are they which testify of me. (John 5:39)

Perhaps a word of warning would not be amiss here: It is that we beware the common habit of putting confidence in books, as such. It takes a determined effort of the mind to break free from the error of making books and teachers ends

354

in themselves. The worst thing a book can do for a Christian is to leave him with the impression that he has received from it anything really good; the best it can do is to point the way to the Good he is seeking. The function of a good book is to stand like a signpost directing the reader toward the Truth and the Life. That book serves best which early makes itself unnecessary, just as a signpost serves best after it is forgotten, after the traveler has arrived safely at his desired haven. The work of a good book is to incite the reader to moral action, to turn his eyes toward God and urge him forward. Beyond that it cannot go.

> Thou therefore which teachest
> another, teachest thou not thyself?
> (Rom. 2:21)

Some who desire to be teachers of the Word, but who understand neither what they say, nor whereof they affirm, insist upon "naked" faith as the only way to know spiritual things. By this they mean a conviction of the trustworthiness of the Word of God (a conviction, it may be noted, which the devils share with them). But the man who has been taught even slightly by the Spirit of Truth will rebel at this perversion. His language will be, "I have heard Him and observed Him. What have I to do any more with idols?" For he cannot love a God who is no more than a deduction from a text. He will crave to know God with a vital awareness that goes beyond words, and to live in the intimacy of personal communion. "To seek our divinity merely in books and writings is to *seek the living among the dead;* we do but in vain many times seek God in these, where His truth too often is not so much enshrined as entombed. He is best discerned by an intellectual touch of Him. We must see with our eyes, and hear with our ears, and our hands must handle of the word of life." Nothing can take the place of the *touch* of God in the soul and the

sense of Someone there. Real faith, indeed, brings such realization, for real faith is never the operation of reason upon
texts. Where true faith is, the knowledge of God will be given
as a fact of consciousness altogether apart from the conclusions of logic.

> For the word of God is living, and
> powerful. . . . (Heb. 4:12,
> *New Scofield Reference Bible*)

I have not said that religion without power makes no
changes in a man's life, only that it makes no fundamental
difference. Water may change from liquid to vapor, from
vapor to snow and back to liquid again, and still be funda-
mentally the same. So powerless religion may put a man
through many surface changes and leave him exactly what
he was before. Right there is where the snare is. *The changes
are in form only, they are not in kind.* Behind the activities of
the non-religious man and the man who has received the
gospel without power lie the very same motives. An unblessed
ego lies at the bottom of both lives, the difference being that
the religious man has learned better to disguise his vice. His
sins are refined and less offensive than before he took up
religion, but the man himself is not a better man in the sight of
God. He may indeed be a worse one, for always God hates
artificiality and pretense. Selfishness still throbs like an
engine at the center of the man's life. True he may learn to
"redirect" his selfish impulses, but his woe is that self still lives
unrebuked and even unsuspected within his deep heart. He is
a victim of religion without power.

The man who has received the Word without power has
trimmed his hedge, but it is a thorn hedge still and can never
bring forth the fruits of the new life. Men do not gather grapes
of thorns nor figs of thistles. Yet such a man may be a leader in
the Church and his influence and his vote may go far to
determine what religion shall be in his generation.

356

And why call ye me, Lord, Lord, and
do not the things which I say?
(Luke 6:46)

The gradual disappearance of the idea and feeling of
majesty from the Church is a sign and a portent. The revolt of
the modern mind has had a heavy price, how heavy is
becoming more apparent as the years go by. Our God has now
become our servant to wait on our will. "The Lord is my
*shepherd,"* we say, instead of *"The Lord* is my shepherd," and
the difference is as the world.

We need to have restored again the lost idea of sovereignty,
not as a doctrine only but as the source of a solemn religious
emotion. We need to have taken from our dying hand the
shadow scepter with which we fancy we rule the world. We
need to feel and know that we are but dust and ashes, and
that God is the disposer of the destinies of men. How ashamed
we Christians should be that a pagan king should teach us to
fear the Majesty on high. For it was the chastened Nebuchad-
nezzar who said, "I lifted up mine eyes unto heaven and mine
understanding returned unto me, and I blessed the most
High, and I praised and honored him that liveth forever,
whose dominion is an everlasting dominion, and his kingdom
is from generation to generation. And all the inhabitants of
the earth are reputed as nothing, and he doeth according to
his will in the army of heaven, and among the inhabitants of
the earth: and none can stay his hand, or say unto him, What
doest thou?"

And he knew not that the LORD was
departed from him.
(Judg. 16:20, ASV)

We bear within us the seeds of our own disintegration.
Our moral imprudence puts us always in danger of acci-
dental or reckless self-destruction. The strength of our flesh is

357

an ever present danger to our souls. Deliverance can come to us only by the defeat of our old life. Safety and peace come only after we have been forced to our knees. God rescues us by breaking us, by shattering our strength and wiping out our resistance. Then He invades our natures with that ancient and eternal life which is from the beginning. So He conquers us and by that benign conquest saves us for Himself.

With this open secret awaiting easy discovery, why do we in almost all our busy activities work in another direction from this? Why do we build our churches upon human flesh? Why do we set such store by that which the Lord has long ago repudiated, and despise those things which God holds in such high esteem? For we teach men not to die with Christ but to live in the strength of their dying manhood. We boast not in our weakness but in our strength. Values which Christ has declared to be false are brought back into evangelical favor and promoted as the very life and substance of the Christian way. How eagerly do we seek the approval of this or that man of worldly reputation. How shamefully do we exploit the converted celebrity. Anyone will do to take away the reproach of obscurity from our publicity-hungry leaders: famous athletes, congressmen, world travelers, rich industrialists; before such we bow with obsequious smiles and honor them in our public meetings and in the religious press. Thus we glorify men to enhance the standing of the Church of God, and the glory of the Prince of Life is made to hang upon the transient fame of a man who shall die.

> But the Comforter, . . . whom the
> Father will send in my name, he
> shall teach you all things. . . .
> (John 14:26)

Whatever men may think of human reason God takes a low view of it. "Where is the wise? Where is the Scribe? Where is the disputer of this world?" Man's reason is a fine instrument and useful within its field. It is a gift of God and God does not hesitate to appeal to it, as when He cries to Israel, "Come now, and let us reason together." The inability of human reason as an organ of divine knowledge arises not from its own weakness but from its unfittedness for the task by its own nature. It was not given as an organ by which to know God.

The doctrine of the inability of the human mind and the need for divine illumination is so fully developed in the New Testament that it is nothing short of astonishing that we should have gone so far astray about the whole thing. Fundamentalism has stood aloof from the Liberal in self-conscious superiority and has on its own part fallen into error, the error of textualism, which is simply orthodoxy without the Holy Ghost. Everywhere among Conservatives we find persons who are Bible-taught but not Spirit-taught. They conceive truth to be something which they can grasp with the mind. If a man hold to the fundamentals of the Christian faith he is thought to possess divine truth. But it does not follow. There is no truth apart from the Spirit. The most brilliant intellect may be imbecilic when confronted with the mysteries of God. For a man to understand revealed truth requires an act of God equal to the original act which inspired the text.

"Except it be given him from heaven." Here is the other side of the truth; here is hope for all, for these words do certainly mean that there is such a thing as a gift of knowing, a gift that comes from heaven. Christ taught His disciples to expect the coming of the Spirit of Truth who would teach them all things. He explained Peter's knowledge of His Saviourhood as being a direct revelation from the Father in heaven. And in one of His prayers He said, "I thank thee, O Father, Lord of heaven and earth, because thou hast hidden these things from the wise and prudent, and hast revealed them unto babes."

> But as he which hath called you is
> holy, so be ye holy in all manner of
> conversation; Because it is written,
> Be ye holy, for I am holy.
> (I Peter 1:15–16)

The Holy Spirit is first of all *a moral flame*. It is not an accident of language that He is called the *Holy* Spirit, for whatever else the word *holy* may mean it does undoubtedly carry with it the idea of moral purity. And the Spirit, being God, must be absolutely and infinitely pure. With Him there are not (as with men) grades and degrees of holiness. He is holiness itself, the sum and essence of all that is unspeakably pure.

No one whose senses have been exercised to know good and evil but must grieve over the sight of zealous souls seeking to be filled with the Holy Spirit while they are yet living in a state of moral carelessness or borderline sin. Such a thing is a moral contradiction. Whoever would be filled and indwelt by the Spirit should first judge his life for any hidden iniquities; he should courageously expel from his heart everything which is out of accord with the character of God as revealed by the Holy Scriptures.

At the base of all true Christian experience must lie a sound and sane morality. No joys are valid, no delights legitimate where sin is allowed to live in life or conduct. No transgression of pure righteousness dare excuse itself on the ground of superior religious experience. To seek high emotional states while living in sin is to throw our whole life open to self deception and the judgment of God. "Be ye holy" is not a mere motto to be framed and hung on the wall. It is a serious commandment from the Lord of the whole earth. "Cleanse your hands, ye sinners; and purify your hearts, ye double minded. Be afflicted, and mourn, and weep: let your laughter be turned into mourning, and your joy into heaviness" (James 4:8–9). The true Christian ideal is not to be happy but to be holy. The holy heart alone can be the habitation of the Holy Ghost.

# David Martyn Lloyd-Jones
## (1900–1981)

When you consider the writings of D. Martyn Lloyd-Jones, and try to make selections, you are astonished by the possibilities. His *Exposition of the Sermon on the Mount* is already a classic, and his six volumes on Romans stand as models of sound and practical exposition. These selections are from the first volume of his series on Ephesians.

Trained to be a doctor, and well on his way to success in that field, Lloyd-Jones entered the ministry in 1927. He is best known as the associate and then the successor to G. Campbell Morgan at Westminster Chapel, London. Lloyd-Jones made Westminster a center for Bible exposition in the Reformed tradition. He was counselor and friend to many people, especially pastors and students.

My wife and I cherish lovely memories of our visits with Dr. and Mrs. Lloyd-Jones whenever we were in Britain. "The Doctor" (as he was affectionately called) was always eager for fellowship no matter how busy his schedule. We miss him, but we give thanks for the riches of his ministry found in the pages of his books.

Having made known unto us the
mystery of his will, according to his
good pleasure which he hath
purposed in himself. (Eph. 1:9)

Incidentally, this truth is the whole basis of missionary activity. It is because of this that you can go to the heart of Central Africa and visit a tribe of people who cannot read or write and who have no learning. You can preach the gospel to them with the same confidence as you preach it in Western society, because God can enlighten them through the Holy Spirit. Most of the early Christians were slaves; the gospel is 'preached to the poor'. Throughout the centuries it has been the same. Thank God for this. If it were otherwise, men of intellect would have a great advantage over others; but here we are all one. 'There is none righteous, no, not one.' 'The world by wisdom knew not God.' 'It pleased God by the foolishness of preaching to save them that believe' (I Corinthians 1:21). How we should thank God that He has made the riches of His grace to abound toward us 'in all wisdom and prudence, having made known unto us the mystery of his will, according to His good pleasure which He hath purposed in himself'! Let us join the Apostle Paul in saying, 'O the depth of the riches both of the wisdom and the knowledge of God! how unsearchable are his judgments, and his ways past finding out'! (Romans 11:33). Who but God would ever have contrived such a way of salvation, such a perfect way of salvation? 'For of him and through him and to him are all things, to whom be glory for ever. Amen.'

> . . . being predestinated according to
> the purpose of him who worketh all
> things after the counsel of his own
> will. (Eph. 1:11)

How, then, do we approach the truth? First of all without prejudice. We all start with prejudices; we take up positions, and having taken them up, we argue for them and we defend them. We say 'I have always said this; my parents said it before me; I have always been taught to believe this; therefore I stand . . .' So it often happens that we have never really considered the Scripture teaching concerning these matters. We may never have read a book on the subject, or considered what those whom God has called and appointed as leaders in

362

the Church throughout the centuries have said and taught concerning it. We start with a prejudice and we hold on to it, and feel that it is a part of our personality. We must defend it! Our minds are so shut and closed that we do not even consider the question. It is surely unnecessary to point out that that is a totally un-Christian attitude. Nothing is further removed from the Christian position. This was the attitude of the Pharisees, and it was the reason why they hated our Lord and His teaching. It was the same attitude that opposed the Apostles wherever they went to preach. This new theory, this new idea and teaching offended people's prejudices. May God give us grace to rid ourselves of the prejudices to which we are all liable, and to which we are subject as the result of sin.

> Which is the earnest of our inheri-
> tance until the redemption of the
> purchased possession, unto the
> praise of his glory. (Eph. 1:14)

In other words the Apostle's teaching is that the Holy Spirit within us gives us what we as Christians should be enjoying— a foretaste of heaven! Our coming together in public worship should be a foretaste of heaven. As we meet to consider these things, and to talk about them, and to discuss them, we are having a foretaste of heaven. Public worship should be a gathering of the firstfruits, a sampling of what is to be our lot in heaven. These New Testament Epistles constantly urge us to look forward to the enjoyment of heaven. We know little of what that means, and we are told but little about it in the Scriptures, but we can safely say that the two chief blessings in heaven will be to see our blessed Lord and Saviour, and to become like Him. 'Blessed are the pure in heart, for they shall see God' (Matthew 5:8). 'Beloved, now are we the sons of God, and it doth not yet appear what we shall be; but we know that, when he shall appear, we shall be like him, for we shall see him as he is' (I John 3:2). To see our blessed Lord and Saviour face to face, to see God; this is beyond our comprehension, and we cannot grasp it because it is so glorious. But in heaven we shall see God, and look into the face of our blessed Saviour who died for us. All we have at present, even our highest experiences, are the firstfruits; they are only the foretaste of bliss.

Wherefore, I also, . . . cease not to give thanks for you, . . . that the God of our Lord Jesus Christ, the Father of glory, may give unto you the spirit of wisdom and revelation in the knowledge of him. (Eph. 1:15–17)

The Apostle, however, does not pray to 'the God of Abraham, of Isaac and of Jacob'; he prays to 'the God of our Lord Jesus Christ'; and he does so because there is a new covenant. God has now made a covenant with man in the Person of our Lord and Saviour Jesus Christ. This is the 'Covenant of grace', the 'Covenant of Redemption' appearing in a new form. It is the same Covenant in essence as the old one, but now it is in the Person of the Son, the Second Adam, the new Man. The representative of the human race is the Lord Jesus Christ, and God has covenanted with Him for His people. So when Paul reminds himself that he is praying to 'the God of our Lord Jesus Christ' he reminds himself that he is praying to the God of our salvation, he is praying to the God who has originated and brought to pass all the things we have been considering from verse 3 to verse 14 in our chapter. He is praying to the God who has, before the foundation of the world, chosen and elected us and planned His glorious purpose in Christ for our final complete salvation. What a difference it makes to prayer when you begin in that manner! You no longer go to God uncertainly, or with doubts and queries as to whether He is going to receive you; you remember and realize that you are praying because He has done something to you, and drawn

364

you to Himself in and through 'our Lord Jesus Christ'. You realize that you are approaching 'the God of peace that brought again from the dead our Lord Jesus, that great Shepherd of the sheep, through the blood of the everlasting covenant' (Hebrews 13:20).

That I may know him. . . . (Phil. 3:10)

Do you know God? I am not asking whether you believe things about Him; but have you met Him? Have you known yourself for certain in His presence? Does He speak to you, and do you know that you speak to Him? *The Practice of the Presence of God'* by Brother Lawrence tells us that this is possible in the kitchen while you are washing the dishes, and performing the most menial tasks. It matters not where you are as long as you know that this is possible, that Christ died to make it possible. He died 'to bring us to God', and to this knowledge. Is your fellowship 'with the Father and with his Son Jesus Christ'? O that we might know God! Begin to cry with Job, 'Oh, that I knew where I might find him', and you will soon find yourself desiring, hungering to know Him. The most vital question to ask about all who claim to be Christian is this: Have they a soul thirst for God? Do they long for this? Is there something about them that tells you that they are always waiting for His next manifestation of Himself? Is their life centred on Him? Can they say with Paul that they forget everything in the past? Do they press forward more and more that they might know Him and that the knowledge might increase, until eventually beyond death and the grave they may bask eternally in 'the sunshine of His face'? 'That I might know him!'

> The eyes of your understanding
> being enlightened. . . . (Eph. 1:18)

We should be constantly praying for this enlightening of the eyes of our understanding. This again can be stated in the form of a question. Do we day by day pray to God, the God of our Lord Jesus Christ, the Father of glory, to enlighten the eyes of our understanding? It should be our constant daily prayer. We should always preface our reading of the Word by praying for this enlightenment. The constant desire of our lives should be that we might 'grow in grace and in the knowledge of the Lord'. The trouble with so many of us is that we have never awakened to this realization. We seem to think that we have 'arrived', that we 'know'. We know more than those liberal theologians, those modernists, and people who are not Christians; so we seem to think that we have encompassed the whole of Christian knowledge. The fact is that we are but tyros, we are babes, we are merely at the very beginning. We must press on unto perfection. Are we interested in Christian doctrine? Do we really see the importance of it, or do we find it rather boring and dull? Do we always seek some excitement, something to entertain us? Do we realize that, having been saved and called and placed in Christ, what God desires is that we should grow in our understanding of truth and of doctrine, that we should become more concerned about this than about anything else, that the 'eyes of our understanding', our comprehension, may be enlightened to that end.

> . . . and gave him to be the head
> over all things to the church, Which
> is his body, the fulness of him that
> filleth all in all. (Eph. 1:22–23)

The Lord Jesus Christ as the eternal Son of God is eternally self-sufficient and independent and has no need of us. But when we think of the Lord Jesus Christ as the Mediator, as the

God-Man, as the One who has come to achieve redemption and to present His people to His Father, then in that sense He is joined to the body and needs it. A head alone is not complete. A head needs a body, and you cannot think of a head without a body. So the body and the head are one in this mystical sense. As such we Christian people are a part of the 'fulness' of the Lord Jesus Christ.

This is the amazing New Testament conception of the Church, and since the Lord Jesus Christ ascended and returned to heaven, this body of His, the Church, is being perfected. Think of a new-born babe. In a sense the child is perfect; but it can grow and develop, and it will attain to a certain maturity. The same is true of the Christian Church. From the Ascension to the Second Advent the body of Christ has been growing and developing; and there is a day coming when she will be complete and perfect. Then the 'fulness' of the Gentiles will have come in, and the fulness of Israel will also have been saved. Then the body will be complete and entire and will have attained its fulness. So I must learn to think of myself, humble unworthy insignificant Christian as I am, as someone who is essential and vital to the 'fulness' of the mystical body of Christ. What an idea! To the extent to which we grasp this idea we shall receive strength not to sin. It will enable us to see sin in a new light. A member of this mystical body continuing in sin? Impossible! There is no way which leads so directly to holiness and sanctification as the understanding of this New Testament doctrine of the Church as the body of Christ. We are a part of 'his fulness', of His mystical completeness as the Mediator, as the One given to the Church by God to be its Head.

# *Epilogue*

Truth is a power. But one can see that only in rare instances, because it [truth] is suffering and must be defeated as long as it is truth. When it has become victorious others will join it. Why? Because it is truth? No, if it had been for that reason they would have joined it also when it was suffering. Therefore they do not join it because it has power. They join it after it has become a power because others had joined it.

Sören Kierkegaard

From William Hubben, *Dostoevsky, Kierkegaard, Nietzsche, and Kafka* (New York: Collier, 1962), p. 9.

# List of Sources

Hugh Black, *Edinburgh Sermons* (London: Hodder and Stoughton, 1906), pp. 36–37, 42–43, 69–70, 75–76, 81–82, 221, 272–273.

*Andrew A. Bonar, Diary and Letters* (London: Banner of Truth Trust, 1960), pp. 84–85, 98–99, 118–119, 198–199, 225, 234, 371.

Frank W. Boreham, *The Heavenly Octave: A Study of the Beatitudes* (1935; reprint ed., Grand Rapids: Baker, 1968), pp. 27–28, 43–44, 78–79, 82–83, 99–100, 106–107, 109–110.

*The Life and Diary of David Brainerd*, in vol. 3 of the *Complete Works* of Jonathan Edwards, ed. Philip E. Howard, Jr., (Chicago: Moody Press, 1949), pp. 78–79, 81–82, 102, 116, 126–127, 139–140, 352–353.

Phillips Brooks, *Sermons* (London: Richard D. Dickinson, 1879), pp. 62–63, 66, 71, 72–73, 17–18, 141, 272–273.

John Bunyan, *The Works of John Bunyan*, ed. George Offors, 3 vols. (London: Blackie and Son, 1875; reprint ed., Grand Rapids: Baker, 1977). Individual selections are from volume 2, *The Pharisee and the Publican*, p. 260; *The Saint's Knowledge of Christ's Love*, p. 37; *An Exposition of the First Ten Chapters of Genesis*, p. 419; *A Holy Life the Beauty of Christianity*, p. 532; *Advice to Sufferers*, pp. 707–708, 720, 732.

John Calvin, *Institutes of the Christian Religion*, ed. John T. McNeill, 2 vols. (Philadelphia: Westminster Press, 1960), vol. 2, pp. 851, 853–854, 874–875, 1013–1014, 1024, 1025–1026, 1026–1027.

*Sermons by the late Robert S. Candlish* (Edinburgh: Adam and Charles Black, 1874), pp. 91–92, 98, 121, 122–123, 200–201, 246–247, 309–310.

Oswald Chambers, *My Utmost for His Highest* (New York: Dodd, Mead and Company, 1935), pp. 87, 122, 130, 135, 139, 137, 243, 165.

William M. Clow, *The Secret of the Lord* (London: Hodder and Stoughton, 1911), pp. 1, 111–112, 169–170, 182–183, 196–197, 240–241, 292–293.

R. W. Dale, *The Epistle of James, and other discourses*, ed. Sir Alfred W. W. Dale (London: Hodder and Stoughton, 1895), pp. 34–35, 24, 99–100, 108–109, 118–119, 258–259, 302–303.

Philip Doddridge, *The Rise and Progress of Religion in the Soul* (reprint ed., Grand Rapids: Baker, 1977), pp. 121, 125, 224–225, 226–227, 198–199, 235, 252–253.

Marcus Dods, commentary on John, in the *Expositor's Bible*, 6 vols. (Grand Rapids: Eerdmans, 1940), vol. 5, pp. 123, 126, 132, 166, 204–205, 222, 228.

James W. Kennedy, ed., *Henry Drummond: An Anthology* (New York: Harper and Row, 1953), pp. 88, 111, 112, 116–117, 138, 139, 175–176.

Frederick William Faber, *Spiritual Conferences* (1859; London: Burns and Oates, 1888), pp. 2–3, 19, 36–37, 151, 190–191, 282–283, 296. This book is a collection of addresses Faber gave at the oratory during special holy seasons.

H. H. Farmer, *Things Not Seen: Studies in the Christian Interpretation of Life* (London: Nisbet and Company, 1927), pp. 48–49, 96–97, 102–104, 137–138, 170, 176, 194.

François Fénelon, *Christian Perfection*, ed. Charles F. Whiston, trans. Mildred Whitney Stillman (New York: Harper and Row, 1947), pp. 35, 41–42, 53–54, 57–58, 93, 95–96, 103.

P. T. Forsyth, *The Soul of Prayer* (London: Charles H. Kelly, 1916), pp. 9–11, 15, 27–28, 58–59, 88–89, 95–96, 117–118. This book is the best "theology of prayer" I have ever read.

A. J. Gossip, *The Hero in Thy Soul* (New York: Charles Scribner's, 1930), pp. 58–59, 85–86, 108, 142, 168–169, 226–227. This book, a superb collection of Gossip's sermons, includes "But When Life Tumbles In, What Then?"

Robert Haldane, *Exposition of the Epistle to the Romans* (1835; reprint ed., London: Banner of Truth Trust, Geneva Series Commentary, 1966), pp. 274–275, 324–325, 325, 344, 392–393, 559, 565–566. I recommend this book as a commentary that blends evangelical doctrine and devotional warmth.

J. Stuart Holden, *A Voice for God* (London: Hodder and Stoughton, 1932), pp. 92–93, 111–112, 115–116, 120, 128–129, 186, 211–212.

*Lectures on Colossians* by H. A. Ironside, published by Loizeaux Brothers, Neptune, New Jersey, pp. 27, 29–30, 38–39, 71–72, 89–90, 119–120, 166–167.

J. D. Jones, *The Inevitable Christ* (London: Hodder and Stoughton, 1928), pp. 38–40, 41–43, 46–48, 74–75, 106–108, 125–126; *The Gospel According to Mark*, in the Devotional Commentary (London: The Religious Tract Society, 1919), vol. 3, pp. 118–119. *The Inevitable Christ*, a book of Jones's sermons, was dedicated "to my church and congregation at Richmond Hill, in gratitude for 30 happy years."

John Henry Jowett, *Things That Matter Most* (New York: Revell, 1913), pp. 74–75, 33–34, 49–50, 99–100, 164–165, 199–200, 203–204.

Thomas R. Kelly, *A Testament of Devotion* (New York: Harper and Row, 1941), the chapter "Simplification of Life," pp. 113–114, 114–115, 116–117, 118, 120–121, 122, 122–123.

John Ker, *Thoughts for Heart and Life* (Edinburgh: David Douglas, 1888), pp. 24, 102–103, 110–111, 111, 120–121, 127–128, 239–240.

D. Martyn Lloyd-Jones, *God's Ultimate Purpose* (Grand Rapids: Baker, 1979), pp. 195, 223, 308, 331–332, 348–349, 368–369, 431.

George MacDonald, *Life Essential: The Hope of the Gospel*, ed. Rolland Hein (Wheaton, IL: Harold Shaw Publishers, 1974), pp. 14, 16, 17, 31, 38, 46–47, 69–70. This is a careful condensation of the edition originally published in 1892.

C. H. Mackintosh, *Notes on the Book of Genesis* (New York: Loizeaux Brothers, 1880), pp. 2–3, 89–90, 127–128, 143–144, 151–152, 195–196, 231–232. Also available is *The Mackintosh Treasury: Miscellaneous Writings of C. H. Mackintosh*, rev. ed. (Neptune, NJ: Loizeaux, 1976). This was republished in 1972 in *Genesis to Deuteronomy: Notes on the Pentateuch*, complete in one volume.

Alexander Maclaren, *Expositions of Holy Scripture*, 17 vols. (Grand Rapids: Baker, 1975), vol. 4, pp. 98–99A, 210A, 291–292A, 308–309A, 120–121B, 160–161B, 181–182B. These are double volumes, and the letters indicate whether the selection is from the first or second part of the volume. *Expositions of Holy Scripture* was originally printed in thirty-two volumes, 1904–1910.

Thomas Manton, *An Exposition of John XVII* (London: Banner of Truth Trust, 1959), pp. 146, 152, 169, 181, 193–194, 390, 357–358.

George Matheson, *Rests by the River: Devotional Meditations* (London: Hodder and Stoughton, 1907), pp. 1–2, 44–45, 75–77, 95–96, 169–171, 282–283, 344–345.

Andrew A. Bonar, *Memoir and Remains of Robert Murray McCheyne* (reprint ed., London: Banner of Truth, 1966), pp. 346, 389–390, 412, 457–458, 469–470, 472–473, 502. This is reprinted from the enlarged edition of 1892.

F. B. Meyer, *Christian Living* (New York: Revell, n.d.), pp. 18–19; *The Future Tenses of the Blessed Life* (New York: Revell, 1892), pp. 12–13, 29–30, 44–46; *The Present Tenses of the Blessed Life* (Chicago: Revell, n.d.), pp. 86–88, 102–103, 131–133.

Ralph G. Turnbull, ed., *The Best of Dwight L. Moody* (Grand Rapids: Baker, 1971), pp. 33–34, 85–86, 197, 235, 235–236, 241, 244–245.

G. Campbell Morgan, *The Westminster Pulpit*, 10 vols. (London: Pickering and Inglis, Ltd., 1955–1956), vol. 8, pp. 13, 18–19, 46, 77–78, 98–99, 197–198, 290–291.

371

George H. Morrison, *Sun-rise: Addresses from a City Pulpit* (London: Hodder and Stoughton, 1903; reprint ed., Grand Rapids: Baker, 1971), pp. 19–20, 35–36, 77–78, 170–171, 179 and 184–185, 226–227, 254–255.

Andrew Murray, *Humility, the Beauty of Holiness* (1895; Old Tappan, NJ: Revell, 1974), pp. 14–15, 20–21, 27–28, 38–39, 44–45, 53–54, 64–65.

John Henry Newman, *Parochial and Plain Sermons*, 8 vols. (London: Rivington's, 1887), vol. 1, pp. 36–37, 45–46, 127–128, 173–174, 188–189, 248–249, 303–304.

*The Letters of John Newton* (London: Banner of Truth Trust, 1960), pp. 17, 25–26, 30, 33–34, 105–106, 132, 150.

Joseph Parker, *The People's Bible*, 25 vols. (London: Hodder and Stoughton, 1899), vol. 21 (the Gospel of John), pp. 34–35, 59–60, 105, 116–117, 148–149, 199, 283–284.

F. W. Robertson, *Sermons, Second Series* (London: Kegan Paul, Trench, Trübner and Company, 1898), pp. 218–219; *Sermons, First Series* (London: Kegan Paul, Trench, Trübner and Company, 1898), pp. 230–231, 271–273, 286–287; *Second Series*, pp. 101, 111, 151–152.

J. C. Ryle, *Practical Religion* (reprint ed., Grand Rapids: Baker, 1977), pp. 45–46, 54–55, 78–79, 121–122, 192, 292–293, 343–344.

Ralph G. Turnbull, ed., *A Treasury of W. Graham Scroggie* (Grand Rapids: Baker, 1974), pp. 24–25, 45, 79, 119, 128, 131, 161. This volume is the best introduction to Scroggie's varied works that a reader can find.

*The Pastor in Prayer* (London: Elliot Stock, 1893), pp. 23–24, 27, 61, 66, 68–70, 85–86, 93, 116–117.

James Stalker, *The Four Men* (London: Hodder and Stoughton, 1892), pp. 35–36, 38–40, 40–41, 67, 77–79, 80–82, 145–147. The book is a collection of Stalker's sermons.

J. Hudson Taylor, *Hudson Taylor's Legacy*, ed. Marshall Broomhall (London: China Inland Mission, 1931), pp. 15, 34, 35, 54, 67, 79, 104. This is a collection of Hudson Taylor's devotional writings.

W. H. Griffith Thomas, *Studies in Colossians and Philemon*, ed. Winifred G. T. Gillespie (Grand Rapids: Baker, 1973), pp. 27, 26–27, 33–34, 78–79, 90, 103–104, 115–116.

Thomas à Kempis, *The Imitation of Christ*, World Classics edition (Oxford: At the University Press, 1903), pp. 1–2, 11, 14–15, 26–27, 66–67, 105–106, 217–218.

A. W. Tozer, *The Divine Conquest* (Old Tappan, NJ: Fleming H. Revell, 1950; reprint ed., Harrisburg, PA: Christian Publications, 1950), pp. 14–15, 25–26, 33–34, 51, 57–58, 78–79, 99–100.

John Wesley, *The Works of John Wesley,* 14 vols. (reprint ed., Kansas City, MO: Beacon Hill Press, 1979), vol. 5, pp. 21, 78, 80–81, 204, 232, 385–386, 486.

Alexander Whyte, *In Remembrance of Me* (1906; reprint ed., Grand Rapids: Baker, 1970), pp. 13–15, 28–29, 41–43; *The Apostle Paul* (1903; reprint ed., Grand Rapids: Baker, 1977), pp. 92–93, 100–101, 211–212; *The Walk, Conversation, and Character of Jesus Christ Our Lord* (Edinburgh and London: Oliphant, Anderson and Ferrier, 1900), pp. 186–187.